KU-661-352

FALSE INHERITANCE

Also by Michael Rice

Dilmun Discovered:
The First Hundred Years of Bahrain's Archaeology

The Temple Complex at Barbar, Bahrain

The Search for the Paradise Land:
An Introduction to the Archaeology of Bahrain and the Gulf

'Bahrain Through the Ages' (Joint Editor):
Vol. I The Archaeology
Vol. II The History

Egypt's Making:
The Origins of the Egyptian State, 5000–2000 BC

The Archaeology of the Arabian Gulf: 7000–323 BC

The Power of the Bull

FALSE INHERITANCE

Israel in Palestine and the Search for a Solution

Michael Rice

KEGAN PAUL INTERNATIONAL
London and New York

First published in 1994 by
Kegan Paul International Ltd
UK: P.O. Box 256, London WC1B 3SW, England
USA: 29 West 35th Street, New York, NY 10001–2299, USA

Distributed by

John Wiley & Sons Ltd
Southern Cross Trading Estate
1 Oldlands Way, Bognor Regis
West Sussex, PO22 9SA, England

Routledge, Inc
29 West 35th Street
New York, NY 10001–2299, USA

© Michael Rice 1994

Set in Palatino 10 on 12 pt
by Intype, London

Printed in Great Britain by
TJ Press, Padstow, Cornwall

All rights reserved. No part of this book may be reprinted
or reproduced or utilized in any form or by any electronic,
mechanical or other means, now known or hereafter
invented, including photocopying and recording, or in
any information storage or retrieval system, without
permission in writing from the publishers.

British Library Cataloguing in Publication Data

Rice, Michael
    False Inheritance: Israel in Palestine
    and the Search for a Solution
    I. Title
    956.04

    ISBN 0–7103–0473–0

US Library of Congress Cataloging in Publication Data

Rice, Michael, 1928–
    False Inheritance : Israel in Palestine and the search for a solution /
    Michael Rice.
    240 pp. 21cm.
    Includes bibliographical reference and index.
    ISBN 0–7103–0473–0
    1. Zionism—Controversial literature.   2. Israel—History.
3. Jewish-Arab relations.   I. Title.
    DS149.R46   1993
016.3225'4'095694—dc20   93–28499
                                                              CIP

This book is dedicated
to all peoples who suffer
at the hands of others.

CONTENTS

'If I was an Arab leader I would never make [peace] with Israel. That is natural: we have taken their country.'

David Ben Gurion, quoted in Nahum Goldman, *The Jewish Paradox*, Weidenfeld & Nicolson, 1978, p. 99

'If this is Palestine and not the land of Israel, then you are conquerors and not tillers of the land. You are invaders. If this land is Palestine, then it belongs to a people who lived here before you came.'

Menachem Begin, *Yediot Aharanot*, 17 October 1969

PREFACE

This book was in proof when the announcement was made of the resumption of the talks between the Israelis and their Arab antagonists, including the Palestinians, and the subsequent revelation of the independent and secret meetings between representatives of Israel and the Palestinians directly, held under the auspices of the Norwegian government. It was a startling though not wholly unforeseen development; there had been speculations, of which the Middle East is seldom deprived for long, that an agreement of some sort would materialise in the current political phase. For some time past and for reasons which *False Inheritance* explores, the situation in Israel as much as amongst the Palestinians and their supporters had been tending in this direction. This preface is the result.

False Inheritance is highly critical of the policies and actions of the successive administrations which have governed Israel since the formation of the state in 1948. It is largely historical in its approach, since it has long been my conviction that the confrontation between the Palestinians, the Arab states and Israel cannot be understood unless the historical parameters are firmly established. Equally, it is the purpose of *False Inheritance* to demonstrate what seem to me to be the manifest consequences of the deceptions, manipulations and cruelties which have been practised on the Palestine people in the names of Zionism and the Israeli state over the past half-century and more.

The book argues that the Jewish inhabitants of Israel for whom the state was principally created, those of European or Western origin, have no historical, legal or moral claim to the land of Palestine. It maintains that justice will not be done nor

xi

will peace survive unless Israel is de-Zionised and its Jewish population becomes part of a secular federal state. This, the book's basic thesis, is unchanged by the latest events. Whether its arguments are perceived to be valid, when judged against these developments as much as against the backdrop of history, must be the reader's decision.

Having set myself up to write in a primarily historiographical format, it is not really for me to comment on the unfolding of a political drama day by day, still less to offer advice, unsought and no doubt unwanted, to the principal actors in the drama. The Middle East has never been short of those who are prepared to offer advice, at least since the days of Job.

That part of the world has also been well known for the appearance of prophets, forecasting doom and, not infrequently, punishment for a back-sliding people. It is not my purpose to join their number, either. On the other hand, it would be disingenuous to overlook entirely the fact of the dialogue (if that is truly what it turns out to be) between those who have been engaged in a dispute which has for so long perplexed the world community. Other considerations apart, the very fact of the Israelis and their apparently implacable enemies talking to each other is another of the sequence of otherwise wholly unthinkable events (the destruction of the Berlin Wall, the collapse of international communism, a civil war of bloody proportions in Continental Europe) which seems to be one of the hallmarks of this political generation.

Why this development has happened at this particular time is clearly the stuff of historical analyses of the future. I have my own views, which are set out in the text which follows. My principal conclusion, which became inescapable during and after the Gulf War, is that Israel has become marginal to the strategic interests of America and the West; the realisation of this awkward fact has made it necessary for the government of Israel, I believe, to countenance courses of action which hitherto would have been unthinkable. Israel, I suggest, is also under great threat from the various disparate pressures which are boiling up in its society – profound demographic changes, internal security and the fracturing of its political and moral purpose. It is entirely to be expected therefore that Israel should try and take the initiative in neutralising its enemy even if, in the process, it appears to be making concessions to that enemy, the very possibility of which have always roundly been denied.

It is also entirely in keeping with Israel's past actions that it should now set out to achieve maximum favourable exposure in the world's media, which will confuse its opponents and provide it with the opportunity to manipulate events, to protect what are seen to be the Jewish state's long-term interests. Whether Israel will be successful in achieving such objectives remains to be seen. What is certain is that the Arab states, when they have recovered from their immediate reaction to the present chain of events, will look on any and all of Israel's future acts with the deepest reserve.

It should not, however, be a matter of surprise that the protagonists in the Israeli–Palestinian dispute, faced with a world order profoundly different from that with which they have grown up (for politicians are subject as much as anyone else to bafflement by unforeseen events) should seek a respite or even disengagement from the past. After nearly half a century of confrontation many of the people of Israel, as much as most Palestinians, must long for an ending to the conflict which has bedevilled their lives. The desire to achieve an end to the dispute will be strong, with every reason, except amongst the most implacably committed on either side.

For the Palestinians the prospects of even a limited understanding with Israel are tempting. To the leaders of the Palestinian community, self-appointed though generally acknowledged by their people, it brings the possibility of improved international recognition, albeit of a limited and constrained sort, and something approaching the level of political acceptance to which they have for so long, and often so fruitlessly aspired. For the Palestinian people living in the Occupied Territories, an understanding with Israel, no matter how limited, should mean an end to the killing, the night-time arrests, the disappearance of family members into prison camps and the arbitrary destruction of homes on grounds of 'collective responsibility'. The Israelis, too – except perhaps the most entrenched Zionists for whom peace with the Palestinians would promise, I believe, ultimate extinction – will rejoice: the dreadful responsibility which Israel has borne over these years will be seen to be lightening at last.

Thus far, only one thing about the emergence of a level of understanding between the two parties is certain: expectations will be substantially higher than can possibly ever be achieved. In this condition lies the first grave danger for the prospects for lasting peace.

The agreement in real terms is hardly even a beginning when judged from the standpoint of the Palestinians and of the struggle in which they have been engaged. It gives them a humiliatingly limited degree of 'autonomy' over the Gaza Strip – the least significant and most intractable of Israel's captured territories – and the town of Jericho – which has great archaeological and historical significance (it is spoken of as the oldest city site in the world) but no immediate political value. (Coincidentally I proposed Jericho as a possible location for the capital of the federal state which I believe to be the only viable structure for a future Palestinian entity – page 194.) But if the Palestinians were so naïve as to establish their headquarters there in the present phase, they would place themselves at great risk, for it would be the simplest of military operations for the Israelis to sweep into Jericho at whim. The advantages of the latest agreement to the Palestinians are at best illusory. The implications of the agreement are clear: the Palestinians are not considered by the Israelis and their partisans fit to be allowed their own state but must, for the foreseeable future, exist at best as clients of Israel. The power which will be devolved upon the Palestinians in Gaza and Jericho will be somewhat less than that enjoyed by an English County Council.

If negotiations between the Israelis and the Palestinians proceed along the lines on which they have begun, Israel will doubtless represent itself at every stage as having surrendered the absolute maximum of territory and political control to the Palestinians. Any further promptings to make the terms more acceptable to the Palestinians will provoke the Israelis to protest how generous are the terms which they are being forced to accept. The Palestinians, anxious for a settlement, will be presented with a meagre offering of land, part of the whole which was once theirs, and with such restrictions on their rights as to negate any real political responsibility for their future. Such humiliating terms will achieve nothing and I am fearful that they will only serve to build up deeper resentment and bitterness in the years to come.

The Palestinians are under comparable pressures to those exerted upon Israel to come to a settlement, however tentative and however inadequate. Partly as the consequence of the Palestinian leadership's own maladroitness and the divisions between the various factions which make up the Palestinian opposition to Israel's occupation of their territory, the Arab states, particularly those in the Arabian peninsula and the Gulf, are heartily tired of the constant demands made on their generosity. Such demands have only been equalled or excelled by the abuse which has been heaped on the 'oil-rich states' by those who have benefited most from their largesse. The oil-producing states have been uncommonly forbearing; they have been told that they are lackeys of the West and of Zionism and that the fossil hydro-carbons which lie beneath their territories represent, in some transcendental way, 'Arab oil'.

The final straw for the Arab states came with the Palestinians' response to the invasion of Kuwait. The PLO leadership's political ineptitude was never more visibly portrayed and the Arab states' response was immediate, angry and hurt. They will never again open either their coffers or their hearts to the Palestinians' present leadership and the Palestinians realise that they will not be able to continue to finance even the level of opposition to Israel which they have managed to sustain in the past.

The world community will do all that it can to bring about a rapprochement between the Palestinians and the Israelis. The PLO leadership's rapid acceptance of what little it was offered by Israel will have convinced many that 'if that is what the Palestinians want, then let them have it'. The world community will feel free to turn its attention to the other issues, still unresolved, on its agenda.

In this attitude, of those who have been either vicariously involved in the conflict or merely onlookers, lies a further danger for the future. Nothing in the agreements thus far revealed (though already there are dark hints of secret protocols, likely to work to the disadvantage of the Palestinians) gives any hope to the Palestinian refugees, nor for the many more Palestinians who are dispersed around the world as a result of Israel's existence. The 'Law of Return' still applies only to Jews; it does not apply to Palestinians, even those who can prove their ancestry over generations.

The indifference of the world community – which can be expected to become more and more evident as the early euphoria begins to die away – will enable Israel to continue to plant settlements in the Occupied Territories, to create 'new facts' without the inconvenience of constant observation by television and the press. If the Palestinians or their friends protest they will be told to remain silent for they may otherwise risk the agreement between the Israelis and the PLO being prejudiced.

It is a fair assumption that Israel will attempt to 'farm' the Occupied Territories, Gaza and Jericho, by exerting pressure on its allies (and, no doubt, on most of the hapless oil producers) to invest in industrial enterprises which can be used not primarily for the benefit of the Palestinians but to bolster Israel's collapsing economy. It is more than ever likely that Israel has come to recognise that it will not be able to rely indefinitely on the subventions either of the United States or of dispersed Jewry. What better alternative source of funding for Israel's expansion than the international oil producers and the economies of the states which are based on the extraction of the Arab world's one real resource? It may seem fanciful to advance such a concept now but it may all look very different in a few years' time. The pull of the prophetic gene is sometimes difficult to resist.

There is evidence already of a move afoot by Israel to present itself as the only bulwark against what it represents as the rising tide of Muslim fundamentalism. The existence of Israel and its behaviour over the past half century is one of the principal causes of the growth in corporate feeling in the Muslim world, especially in the Arabic-speaking states and in Iran, which is now called by the name of fundamentalism. It is another bogey, of the same puffed-up quality as 'Arab Nationalism' in the 1950s and 1960s, which Israel will try to use to frighten its allies into continuing their uncritical support for its policies.

Nothing is essentially changed by the latest developments. Israel will find it increasingly difficult to sustain her political economy, for reasons which I explore, but, despite the pessimism with which I view the handing back of the very limited direction of the affairs of Gaza and Jericho, it *is* a beginning of sorts. Yitzhak Shamir, the once-upon-a-time gunman who became Prime Minister of Israel, believed that any concession to the Palestinians which involved territory was the beginning of the end. I believe this to be true.

To admit any part of the Palestinians' claim to their land must lead inevitably to the admission of the totality of their case. For reasons which this book explores in some detail, the existence of the Israeli state is based upon a structure of false premises, invented 'history' and a series of responses to the problems not of the Middle East but of Europe, which resulted in the acceptance of Israel's claim to statehood. That claim has, it seems to me, no substance in law and certainly none in justice. If the Palestinians are steadfast and if they manage the politics of the situation with which they are now presented with skill and sophistication, they may yet see their land restored to them and, in the form of political structure which *False Inheritance* proposes, a true peace established between the Jewish and non-Jewish populations of the Eastern Mediterranean. On so many occasions in the past the Palestinians have chosen the wrong path, to their own disadvantage; this time they must make their way, not with force of arms but with the careful management of high politics.

1

A GREAT WRONG

For many years past I have been engaged in the analysis and presentation of the history of that part of the world in which the confrontation between the Arabs and the State of Israel has festered for the best part of the last half century. Admittedly the times with which I have been primarily concerned are long before the present – though not exclusively so since, by a curious and rather fortunate set of circumstances I became involved with the politics and affairs of the Middle East in the present day too. However that may be, it seemed clear to me that it was not before time for someone, however inadequately, to attempt to set the present politics of the matter of Palestine and Israel into some sort of historical perspective and, in doing so, to express some of the realities which inform the confrontation of Palestinians and Israelis, shorn of the overgrowth of fable, myth and downright untruth which have, I am quite certain, obscured it so totally for so long.

What follows here is an attempt, however presumptuous, to provide a counterbalance to the often strange (and to me distressing) uses which have been made of history, myth and language in justifying the existence of the State of Israel and its continued presence in Palestine. So many of the arguments deployed to give warrant to the existence of a Jewish state in that part of the Levant which has generally been known as Palestine depend upon the interpretation – or occasionally the unashamed invention – of historical precedents plastered over an exceptionally long surviving tribal myth. It is necessary, it seems to me, to review the historical paradigms, examine the myths and to see whether they do contribute meaningfully to the conclusions which have been claimed for them. I am certain

1

that they do not; I believe that an understanding of what I am certain *are* the realities has never been more important than now.

The latest dramatic developments, which some – more optimistic than I – will see as the first real prospects for peace between the Palestinians and the Israelis, make it more necessary than ever to understand the essential underlying realities which have dogged the last forty years and more of Israel's existence. Unless the truth of Israel's nature and history is understood and the conclusions, which seem to me to be inescapable, drawn from it, the Palestinians will ultimately not achieve justice nor the Middle East peace and stability.

The essential elements are these: the Jewish migrants, largely of European origin, to the land which was once part of Palestine and is now called Israel, claim that they are the direct lineal descendants and heirs of the occupants of the land which was promised to a group of semitic-speaking clans early in the second millennium BC, by the God of Abraham, Isaac and Jacob, three of those putative ancestors from whom they and other 'semites' claim descent. Further, it is claimed that those who have adopted Judaism as their religious belief, becoming in the process 'Sons of Abraham', have an equal title to live in the land of Israel. In light of this alleged descent or inheritance every Jew, from wherever he or she may come, can claim the right of 'return' to Israel and to citizenship of the state.

In contemporary terms Israel relies for the legal warrant for its existence as a state upon a vote of the General Assembly of the United Nations in 1948 which, by proposing a form of partition for Palestine, recognised the right of a then unnamed country to exist as a specifically Jewish entity. That entity became the state of Israel though not, evidently, quite in the way that the United Nations intended.

The Palestinians, who regard themselves as part of the larger Arab community (Arab is a term as difficult of precise definition as is, apparently, the term Jew) are mainly Muslim by religious affiliation, but with an important Christian component in their population. They see themselves, on the one hand, as the descendants of the Muslim warriors who conquered the Levant in the aftermath of the Prophet Muhammad's mission, outpouring from the Arabian peninsula and, on the other, as the aboriginal inhabitants of Palestine, present there from time immemorial. It will be readily apparent that a degree of confusion exists in these images which the Palestinians hold of themselves.

To those who know something of the Arab world and its peoples, the Palestinians may seem to be less approachable, in many ways less appealing than, say, the Egyptians (doubtful Arabs though they are, other than in a linguistic and cultural sense) or the more Europeanised Levantines of Syria and Lebanon. They are more reserved, even dour; they are also resourceful, able, hard-working and talented. Though many of them still follow the way of life of their ancestors – small farmers and peasantry, simple townsfolk living in small communities with clearly defined loyalties and generally rather inward-looking – many others have been able to obtain positions of profit and respect in the Arab states and in the world outside the Middle East, when they have been forced to seek their livelihoods beyond Palestine. They are successful and respected academics, administrators and entrepreneurs; as such it has not always been easy to portray them as a people, victims of a great misfortune, whose suffering and deprivation should move the world's conscience.

Perhaps facetiously, the Palestinians have sometimes been called 'the Jews of the Arab world'. Certainly they are often high achievers, distinct in their manners, in many of their customs and in much of their culture, given to scholarship and now, more sadly, accustomed to exile and persecution. But, at the time of Israel's creation and their dispossession, they were a small people, friendless and bewildered by the disaster to which fate had exposed them.

The Palestinians were politically unsophisticated and unaware of the cardinal importance, so brilliantly realised by their opponents, of seeking friends in the cabinet rooms and counting houses of an industrialised world of which few of them had any understanding or contact. Even after the creation of the State of Israel, for a crucial period of a generation or more they wasted time on internecine disputes, tossed from party to party in inter-Arab rivalries and in a succession of minor, often pointless forays against Israeli targets. These were invariably always batted away with calm assurance by their vastly more sophisticated opponents, who had all the most advanced weaponry and intelligence techniques supplied by misguided, and often deliberately misled, Western allies. The Palestinians' want of success on the battlefield was duplicated by their failure to convince the world outside the Middle East of the justice or, more poignant still, even the relevance of their cause.

The Arabs and their supporters have frequently, even if understandably, demonstrated marked symptoms of paranoia when faced with the Israelis' skills in exploiting the centres of influence and the international media. Israeli penetration of European and American political society in particular was, until the middle of the 1980s, remarkable indeed. It was not only, as the Arabs seemed often to believe, the consequence of a predisposition of such societies towards the Israeli case nor, as they similarly often insisted, the consequence of Israeli manipulation of Jewish financial and commercial influence. Such a predisposition was indeed sometimes evident and did, as I can testify, sometimes occur. But the political and propaganda victories which the Israelis and their friends achieved were almost invariably the result of careful organisation, the skilful marshalling of their supporters and their provision with well presented arguments to apply to any case, whether it was to draw outraged attention to some 'atrocity' by the Arabs or to justify what might otherwise be thought to be an act of repression or coercion by the Israeli authorities themselves. The mental and moral convolutions undergone by Israel's protagonists in the wider world were sometimes remarkable to observe.

In every major community in the Western world pro-Israeli action committees were formed whose function was to monitor the media – press, radio and television – as well as debates of political assemblies and to respond immediately to any action or comment critical of Israel or favourable to its opponents. Gradually such a response mechanism came to work autonomously and often with a cavalier regard for truth, so overwhelming was the need to respond on the part of those who formed the groups charged with this duty. Before the invasion of Lebanon in 1982, any journal which attracted the attention of Israeli propagandists would be deluged with letters and telephone calls from pro-Israeli activists (by no means only Jewish ones) demanding support for the Israeli point of view, and threatening dire consequences, notably the loss of advertising revenues, if such support was not instantly and uncritically forthcoming. Members of national and regional political assemblies were similarly targeted and were in consequence understandably cautious about expressing opinions on issues

4

which frequently seemed unlikely, at best, to enhance their electoral interests and at worst could see them identified as 'anti-semitic' and therefore fit to be cast into the fires of political perdition. Powerful men in the United States Congress had occasion to rue the day when, innocently or from conviction, they might speak kindly of the Palestinian case or in mild reproof of the Israeli position. After the invasion of Lebanon, when the mask began to slip from the Israelis' public face, matters began to change. But that change was slow in coming.

In the United States the activities of the AIPACs (American-Israel Political Action Committees) were particularly ferocious. Large amounts of money were deployed to support the election campaigns of Israel's friends whilst any politician who might be critical of the United States' perpetual support of Israel, even in the teeth of universal condemnation, found himself exposed to a barrage of abuse and calumny, and the direction of formidable amounts of money and influence against his re-election and to the support of his opponent. The widespread use of the McCarthy technique of the black-list, or even the threat of inclusion on the black-list of the enemies of Israel, was often enough to discourage many American politicians from associating themselves with a position even mildly critical of Israel, let alone one which was condemnatory, or which was supportive of the Palestinians. This inheritance of the McCarthy era, when so many Jewish intellectuals were themselves the victims of the Wisconsin Senator's campaigns, has been well demonstrated in publications such as *The Campaign to Discredit Israel*, published by AIPAC in 1983. This contained the names of officials and elected politicians alike whose views or actions had displeased the supporters of a foreign country, whose interest its authors had chosen to elevate above the interests of their own nation.

Even at a far more modest level of personal experience, anyone who has been identified politically with a position which might be considered to be inimical to the interests of the State of Israel will have experienced abusive telephone calls or even the threat of violence. Such activities, unacceptable though they are in free societies, were the inevitable consequence of the orchestration of the campaigns of hatred and vilification which were directed against the opponents of Israel. To the Arabs' own feelings of paranoia was often added the reluctance of their friends to be counted amongst them.

5

In the crucial years after the 1967 War, when for the first time some people who had hitherto been well disposed towards Israel began to question her policies in the aftermath of the occupation of parts of the West Bank of the Jordan, the Golan Heights and the Gaza Strip, the Arabs did little themselves to advance their cause. All too readily their squabblings and internal disputes (which not infrequently assumed murderous proportions) deflected attention from Israel's further penetration of the centres of power and influence in the countries of the industrialised West.

My own professional involvement with the Middle East began at the end of the 1950s and, aptly enough, it began with Egypt: aptly because Egypt is the most ancient of nation-states and has exercised a profound influence – though much of it is buried under the accretions of the millennia of other influences – on the development of the world in which we live today. Although diplomatic relations between Britain and Egypt were suspended at the time of the Suez crisis in 1956, they were resumed some three years later. The Egyptians decided that they would seek the services of a consultancy which could assist them in their relations with media, parliament and, to a lesser degree, industry. We were proposed, approached and appointed by the somewhat Orwellian-styled 'Ministry of Culture and National Guidance' of the Arab Republic of Egypt.

Our principal task, at the outset, was advising on the planning and management of a campaign to promote tourism to Egypt. In the period of political uncertainty following Suez and the hectic anti-Egyptian propaganda disseminated both by some British interests, particularly in the press, and by the Israelis and their supporters, this proved quickly to be a more overtly political task than might at first have been anticipated. To our surprise we found ourselves, willy nilly, being drawn into the Arab world's most absorbing concern, Palestine and the confrontation with Israel.

Until 1960, apart from a considerable reservation about the purpose and sense of the Suez invasion, which had led to my own not very significant withdrawal from active political involvement, I had accepted, I suppose, much of the propaganda line representing Israel as a gallant little Western enclave surrounded by a monstrous and overwhelmingly numerous enemy. I experienced a sharp change of view one night in Malta. During

6

dinner news of Eichmann's kidnapping by the Israelis broke. Eichmann was a pernicious creature, the stereotype of the small official suddenly given the power of a Tartar Khan and the tastes to indulge the destruction of those of his fellow humans whom he saw as the enemies of whatever it was in which he believed, or who opposed those whom be believed he was serving. I had listened, as a boy, to the broadcast of the sentences passed on the principal defendants at Nuremburg. Though they had placed themselves beyond humanity's pale, they were, it seemed to me, no more (though certainly no less) guilty than most defeated enemies in all conflicts past. I thought then and I think still that the Nuremburg verdicts were deeply misconceived, the trials and their inevitable outcome unjust and contaminating to the victorious Allies in whose name they were conducted. As I listened to the account of Eichmann's kidnapping, an act of unequivocal illegality given that Eichmann was living at the time in a sovereign country with its own laws and practice, I was appalled. The kidnapping, no matter how vile a man was Eichmann, was a flagrant act of terrorism. I hoped that Israel, with its professed high code of individual and political morality, would understand that to hang Eichmann would be to smear itself with the same foulness that seeped out of Germany and its conquered lands during the Second World War. If Israel had tried Eichmann and then let him out into the world, a scapegoat branded with a mark like Cain's, then I believed that something of what I had understood to be historic Jewish values and ideals would have been vindicated.

Eichmann was hanged by the Israelis, certainly not the only one to be put to death by the Israeli system, but the only one to be executed with, as it were, public acknowledgement of the event. By that act I believe that Israel set itself upon a course from which it has never recovered.

When our work for Egypt began, in 1960, the year of Eichmann's kidnapping, we found that the few foreign tourists who ventured to Egypt, beset by a stifling bureaucracy and the dead hand of an oppressive state system, were exposed, beside their innocent hotel beds, to a barrage of incompetently produced and crassly expressed propaganda about Palestine. Quite apart from the ineptness of the material's presentation, tourists visiting the lands of the Pyramids did not, we argued fairly forcefully, wish to be exposed to the hectic presentation of a political issue about which they knew little and cared less. It was not the way to do it, and we were successful in persuading the Egyptians to remove from the tourists' bedsides the piles of booklets and leaflets which undoubtedly did more harm to the cause that they advocated than any good at all.

The years went by. In 1967 Israel again provoked a war with Egypt, Jordan and Syria.[1] The result was a disastrous defeat for the Arabs. Nasser, to a large degree responsible for the débâcle, offered to resign; predictably, but none the less a little touchingly, the Egyptian mob, or at least that part·of it which was in Cairo, refused to allow him to go, though he was demonstrably a broken man.

In the weeks following the June War of 1967 I was perturbed at the grotesque – as it seemed to me – way in which all the channels of opinion accepted the Israeli line and gloated, with an unconcealed delight, at the humiliation of the Arabs. That the response was so violently pro-Israeli and anti-Arab seemed to me, and to the others who thought like me, to be wholly unreasonable and against the grain of political dispute. There is hardly a political issue in the world on which right is wholly concentrated on one side of the argument. Shortly after the end of the Six Day War I wrote and published what I believe was the first statement of the Arab case in book (or, more precisely, pamphlet) form. *The Need for Understanding the Arab Case* was politely received in Britain and with enthusiasm in the Arab press. It made, I suspect, little difference to anyone.

At this time, prompted by the unease which the extreme unfairness of the media and political response to the Arabs' position evoked, a number of prominent people in the Anglo-Arab·community in London – politicians, retired diplomats, academics and others – came together to try to counter the unremitting flow of anti-Arab propaganda which was being directed at the political arena as much as to the organs of opinion. A prime mover in the proposal was Elizabeth Collard, the founder of the journal, *Middle East Economic Digest*,[2] who frequently sought our help in matters of mutual interest and concern. The first meetings were, as I recall it, held in our offices; from them emerged the Council for the Advancement of Arab-British Understanding (CAABU),[3] a somewhat cumbersomely named but very creditable organisation which, over the intervening years, has done much to improve awareness of the Arab position, not only in relation to Israel and Palestine, but on other issues, not the least of which is the mutuality of interests and history which much of the Arab world shares with Europe and, in particular, with Britain.

At the beginning of the 1970s we were retained by the Arab League, to whose Information Department a number of the Egyptian officials with whom we had worked in the past had transferred themselves. Our brief was to assist the League's office in London. We set about trying to devise a coherent plan for the Arab states, in the process producing a series of information briefs for the press and others on the political character, size and economies of the various states, in an attempt to minimise the more arcane statements made about them, the product as often of imagination as of malice. We also produced a film on the origins of the Palestinian-Israeli confrontation; this was based largely on archive material and I believe that it was amongst the best of its kind at that time. As it was largely historical in content and coolly expressed in argument, it was not well regarded by some of the more vociferous Palestinian activists. It did, however, receive a very good showing in universities and to other influential audiences throughout the country.

One proposal which we made to the League was that it should sponsor a supplement or advertisement feature in *The Times* to draw attention to the deterioration of the situation in Palestine in the early summer of 1969. Such supplements were a device, primarily intended as a revenue-earner for the larger and more prestigious newspapers, by which an advertiser might be given an extensive editorial treatment over a number of pages supported by advertising from the interest concerned, or, similarly, a foreign country would be given publicity for its potential as a source of investment, the promotion of its exports or tourism, or the expression of a more politically directed message.

We proposed that the League should sponsor such a feature and use it as the highlight of the Palestinian event. The readership of *The Times*, after all, was precisely that, we argued, which the Palestinians needed to convince of the justice of their cause. For once, our advice was accepted by the League, a circumstance which was by no means always the case; even the Palestinians in Britain acquiesced, though at the time their leadership would probably have considered the readership of

9

the *Daily Worker* (as it was still called) more to their taste than that of *The Times*.

The newspaper itself accepted our proposals for the League to sponsor a feature. This was by no means a foregone conclusion, despite *The Times'* natural enthusiasm for the additional revenue which it represented. But the contract was agreed, with the unusual proviso that each page should carry the rubric 'Advertisement', a condition which appeared not to have been applied in other cases of a feature with a political content. Further, *The Times* required a 'box' to appear prominently at the head of the first page of the supplement which carried this remarkable and, as far as I know, unprecedented disclaimer, 'These pages are a political advertisement sponsored by the London Office of the League of Arab States. *The Times* has accepted its publication in accordance with its traditional policy, but does not vouch for any of the facts or opinions expressed.'

This statement, which if it appeared in a less distinguished context, might well seem to be distinctly mealy-mouthed not to say time-serving, was supported by yet another, also appearing on the first page: 'The authors of these articles have accepted the invitation of the London Office of the League of Arab States to contribute to this feature.'

The Times, apparently seeking to distance itself from a major editorial feature appearing in its own pages, had clearly become quite paranoid about the whole enterprise; this did not, however, prevent them from feeling able to accept the Arab League's cheque. To all of *The Times'* conditions, though they were, to say the least, unusual, the League, again on our advice, agreed.

The Times asked us to propose the names of writers who would be acceptable to the League and to submit an editorial outline. This we did and it was agreed without marked discussion, since the League was at pains to present its case in a manner which would be acceptable to *The Times'* readers. Many of the contributors were active in CAABU; several were amongst its founders and all were distinguished in their particular fields.

As the date of publication neared I was invited to call on the Editor, at *The Times'* offices, then still located in Printing House Square. I went to see him, accompanied by one of my colleagues. The Editor was seated, almost too much in character, in a rocking chair, in which he rocked himself sedulously throughout the interview; it was as though Central Casting had been asked to provide an appropriate *mise-en-scène* for the Editor of the world's most prestigious daily newspaper. He asked me, with considerable courtesy, if I would in turn ask the League to forego the publication of the feature which was planned; I enquired why it was considered appropriate to put such a request to an advertiser. I received no clear reason why the League should give up a promotion of its case, by which it placed some store. I said that of course that I would convey the Editor's request to the League, but that I would feel bound to advise them against agreeing to it.

The Editor then, in a voice which, if it had come from other lips might have been thought to have been heavy with menace, asked me to inform the proposed contributors, all of them men distinguished in public life or in their professional fields, that, if their names appeared in the proposed supplement, they would never again be asked to contribute to *The Times*. I invited the Editor to repeat or perhaps to withdraw this, to me, startling statement; he declined to do either. We withdrew with mutual expressions of regard.

The Editor went on to achieve respectability as an antiquarian bookseller and celebrity as Chairman of the Arts Council. I returned to my office and at once wrote a record of the meeting, a copy of which no doubt lies somewhere in the League's archives to this day. The contributors were all honourable men and, predictably, none of them was influenced by the Editor's curious request. Equally predictably, none of them was victimised in the way that the Editor had chosen to suggest might be the case.

The Times' fears had been prompted, evidently, by some of their larger advertisers whose sympathies lay with Israel, having got wind of the supplement and threatening to withdraw their advertising support from the paper if *The Times* was so ill-advised as to allow the presentation of a point of view on Palestine other than that promoted by Israel and its supporters. To the best of my knowledge that threat was not carried into effect either. In the event the supplement appeared to general approval.[4]

Another episode involving *The Times* is perhaps worth recounting for it may go some way to compensate for the otherwise rather negative impression which this anecdote might convey. The paper is, after all, a journal which has often taken a clear and objective line in reporting the affairs of the Middle East.

In August 1969 a man, described somewhat exotically as 'a deranged Australian', was arrested in Jerusalem and accused of attempting to set fire to the Haram as-Sherif, the Dome of the Rock, the third of Islam's most sacred shrines. The Arabs were generally sceptical of the Australian's involvement, as much as they were of his alleged derangement. The League consulted my colleagues and I as to what course of action they might take, to bring home the horror and distress which this act of sacrilege had provoked in the Muslim world. We suggested that, to ensure that they got their message across accurately and without distortion (a condition which could not otherwise always be relied upon) they should take advertising space to relate the story of the Mosque's desecration.

Showing what might be thought to be considerable forebearance we proposed, and the League accepted, that the advertisement should appear in *The Times*. This time there was no objection from the paper. The full-page advertisement which we prepared appeared,[5] and if it roused anger amongst other of *The Times* advertisers, we did not hear of it.

What we did not know was that the advertising industry at that time promoted annual awards for outstanding advertisements. To our considerable surprise and pleasure our advertisement on the burning of the Mosque won an award. Its inclusion amongst the winners must also have surprised some of the other advertisers, who would not generally have been accustomed to advertising critical of Israel appearing in Britain's leading daily newspaper, and being commended by a panel drawn from the industry itself.

At this time I had become accustomed to being on the receiving end of threatening telephone calls. One caller regularly telephoned my flat in Arlington House, often whilst I was at lunch; for reasons best known to himself he usually addressed me as 'Monty Rice' and expatiated on what he felt to be the reasons for my concerning myself with the Arab case. He had, apparently, read my defence of the Arab case, and didn't like it. From time to time similar calls would be received at my office; a bomb had been planted in the basement, we were told, and my staff were in consequence at mortal risk. We learned to treat these and similar occasions with contempt, though this did not diminish the distaste which such behaviour aroused.

But this is all long in the past. My concern with the Middle East over more recent years has largely been the planning of museums in the Arabian peninsula states and, more generally, with the development of the practice of archaeology in the Gulf and Saudi Arabia, making the region more accessible both to scholarly as much as to lay audiences.

My involvement with the Arab world has extended over much of the lifetime of the State of Israel. I have travelled widely, listened and observed. I have lived through the events of 1967, the War of 1973, which marked a very significant change in the fortunes of Israel, and the catastrophe of the invasion of Lebanon. No longer was Israel believed to be invincible, no longer were its politicians seen as men of exceptional skill and power. Gradually the image which Israel had achieved over the previous generation and on the fabrication of which the state and its protagonists had expended such effort and so much treasure, began to crack and dissolve.

The invasion of Lebanon, prompted by that ageing, bitter high-priest of urban terrorism, Menachem Begin, resulted in a further substantial change in Israel's fortunes in the larger political world. For the first time Israel's policies were no longer to be concealed and it became evident, even to its most besotted supporters, that its actions were far removed from the lofty moral virtues which its protagonists had always claimed for it.[6] As a consequence, the history of the Israeli state as a whole was subjected to more scrutiny than it had ever been before and a sorry record of duplicity, exploitation and deceit was brought increasingly into the light.

In recent times, no circumstance has more directly put the policies of Israel under intense scrutiny than has the *intifada*,[7] the uprising of ordinary Palestinians in the Occupied Territories. The daily record of repression and killings, though it would provoke world-wide outrage had it occurred in, say, South Africa or in a country under communist domination, at least raised distaste and dismay amongst many of Israel's supporters, including very many Jews both inside and outside Israel.

The *intifada* came about at a time when the nature of the confrontation between the Palestinians and the State of Israel changed profoundly. The factors which contributed to this change were several and various. First, there was the with-drawal of the Egyptians from direct military confrontation with Israel which, though it happened years rather than months ago, must yet be considered as part of the process of essential change. The withdrawal of Egypt effectively put a stop to a situation which had persisted since the foundation of the Israeli state in 1948; more than any other single event it reduced Israel's political credibility internationally, for she lost at a stroke the one enemy to which she might always convincingly point as most threatening to her survival.

More recent still was the change of political direction by Russia and the remarkable series of convulsions in Eastern Europe. The Soviet Union had always seen the tensions in the Middle East as worth sustaining, since its principal opponent on the international chess board, the United States, was clearly so inextricably identified with the State of Israel that Russia felt bound, both by inclination and by the dictates of self-interest, to assume the part of the Palestinians. But suddenly a new posture was adopted by Russia; no longer could revolutionary regimes or liberation movements around the world depend upon Russian support, merely because they declared themselves to be revolutionary, or committed to the cause of liberation. All at once the Russians realised that the world is now too small to allow two great powers to be drawn into a conflict which, in this case, is not primarily of their own making, because of ideology or the hectoring of a small people, demanding support and increasingly costly aid. Whilst at first sight the radical Arab regimes might seem to be the losers by the Russian change of position, in reality it was Israel's position which was weakened for she was no longer able to present herself as the only credible Middle Eastern alternative to an otherwise general tendency for the Arab world to embrace communism. Despite the idea's patent improbability the Israelis, with extraordinary skill, had managed to persuade the Americans and not a few Europeans (who really ought to have known better) of the plausibility of this fatuous assertion.

However, one dangerous element remained in the aftermath of the apparent collapse of international Marxism as a force binding together Russia and those states which have been her clients. Whilst the United States remained firmly entrenched behind Israel (though under the Bush administration it was possible to detect some qualification of the otherwise unreserved support which America had been expected to bring to Israel),

14

the Arab states would seem to have no super-power godfather to stake their claims to justice in Palestine.

The most significant development in this confrontation between the two antagonists was a purely local one, when the Palestinians, after decades of the most incompetent political management of their affairs, took their direction, quite literally, into their own hands. The *intifada*, an exceptionally well disciplined uprising which in its origins owed little to the manipulations of politicians, proved the undoing of Israel, since no state so dependent on external support can allow itself to be seen as set upon the destruction of a desperate people whose front line is composed of stone-throwing children.

The 1988 election in Israel which coincided with these complex and often perplexing events resulted, as it was almost bound to do, in an impasse. In its aftermath, having learned the rudiments of political wisdom, the Palestinians seized the occasion to proclaim the creation of a Palestinian State and to declare that state's preparedness to recognise the right of all states in the region to a settled and peaceful existence, and to renounce the use of terrorist tactics.[8]

This declaration by the Palestine Liberation Organisation, at that point the undeniable representative of the Palestinian people, was in line with the position which it had been evolving since the early 1970s. It was, predictably, greeted by Israel with contumely and abuse; such was to be expected. But it changed radically the position of many pieces on the board of the deathly game in which the two principals were engaged. Israel was reduced to asserting that, despite whatever the Palestinians might say, they still really believed in the destruction of Israel. The Palestinians, in their turn, found themselves having to connive in the occupation of their land and thus for the first time giving some legal substance to Israel's occupation of it.

It would have been a bold political commentator who, twelve months before this happening, would have predicted such a constellation of events, or even any combination of them. As a result of their occurrence, however, the situation in the Middle East was entirely turned upside down; the dimensions of the crisis which the Middle East had faced since the creation of the State of Israel were never to be the same again.

However, it is well to remember that, although the political environment has changed profoundly, the realities remain the same. There is still a large dispossessed body of Palestinian nationals driven from their homeland, which is occupied by a people whose title to occupation is, in the view of this writer, wholly without historical or legal validity. There is still a powerful pro-Israel lobby in America, rallying support for a government in Israel which not only occupies territories seized in war but which also permits, in arrogant disregard of clearly defined international law, the existence of settlements in these lands by its own nationals. There are still the appalling refugee camps, filled with the most unfortunate of all Israel's victims – those that are still living, at least. Above all, there remains unaltered the profound sense of deprivation and humiliation experienced by Arabs of all classes and nationalities at the continued occupation of Arab land by predominantly European settlers. No matter what may be the short-term changes which may be produced by the PLO's declaration and Israel's eventual response to it, the attitude of the settlers to the Palestinians will not change.

What follows here is an attempt to review the historical and political factors which seem to me to have remained constant and which underlie this tense and dismal situation. It attempts, however tentatively, to indicate the essential conditions which must precede the prospect of establishing a lasting solution and sets out some of the conditions by which such a solution might be realised. It will not make comfortable, nor in many cases acceptable reading, perhaps to most of the parties involved. Further, writers who set themselves up to pronounce on matters of the day may find that events and situations which they seek to analyse have an uncomfortable habit of rearing up, as it were, and knocking away all the careful structures which have been erected to support whatever contention it is that the writers may be disposed to advance. A revolution, a modest local war or the unforeseen actions of an unpredictable tyrant can undo years of patient research and thoughtful analysis. The latest developments are a cogent witness of this principle.

When the Iraqis invaded Kuwait, a country with which I had had little to do professionally but which had an important part in the Gulf's ancient history and about which I had written, I was naturally enough concerned for the safety and welfare of my friends in other parts of the peninsula. The Arab world was convulsed, its loyalties and political instincts torn all ways; for once, doubtless because their own vital interests were involved, the world community reacted with something approaching unanimity in condemning Iraq's annexation of a harmless neighbouring state. The United States, its allies and some of the more mature Arab states acted swiftly to send what soon amounted to a formidable defensive force to Saudi Arabia; there can be little doubt that by so doing they baulked the plans of the Iraqis for further opportunistic expansion in the Gulf, however carelessly assembled – for seldom can so great a threat to the peace of an important part of the world have been put together with such blinding incompetance as were Iraq's plans for the annexation of Kuwait.

However, it was not only the most besotted protagonists of the Palestinian cause who enquired why the world had not reacted with the same rapid purposefulness when Israel entered southern Lebanon, arguing, just as Iraq did, that her own vital interests made such an excursion necessary. More voices were raised to enquire why the world community had been prepared to allow Israel to remain in occupation of lands seized after the War of 1967, despite the repeated and universal condemnation of such action by the United Nations and practically every other political assembly of substance anywhere in the world, with the exception of the Congress of the United States.[9] Very quickly Western leaders began to speak of the necessity for trying to resolve all the disputes in the region, not merely the invasion of Kuwait. First amongst these issues was the question of the relationship between the Israelis and the Palestinians.

As the often confusing and unpredictable events of the early weeks of the Kuwait crisis evolved it became clear to me, as it did to many other observers, that the invasion of Kuwait threw into the sharpest of relief the fragility of the political structures of the Middle East as a whole. This characteristic fragility was the consequence of some singularly uninspired politicising by the European powers in the aftermath of the First World War, as irresponsible a record of interference as was the creation of the Israeli state after the Second.[10]

It now seems to be inescapable that whilst the presence of Israel as an alien implant in the Middle East (a contention argued with some vigour in these pages) is the root cause of much of the instability which has plagued the area in the past forty years, and sets at risk the vital interests of much of the industrialised world, it is not the only issue which urgently demands resolution. The events in the northern reaches of the Gulf have shown that issues such as the proper concerns of the oil-consuming nations, the question of national boundaries from Lebanon to the Shatt al-Arab, the role of nation-states in the region and their relationship with their other more recent peers, the issue of consensus government and the expression of dissent in societies which have no history of such awkward political imperatives, all need to be faced and resolved. The invasion of Kuwait may have served, like no other occasion in recent times, to throw these and other similar issues into sharper relief.

Whatever is the eventual outcome of the crisis in the Gulf the pieces are not going to fall again in precisely the same order that they did before the invasion. Unwittingly Saddam Hussein may have done us all a service in reminding those of us who ought to have known better of the realities of politics in the Middle East.

It will be the conclusion of this survey that the invasion of Kuwait and its aftermath will be seen, when the histories are written, as absolutely crucial in bringing about a sea-change in the affairs of the Middle East. Saddam demanded 'linkage' of the withdrawal from Kuwait with the withdrawal of the Israelis from the Occupied Territories. This was, of course, simply the most cynical opportunism, but the readiness of the Israelis now to speak with the PLO, however reluctantly, is, I believe, the direct result of the recognition that the crisis in the Gulf revealed how marginal had Israel become to the interests of the industrialised world, including the United States. This point will recur in this narrative.

In attempting to bring what I have written about Palestine into the context of recent events in the Gulf, one awkward factor has to be counted into the equation. The persistent reader will discover that I believe that reparation must be made to the Palestinians for the occupation of their land by Israel. The argument is not immediately likely to be a popular one. Its prospects for ready acceptance have hardly been improved by the stance adopted by the Palestinians themselves in responding to the crisis in the Gulf. After some prevarication in the first days after Iraq's invasion of Kuwait, the official leadership of the Palestinian Liberation Organisation declared itself in full support of President Saddam Hussein and his annexation of Kuwait. This dismayed many of the Palestinians' supporters, for three principal reasons.

First, there was the evident absurdity of the organisation which was supposed to exist to achieve the recovery of land seized, according to their most basic tenets, by a ruthless oppressor, acquiescing in the seizure of another people's land by an oppressor as ruthless. No amount of rationalisation could conceal this abdication of high principle, certainly not the entirely specious arguments of an historic claim to Kuwait which Iraq advanced and which the Palestinians so readily and uncritically accepted. Then, second, there was the altogether unworthy rejection of all the Kuwaitis, and other Gulf states, had contributed to the Palestinian cause over the years. Palestine has indeed been the Arab cause par excellence, but it is not the only object for the use of the oil-producing states' revenues. The abuse which some parts of the Palestinian leadership poured on the Kuwaitis and other Gulf benefactors was disgraceful and it will be a long time before the Arabs of the peninsula, though they are not a people to harbour grudges, will entirely forget the dereliction of the Palestinians, whom they had so often supported, in their own time of crisis.

Third, there was the unhappy spectacle of the Palestinians allying themselves with Saddam Hussein in the belief that he would somehow effect the liberation of Palestine and, in the process, share the revenues of the Gulf oil producers with its people. If they really believed either of these propositions then the Palestinian leadership had learned nothing after decades of being tossed about as the plaything of whatever dictator or demagogue happened to rise to power in the region.

This, indeed, is the lesson of the Kuwait crisis, as it touches Palestine and its people. The leadership of the Palestinian people is rightly vested in the Palestine Liberation Organisation; it must be questioned, however, whether the leadership itself is of a quality either to direct an armed struggle, which past experience would suggest that it is not, or to have the foresight and political skill to represent its people in the complex, demanding and often publicly unrewarding negotiations which are still the most enduring way in which to achieve political change. The inevitable rising to the surface of the Palestinian guerrilla or terrorist groups (call them what you will) demonstrated again the almost limitless capacity which Middle Eastern communities have for bombast and empty rhetoric on the one hand and, on the other, mindless violence, invariably more damaging to their own cause than to their enemy. In this, they are only too similar to other 'liberation' movements spawned out of urban despair or the political misjudgements of the past.

But none of the irresponsibilities of the Palestinians themselves must be allowed to obscure the absolute justice of their cause. Nothing can alter the fact that they have been betrayed, dispossessed and exposed to a cruel and unwarranted persecution.

It is a matter of the greatest significance that in the ill-omened negotiations which have been held on the relations between the Palestinians and the Israelis in the aftermath of the conflict, the Palestinian delegation has conducted itself with such distinction and authority. It has won every public confrontation with the Israelis; it has dominated the media reporting of the events. It has aroused the thus far impotent fury of the Israeli spokesmen who have seen their previously unquestioned management of the international media melting away as swiftly as the snows in summer. No longer, indeed never again, will Israel's assertions be accepted as anything other than partial expressions of view.

Israel is in an unhappy case. She may try to draw comfort from the upheavals in the Arab world which the crisis has induced, but it will now be clear that as a consequence of the Iraqi-Kuwaiti crisis, Israel is seen to be simply no longer relevant to the West in the way that once she was. The centre of affairs has shifted from the eastern Mediterranean eastwards and south. Israel is now marginal to the United States and the nations of the West. It will be of less and less importance to the West to maintain a European enclave in that part of the Near or Middle East, the more so if its presence, especially as an exclusivist Jewish state, is in danger – as indeed it must be – of acting as a continuing provocation to the Arab population, on whose goodwill, to a greater extent, the industrialised world will long rely for the uninterrupted flow of its principal energy supplies.

Observing the course of the world's reaction to Iraq's invasion of Kuwait, it is inevitable that, given the way that I have earned my living for most of my adult life, I should reflect upon the role which propaganda and the manipulation of the media plays in the contemporary political world. My reflections are neither comforting nor particularly elevating. Now that I have turned more to writing for myself rather than for others I have recovered a concern for words and for their own fragile integrity which the preoccupations of politics do not invariably respect. Language is a delicate instrument. In the dispute of the Arabs with Israel it has been obliged sometimes to undergo the most remarkable and indelicate contortions.

As this book is intensely critical of the part which Israel has played in the politics of the Middle East over the past four decades, and still more critical of Zionism, the philosophy in the name of which so much of it has been carried out, no doubt I will be represented as an inveterate and unrepentant anti-semite. I deal at some length with the abuse – as it seems to me – meted out to language (an innocent victim if ever there was one) in the dispute and of the generous, even extravagant, use which is made of the term 'anti-semite' and its cognates. It is inevitable that I shall be so described, I suppose; I can only shrug sadly and reflect that those who know me and for whose opinions I care will know that I am in no sense whatsoever anti-Jewish, but remain unashamedly anti-Zionist. I have, let it be said, a profound and invincible contempt for the sort of prejudice which judges any man by considerations other than of the ways in which he behaves towards his fellows.

Similarly, I recognise that there will be some people who regard the Bible as the revealed word of an eternally existing god. Such people will be persuaded of the validity of the Jewish claim to be the Chosen People, the Elect of God, to whom, by a covenant between them and Himself, was awarded the land of Palestine and indeed other lands, 'from the Great River to the brook of Egypt'. It will be readily apparent that I do not share that particular view of the world; it seems to me inconceivable that political attitudes today should take as their justification the myths of a small congeries of tribes living in the Near East in the first millennium BC. *Inconceivable*, but yet that is the essential substance of the Israeli claim to rights of occupation in the land which was once Palestine.

Whilst I was preparing the final text of this book, and at the point when I had decided to include a chapter commenting on the anomalies of the archaeological record as manipulated by Israel – and, in consequence, the often highly imaginative way that archaeology had been used to give support to the alleged

21

historicity of the Bible and hence to the Zionist claim to the land of Israel, four books appeared which were especially pertinent to this theme. The Bible, as might indeed be expected from any anthology of folk-tales, myth, poetry and the ill-digested record of historical incident, is shown to be a rich amalgam of muddle, contradiction, anachronisms, misunderstanding and blatant inaccuracy. That this remarkable mélange is expressed in highly poetic language (especially in its English recension) does nothing for its historical value, though much for its acceptance.

One of the works concerned, indeed, had been in print for some time; this was *The Unauthorised Version* by Robin Lane-Fox. Proceeding from the standpoint of a non-believer, Lane-Fox developed an exhaustive, detailed and compelling critique of the essentially literary character of the Judeo-Christian Bible. He demonstrated the inconsistencies and the frequent downright manufacturing of evidence which have been taken into the historiographical apparatus of what has come to be called 'Biblical archaeology'.

At a more popular level and using much of the material on which a successful television series was based, the writer John Romer, well known for his readily communicated Egyptological works, similarly shows that the books of the Old Testament was essentially collections of myth. Both Lane-Fox and Romer were persuaded of the late authorship of the majority of the books of the Old Testament, compiled as we know them to be long after the events which they purport to record had occurred: those, that is, that had some basis in historical reality – a small proportion, in fact, and generally of relative insignificance. The great themes of the Old Testament – the Creation, Abraham's journey, the sojourn in Egypt, the Exodus – are shown to be literary inventions of scribal authors writing, for the most part, in the seventh century BC and later.

Then two candidly academic works, though published in book form and hence available to the non-academic reader as well as to scholars specialising in the disciplines concerned, carried still further the demolition of the argument for the historicity of the Bible and for the early history of Israel which it has been purported to represent.

Donald B. Redford's *Egypt, Canaan and Israel in Ancient Times* (Princeton, 1992) takes as its starting point the relationship of Egypt, from predynastic times to the Assyrian period, with its neighbours to the east and north. In particular he focuses on the 'Asiatics' to whom Egyptian texts frequently refer, with robust disparagement.

Redford's review of the ancient history of the Near East is taken from an Egyptian perspective; he demonstrates that virtually nothing in the Egyptian records and certainly nothing in the archaeology of Egypt lends any support to the existence of a significant group who could be identified with the people of the Bible stories or with a powerful 'Kingdom' in Palestine in Late Bronze Age times, the supposed period of the Davidic and Solomonic Kingdoms. He suggests that the idea of the presence of a body of semitic-speakers in Egypt descends from imperfectly recalled memories of the rule of the so-called 'Hyksos' kings, the fifteenth and sixteenth dynasties in Egyptian chronology, who were in origin semitic-speakers and who probably came from Palestine and whose memory, probably unfairly, was long execrated by the Egyptians.

He expresses the situation concisely when he observes that 'in our sources, both Egyptian and west Asian, there are virtually no references to Israel, its coagents or Biblical associates prior to the twelfth century BC; and beyond that point for four centuries, a mere half dozen allusions can be elicited' (p. 257). He is dismissive of the attempt to equate a foreign people known in the Egyptian texts of the New Kingdom (mid-second millennium BC) as the 'Apiru' with the Hebrews. This identification, once widely held, is now generally discredited. Towards the conclusion of *Egypt, Canaan and Israel in Ancient Times* Redford examines what he describes as 'Four Great Origin Traditions'; he concludes that Genesis, the story of Joseph in Egypt, the Sojourn of the Israelites in Egypt and the Exodus are all literary inventions, the product of post-Exilic mythologising. Redford demonstrates the fragility of the arguments advanced to support the historical nature of many of the Bible stories by suggesting that questions similar to those posed in a Biblical context should be addressed to resolving the Arthurian legends. The example is, of course, exact (p. 261).

The second substantial scholarly work to go over similar ground is Thomas Thompson's *The Early History of the Israelite People* (E. J. Brill, Leiden, 1992). Like Redford, Thompson sees the appearance of the Israelite nation as a post-Exilic phenomenon, the product of the policies of the Persian Empire. He argues that after the Babylonian captivity, the peoples who were brought in to populate Jerusalem and the land around it were a mixture of different ethnic and cultural groups, drawn from all those who were transported to Babylon. He believes that the first temple was built at the initiative of the Persians who wanted Jerusalem to become an important regional centre; it was their custom to encourage the building of temples to important local divinities and into this category Yahweh was seen to fit.

Thompson sees no archaeological evidence for the existence of important population or cult centres at Jerusalem or in its vicinity in the late Bronze Age. He considers Jerusalem insignificant until the seventh century BC (from which period the oldest archaeological remains seem actually to descend); consequently he believes that kings such as David and Solomon never existed, but were conflations of legendary figures given life by the authors of the books of the Old Testament, written after the Exile in an attempt to provide a coherent historical pedigree for those who 'returned'.

Both writers are critical of many of their predecessors in the disciplines with which they are concerned; in a number of cases their comments are distinctly tart. Albright, who did so much to promote the idea of Biblical studies as a specific branch of Near Eastern archaeology and who contributed greatly to the acceptance of the idea of the historicity of much of the Bible, is particularly the target of both writers' criticism.

It is not, of course, the purpose either of Redford or of Thompson to discredit specifically the devices which have been used to give the modern State of Israel, and the people for whom it was created, an historical ancestry in Palestine. However, their work and that of the many other scholars who are now examining the ancient history of Palestine objectively and not from the standpoint of ideological, religious or political preconceptions, is beginning radically to change our understanding of the Bible and, hence, of the stories which it contained. The consequence is, of course, the same: the essential argument upon which the Zionists based their claim to the land of Palestine lies in ruins, though not, it must be said, of the archaeological kind.

No state can predicate its existence and its acceptance in the world community solely or principally on the basis of a collection of myths. No one should attempt to deny the importance of myth in determining attitudes of mind and, most particularly, in the development of the individual personality. But to employ a mélange of myth, most of which can be traced to originals not much earlier than the first millennium BC as the basis on which a claim to territory is justified and, hence, to political recognition by the international community in the second half of the twentieth century AD, is, to put no finer point on it, bizarre. For one community, supported by such arguments, to be permitted to dispossess another is perverse and wholly at variance with the principles of government and the rights of peoples which the world community, however uncertainly, is seeking to realise.

Much of what I argue here will be distasteful to many, wholly unacceptable to not a few, and to some preposterous. Some of the elements of the solution which I advance here will similarly be dismissed as outrageous or absurd. To propose that Israel, the Jewish state, must be de-Zionised if lasting peace is to have a chance will be, I know, greeted by some with derision, as a political impossibility. Yet who, only a few years ago, would have predicted the collapse of communism and the disintegration of the Soviet empire? After that event, all options are possible.

I can only stand by what I have written, with the assertion that I believe what I have written as much as I believe that it needed to be said. If it is written with any eventual reader in mind it is for those who will have a part in the process, now begun as a result of events not in Palestine but in the Gulf, which *might* lead to a resolution of the crisis. All who will be concerned with devising a solution and those who will comment on it, in the media or in political assemblies, must take into account the historical realities and the political imperatives which will determine the attitudes of the Arabs, not only of the Palestinians, perhaps for generations to come.

I can speak of the Arabs with the access of friendship; I have presumed to speak somewhat of the possible attitudes of the Jews of Oriental origin, now living in Israel and drawn predominantly from Arab lands, with whom I have no comparable acquaintance. However, if my book has a conclusion which is in any sense optimistic it is that the Arabs of Palestine and the Oriental Jews differ only in their religious allegiance; in all other essential respects, including that most important of all cultural factors, language, they are effectively branches of the same

25

people. Left to themselves these two communities may represent the only hope for the troubled land in which they now find themselves together, as the third millennium of our era comes into prospect.

I have avoided the temptation to review the course of Arab-Israeli relations in detail, the early wars in the immediate aftermath of Israel's foundation, the deplorable collusion of Israel, France and Britain in the invasion of Egypt at the time of the Suez crisis in 1956, the Six Day War in 1967, the War of 1973, the shameful invasion of Lebanon and all the other dismal events which are the direct consequence of the implantation of a body of European immigrants in the Levant. These events and their implications are described and commented upon in countless books, many written by commentators more qualified than I to judge such issues.[11]

I have tried to understand how it is that Israel appears as the spectre at the feast (a not altogether happy phrase) in every crisis or dramatic turn of events in the Middle East. It happens again now, as I write this in the aftermath of the events in the Gulf, even in so peripheral and grotesque a happening as the death of Robert Maxwell who, after a lifetime of unrepentant and public villainy was treated to a state funeral in Jerusalem. If I have any hope for this text it is that it might act as the voice of the many who feel as I do, at a time when there is at least the prospect of a reassessment of the disastrous policies of the post-war period, and to give expression to the mounting sense, compounded of disbelief, horror and distress at Israeli ruthlessness and intransigence, which so many around the world now experience. I have not tried to give a cool and carefully measured exegesis that would be fair to every side, in every detail, but to advance a purely subjective response to the lies and confusions which have become the currency of the debate over Palestine. Above all I have sought to demonstrate why it is vital at this particular juncture that the Palestinians be not coerced or pressured into conceding vital parts of their patrimony, for if they do, as surely as the night follows the day, the outcome will be a still more bitter, sustained and cruel conflict at some time in the future. Equally, they must not be coerced into accepting any settlement which is less than justice demands and that the arguments of history require.

It is well to consider one's own motivations when approaching a matter of such complexity and intensity of emotional content. I have become exasperated over the years by the example of great injustice being inflicted on a people who have done nothing to deserve it or anything like it, but as a consequence of the exploitation of what I see as a corpus of outmoded and irrelevant beliefs, whose adherants have perpetrated more suffering and anguish than any other group of whom I can think, the Mongols included. Then, too, I resent – and the paradox will not escape those who care to note it – the disparagement of a people of noble achievement, whose contribution to history is set at no value merely because they take a position which counters Israel's in this dispute. That seems to me to be wholly wrong and, whilst I am not so simple as to believe that anything that I may write will make any substantive difference, at least I can tell myself that I have made the attempt.

The arguments of this book may be summarised in the following terms. There is no warrant, of history, law or simple morality for the implantation of a Jewish population, predominantly European in its origins, in the land of Palestine. Only by accepting the de-Zionisation of Israel and the creation of a cantonal or federal structure in which Israel, Palestine and the Kingdom of Jordan are linked can peace be given even the most modest chance of being accomplished.

Further, if the Palestinian people, represented by the PLO or any other body acknowledged by the majority, is persuaded to accept something less than what must be recognised as essential conditions for a just settlement then, at some time in the future the Arab states, though they are heartily tired now of the confrontation with Israel, will again demand restitution, through the means perhaps of a Saddam Hussein of the future, one who is more skilled in war and politically more competent.

There is a clear sense in which the process of the de-Zionisation of Israel has already begun. The Jews of Oriental origin now living in Israel, the Sephardim, who are now moving inexorably towards forming the majority in the state, have few, if any historical links with political Zionism, their experience of its imperatives largely being confined to what they have learned or endured since they migrated from the Arab lands in which they had lived for so many centuries.

The Oriental Jews in Israel have been subjected to great pressures over the past forty years, many of them profoundly destabilising. They have been manipulated by the European settlers to maintain tensions between the Israeli communities and the Palestinians. The animosity which manifests itself between Oriental communities and the Palestinians is not, however, primarily ideological, as is much more the case between the Ashkenazi community and the Palestinians. Violence, when it occurs between the Orientals and the Palestinians, is more likely to be over land, jobs or the pressures which explode when groups of disadvantaged people encounter each other.

If the Orientals do indeed form the majority of the Jewish population of Israel by the year 2000, which seems now certain, then it should not be impossible (it will not of course be easy) to give meaning to the process of extracting Israel from its dangerous and corrupting identification with Zionism.[12] With the Orientals representing the majority of the Jewish population of Palestine, and a more pragmatic approach to policy-making and political action amongst the Palestinians, there could be at least the beginnings of a solution in the creation of a political structure which would have the effect of bringing the prospects of peace amongst the several communities.

It will be said that in international disputes there are no solutions, only compromises. That is as may be, but this book represents a different view; it asserts that, unless there is the most ruthless appraisal of the realities of the situation, seeing it as it really is and not as it has been presented, with all the received myths being stripped away, there is no prospect of a lasting settlement.

I am neither so simple-minded nor so arrogant as to believe that I can dispose of an issue which has bewildered politicians, academic commentators of all sorts and even persons of simple good faith, for so long as the matter of Palestine and Israel. The sheer complexity of the political manoeuvring, over a century and more, the scale of the issues at stake and the sensitivity of the interests involved, all conspire to give any sensible person pause. Despite this evident truth I have written what I have written in the belief that there is some merit, sometimes, in articulating what many believe but few, for whatever reason, are inclined to say.

I am conscious, none more so, that small boys who point out the lack of the Emperor's clothes are unlikely to be thanked for doing so.

2

ZIONISM AND THE WORLD COMMUNITY

The achievement of the Zionist ambition, the creation of a state for the Jews in which they might live as one amongst the community of nations, was the consequence of a long, sustained and skilful campaign conducted over many years. It culminated in a series of actions perpetrated by or through the medium of the United Nations.

The United Nations, which acted as midwife to Israel at the moment of its birth, had come into existence, like its ill-fated predecessor the League of Nations, to ensure the peace, prosperity and stability of the nations of the world. In 1947–8, in those years immediately after the end of the Second World War when perhaps it had its best opportunity to change the course of history for the benefit of humankind, it lent its prestige and authority to a travesty of justice against a small and wholly defenceless people. Seeking to meet the demands for a Jewish state it proposed the partition of Palestine, and in so doing committed itself to the handing over of land which had immemorially belonged to one people to another, wholly alien people, European settlers, who had no claim to it of any substance.

It must be said with all proper emphasis that the United Nations had neither the legal authority nor the political right so to dispose of any part of the Palestinians' land to an invasion of newcomers. Such action had no warrant, either in law or in history. It was the more shameful in that the United Nations had been created to protect the rights of small peoples, to permit their independent survival not their elimination. The vote which resulted in the recommendation to partition Palestine, which in turn led directly to the proclamation of the State of Israel, was entirely without legal force or authority.

29

The United Nations in 1948, when it was responsible for Israel's creation, was a profoundly different body from that which it became subsequently. In 1948 it had 56 members; most of Africa, much of Asia and large portions of the still surviving colonial empires had no place in its Assembly.

The United Nations Resolution of 29 November 1947 must be examined here, by reason of its subsequent use as a warrant by Israel to justify the terms of its existence. As the years have gone by Israel's political leaders have, understandably, preferred to invoke that Resolution than the folk-tales of a special election by a God in whom few of them actually believed. The full text of the Resolution is set out in Appendix 2.

The nature of what actually happened in the United Nations General Assembly in November 1947 needs to be understood clearly, as do the positions subsequently adopted by the Israelis and their supporters on the one hand and the Palestinians and theirs on the other. The first card in the game was dealt by Britain in April 1947, in a letter asking that the matter of Palestine be placed on the agenda of the General Assembly. The Arab states – Egypt, Iraq, Syria, Yemen and Saudi Arabia – asked that at a special session to be called to prepare for the General Assembly, an item to be added to the agenda which called for the termination of the Mandate, hitherto held by Britain since the years after the end of the Great War, and the declaration of Palestine's independence. This request was voted down by the General Committee of the Assembly. However, it did appear for discussion by the General Assembly in May 1947. It was again voted down, though this time by the narrowest of margins (24 to 15, with 10 abstentions). Had this proposal by the Arab states, so early in the game, been accepted, the history of the last forty years would have been very different. But it was not to be.

Britain having renounced the Mandate, a succession of committees was held to study various aspects of the issue and to make recommendations for consideration by the General Assembly. Eventually two plans were put forward; the first was for Partition with Economic Union.[1] This divided Palestine into an Arab state, a Jewish state (it is to be noted that 'Arab' and 'Jewish' are used as analogues, though one has a quite different value from the other) with Jerusalem as an internationalised city

30

and with its environs placed under United Nations jurisdiction. The divisions of land between the two states would be:

- the Arab State, 4,476 square miles or 42.88 per cent of the total;
- the Jewish State 5,893 square miles or 56.47 per cent;
- Jerusalem accounted for 0.65 per cent of the total.

The most extraordinary circumstance of the Partition Plan, however, was that actual Jewish land ownership at the time, even within the territory of the proposed Jewish State, was less than 10 per cent of the total. The Arabs, according to this plan, were thus being asked to acquiesce in the handing over a majority of the land in their ownership to alien, European immigrants.

The second plan, which came to be known as the Federal State Plan, was supported by only a minority of the drafting committee appointed to study the issue.[2] By this plan, an independent State of Palestine would be established, divided into a Jewish and an Arab state with Jerusalem as its capital. The responsibilities of the federal and state governments were to be divided, with the federal government being responsible for matters such as defence, foreign affairs, immigration, currency, waterways, transport and communications.

The Zionists, untiring in lobbying and in exerting pressure on anyone with even a marginal involvement with the committee, received the plan for Partition with enthusiasm; they recognised that it gave them almost all that they wanted at the outset of their aspirations to nationhood. The Arabs rejected both plans: the Partition Plan because of its patently unfair terms and the Federal solution because that too accepted the principle of the partition of their homeland, at the behest of foreigners for the benefit of foreigners.

The Palestinians clearly had no alternative: the choice which they were being offered involved the dismemberment of their land, whichever way they looked at it. Though they had resisted any and all attempts to solve Europe's Jewish problems by the expedient of handing over their land to Jewish immigrants, they lacked the political influence within the United Nations to counter the Zionist pressure which was soon to achieve such spectacular results.

The Great Powers, the United States, Russia and France were evidently already determined on the Partition Plan; China's position was uncertain. Britain remained in the background, in a posture of sadly characteristic ambivalence.

Although Britain had precipitated the situation in bringing the Mandate back to the UN, the policy of the relatively untried Labour government of the day was less resolute than might have been expected of it. The Foreign Secretary, Ernest Bevin, was deeply unhappy about the Partition Plan and, it is clear, himself opposed the movement towards an independent Jewish state in Palestine. However, the Zionists had early on identified the Labour Party as likely to be more tractable and easier to manipulate than the less doctrinaire, more pragmatic Conservative Party which, in any case, they suspected of an endemic anti-Jewishness, despite Churchill's unqualified and unquestioning support of their cause. They succeeded largely in isolating Bevin within the governing Labour Party. In the event, Britain was to remain, not for the first time nor for the last in matters of great moral as well as political importance, on the fence.

The Arabs realised only too clearly that they were being used as part of the process whereby the United Nations was itself to be used to convey some appearance of legitimacy to the rape which it was evident was about to be committed.

The inevitable process drew on. On 29 November 1947 the General Assembly of the United Nations adopted the Partition Plan. Russia, the United States and France, all permanent members of the Security Council, voted for the resolution.[3] Against were ranged five Arab states in membership of the UN – there were only five at the time – other Muslim states and, to their credit, Cuba and Greece. China abstained, as did Britain, maintaining its ignoble indecision to the last.

The final vote saw all the 'white' nations – the British Commonwealth, most of Europe and all those dominated by the two Great Powers – voting for the Resolution. Against were the Arabs and a few states who saw the dangerous reality to which the vote would lead. Ten states abstained.

The story of the vote has been told many times with graphic descriptions of the coercion and intimidation exerted against some of the smaller countries who were inclined to vote against the Resolution. The Zionists and their supporters, particularly amongst the United States delegation, used every tactic, honest or not, to persuade wavering nations to the Zionist camp.

The provisions of the United Nations Resolution make ironic

reading in the light of subsequent events. All civil, political, economic, religious and property rights were guaranteed to the Arabs. The Resolution insisted that there should be no expropriation of land owned by an Arab in the Jewish state ... except for public purposes. Even in such cases, the provision, which opened a substantial loophole for future malpractice, required full compensation to be paid before the expropriation took place. Such provisions, of course, were disregarded by Israel once nationhood had been obtained. Even the stated policy of the United Nations was set at naught.

Neither the British Foreign Office nor the United States State Department wanted Israel to be constituted as a sovereign, Jewish exclusivist entity;[4] the officials were of the right mind but it was the politicians, with an eye to the next election and subject to the overwhelming tactics of the Zionist lobbies, who gave in to Israel's eventual seizure of much of Palestine. Like the Pope, the Arabs, at this time at least, had few battalions.

The vote, when it came, confirmed acceptance of the recommended Partition Plan, representing the consistently held view of the majority of the member countries appointed to the sub-committee charged with the responsibility of reporting to the General Assembly. The members of the sub-committee were controlled either by the United States or by Russia; at this particular time the two antagonists, opposed on virtually every world issue, were united in welcoming the proposal to divide Palestine and hand over the larger part to a European people whom the fortunes of history had identified as a cause for profound guilt in the European consciousness, a guilt apparently shared by those other peoples who derived their cultural inheritance from the European continent.

When the voting on the Resolution which recommended partition of Palestine took place, the votes cast were: for the motion to partition Palestine, 33 votes; against, 13. There were 10 abstentions. Today the vote would undoubtedly be very different; it would be inconceivable that the motion, or anything like it, would be accepted.

It must be emphasised that this Resolution was a *recommendation* – no more – that Palestine should be partitioned. As such, a simple recommendation and not an instruction, which the General Assembly in any case had no power to enact, carried with it no force of law. It gave no authority for Partition nor for anything else, beyond the recommendation to the future action which it proposed. Again, it must be said, the United Nations had no moral or legal right to divide a people's country in so arbitrary a fashion. Even the United Nations itself seems, at this point and however dimly, to have apprehended this fact.

But despite this the Jewish state was proclaimed on 14 May 1948. With a disregard for truth remarkable even in the record of the acts of Israel, the proclamation of Israel's independence stated: 'By virtue of our natural and intrinsic right and of the Resolution of the United Nations General Assembly we hereby declare the establishment of a Jewish State in Palestine.'

The Proclamation of the Independence of Israel is a document of startling effrontery. After asserting the mythological origins of the Jewish people living in and beyond Palestine, it blandly plucks out the reference to a Jewish State in the UN Resolution as a warrant for the creation of Israel, with a wilful disregard of the equally specific recommendation for the creation of a Palestinian State (see Appendix 3 for the text of the State of Israel Declaration of Independence).

Of course, the action of the United Nations must be seen against the events and political currents of the time. The traumata which Europe experienced in the aftermath of the revelation of the Nazi atrocities could hardly be exaggerated. Allied with the intense political activity undertaken by the Zionists before, during and after the war, leading up to the events of 1948, the climate was right for the acceptance of almost any means of assuaging Europe's sense of guilt. That the price demanded was not one which seemed likely greatly to inconvenience Europe made its payment the more acceptable. Thus was Israel born, out of manipulation, coercion and the sense of culpability of a continent.

The peculiar nature of Israel was that it was a state formed not out of territory nor out of the ethnic relationships of its potential population but of religious and societal affiliations. It was not primarily conceived as a geographical entity, a fact which has been emphasised by Israel's continued refusal to define its own frontiers. It was specifically conceived as a state for the Jewish people; as such it was a non-territorial nation, a concept of crucial legal dubiety.

Without the heightened awareness of the founders of the United Nations of the misery of the European Jews brought about by a century of persistent persecutions, first in Russia and then by the Germans, the Zionist claim to this special and peculiar form of statehood would hardly have been countenanced. One thing is certain: without the Nazi persecutions Israel would never so readily have acquired nationhood in the years which immediately followed the end of the war and which were marked by the revelation of Nazi atrocities on a scale which many believed to be without precedent.

The language of Israeli and Zionist propagandists like the language of those militaristic, fascist regimes from which they learned so much and whose simple propaganda techniques they were to develop out of all recognition, is drawn from the vocabulary of bombast and overstatement. The persecution of the Jews by the Nazis has been described (by Menachem Begin, amongst others), as 'the greatest crime in human history'.[5] This patently it is not; the catalogue of such crimes is long indeed and the competition in beastliness is fierce. The arithmetical approach to human suffering is in any case distasteful, but if the deaths of 6 million Jews were so frightful, how much more dreadful must be the computation of the capture, enslavement and death of the 20 million Africans whom Europe sent as slaves to the New World in the seventeenth, eighteenth and nineteenth centuries? Was the killing of 2 million Smyrniots in the 1920s only one-third as evil as the 'Holocaust', or the massacres of the Mongol invaders, estimated by some authorities to have been as high as 18 million people, three times more terrible? Does some special argument make the killing of 6 million Jews somehow worse than the slaughter of 20 million Russians by the communist rulers of that unhappy land under Stalin? It is unpleasing to labour the point, but the immorality of Israel's claim to special consideration because of the suffering inflicted on the Jews by the Nazis must be exposed for the deplorable act of exploitation that it is. Yet whenever Israel's protagonists are faced with arguments which they cannot lightly dismiss, time and time again they will advert to this shameful special pleading.

Few of the actions of the government of Israel and other Zionist factions have been as deplorable as the exploitation of Nazi persecution of the Jews to justify the seizure of the Palestinians' land. This is surely one of the more ignoble episodes in the politics of contemporary Zionism. The appalling suffering

35

of the Jews in Nazi-occupied Europe has been relentlessly rehearsed by every means of propaganda, to drive out any voice of opposition or even criticism which raises itself in the countries of the West, on whose goodwill Israel depends for her existence. To attack the actions and policies of the Israeli state immediately provokes strident reference to the horrors of the Nazi 'Holocaust', a word which has come to dominate the language of Zionist polemic. The essential cynicism of its adoption by Zionism can be detected in the fact that a holocaust, a Greek hybrid word, originally meant a burnt offering of the sort which was so unstintingly offered to Jahweh by his adherents whose myth, fables and history were conflated into the books of the Old Testament. Thus, what was originally an offering to God came to be equated with an act of murder. Particularly after the War of 1967 Israeli propaganda has constantly used the Germans' plan to exterminate the Jews as the justification for their presence in Palestine and to retain the still evidently guilt-ridden support of Europeans and Americans for their own acts of injustice.

To use the dreadful agony of the Jews who died in Europe to give a warrant to the brazen seizure of the Palestinians' land is to debase the suffering of those who endured the death camps and the execution squads. The deaths of those Jews shamed Europe; Zionism now shames the Jews who died. As Emil Ludwig was reported as saying, in what was surely one of the most misguided and off-key observations in this whole sorry tale, 'Hitler will be forgotten in a few years but he will have a beautiful monument in Palestine.'[6]

Some Orthodox Jewish thinkers have seen the 'Holocaust' – and indeed promoted it – as a manifestation of God's will in driving the Chosen People back to the Promised Land.[7] The return of the Jews to Israel is, in this context, represented as the birth pangs of the Messianic Age.

This interpretation, which may well seem peculiarly sinister to those who do not share it, perpetuates the God of Israel as a cruel and implacable divinity whose chief concern for His adherants is to inflict the greatest extent of suffering upon them. It is, however, an interpretation which strikes a chord of recognition amongst some Christian fundamental sects (see Chapter 7) who see the foundation of the Israeli state and the 'return' of the Jews as foreshadowing the Second Coming. That the one idea would seem to be exclusive of the other – the appearance of the Messiah to the Jews and the Second Coming of Christ to the Christians – does not seem unduly to have bothered the protagonists of either.

And what all this has to do with the people of Palestine, no one can say.

The creation of the State of Israel in 1948 was the occasion for much rejoicing in many countries of the world; its entry into the world community was given a largely uncritical reception. After centuries of Jewish suffering at the hands alike of European religious zealots and national leaders, and following many years of unremitting activity in the management of a political campaign of great persistence and subtlety, the Zionist dream was realised at last; the establishment of a homeland to which Jews from across the world could come, to find a refuge from persecution and to fulfil their unique Jewish destiny. The revelation of the horrors which attended the Nazi domination of continental Europe had appalled the Western world. Much of the West was exhausted by the war which had just ended, but it was happy to see one of those peoples now recognised as a small nation, of the sort for whose independent survival the war had, in theory at least, been fought. After all, if there was one group whose sufferings typified the barbarity of the Axis regimes, was it not the Jews of Europe?

Not only Jews shared in the enthusiasm which greeted the new state. Throughout the Christian world, though it had always been deeply ambivalent in its attitudes towards the Jewish people, there was a feeling of something like pride and relief intertwined, that the 'Chosen People' had come home. This fulfilled, it was rather foggily believed, the prophecies of the Bible which, in the case of the books of the Old Testament, the Jewish and Christian faiths shared.

Most politicians in the Western world welcomed the foundation of the Israeli state, for they viewed it, perhaps over-optimistically, as a Western-oriented implant in a part of the world which was otherwise menacing and obscure, the majority of whose peoples, moreover, had a history of deep hostility to the Christian world. The inhabitants of much of the eastern end of the Mediterranean, and still more of its hinterland, adhered to a set of customs and beliefs seemingly far removed from that European culture and tradition which the new Israeli state proclaimed as part of its essential character and heritage. With that identity of cultural values went the possession of much of what Jews and Christians alike revered as the Holy Land, the focus for both of whatever millennial longings.

From the outset, the new state blazoned its commitment to democracy. Indeed, as the years went by it became increasingly insistent on its status as the only true democracy in a region which was represented as being otherwise dominated by despotic hereditary rulers or tyrannous, mainly military, regimes. The new state, it was confidently averred, would surely provide a foothold for Western cultural, political and economic interests in a region which was clearly destined to be of great importance to the industrial societies of the West, which needed desperately to re-gear themselves after the devastation of the war.

The war apart, the years which led to the proclamation of the State of Israel had not been without their difficulties, especially for Britain, which had effectively been the occupying power in Palestine since 1919. These years were marked by violent protests promoted by Jewish zealots against a declining and weary colonial power on the one hand, on the other, an intransigent (if, in the eyes of most observers, a generally contemptible) indigenous population. But there was at least no doubt that the creation of the new state could be seen to be one of the earliest triumphs of the United Nations. This body assisted serenely at Israel's birth, proposing the apportioning of the land then known as Palestine between the immigrant population of the new state and the indigenous Arabs. The latter, admittedly, seemed unconvinced of the advantages of the new state's presence in what they were determined to regard as *their* land. It was obviously not the fault of the United Nations that, as a consequence of Arab incompetence in launching a war against Israel and Arab unreadiness in executing it, the new state was ultimately to occupy more land even than the United Nations had actually intended to give it. The new reality which the Israeli occupation of these lands represented was quickly accepted by most of the important nations of the world. This acceptance was achieved the more easily in the light of evident superiority, military as much as intellectual, of the new-found Israelis over their neighbours. To this might be added the undoubted benefit which Western technology and Western investment, now to be marshalled in the service of Jewish ability and determination, would bring to the barren lands in which the European immigrants were in the process of establishing themselves.

The United Nations, too, found itself in the position that its host country, the United States of America, was an enthusiastic protagonist of the new state; indeed it was quite evidently the most unreservedly enthusiastic of all the nations on earth when contemplating the creation of Israel. Britain readily relinquished the Mandate over the territory which it had held, latterly with extreme unease. Many of the leading members of the United Nations, not least among which was the Soviet Union, joined in the chorus of welcome to Israel.

The Arab states existing at the time of Israel's creation were simply not comparable in influence or skill with their opponents, when set against the real world of politics. The Arab world as a whole had not been well served by the imperial powers in the nineteenth century or afterwards. Following the over-romanticised episode of the otherwise largely irrelevant exploits of T. E. Lawrence in western Arabia in the First World War and the complex machinations of the French in the Maghreb and Syria after it, the Arab world, in the aftermath of the Second World War when much of it had served as a battlefield for European antagonists, found itself required to contribute to a system of world politics for which it had no modern experience. Most of the Arab states which existed in 1945 were clients of European powers; the Arab League, somewhat whimsically brought into existence largely on the initiative of Anthony Eden,[8] gave some shape to Arab identity amongst an otherwise fractious and disparate group of peoples, divided by the arbitrary European habit of determining national boundaries by drawing lines on maps rather than as the consequence of any historical, ethnic or linguistic considerations. Egypt and Iraq were still monarchies, if rather ramshackle ones and with distinctly uncertain support from their own peoples. Even Saudi Arabia, though it was one of the signatories of the United Nations Charter, was still feeling its way tentatively, tied firmly to the apron strings of the United States, which managed its formidable, if newly exploited, oil reserves.

The indigenous Palestinian activists who opposed the new state's existence and its specific and declared Jewish character were not represented amongst the nations which made up the United Nations' membership. Soon it was apparent that the activities of these unrepresented (and thus politically irrelevant) people were as likely to become as troublesome to their Arab neighbours as they ever were to the new Israeli state. But the readiness of the Israelis to deal sternly with the problem of their opposition was widely applauded as sound and prudent law enforcement, the proper recourse of a rapidly maturing state in defending its own interests and security.

Such were the circumstances which attended the formation of the Israeli state: many were the hopes which went with its birth and many were the myths which were quick to grow up around it. The Jews of Europe, indeed of the world, were to return to their original home. Once there they would demonstrate to the world their creative genius in making a modern state out of the desert and, in the process, demonstrate a generosity of purpose and effect to the present inhabitants of the land which would astonish the world.

The reality, however, was something very different. The real consequences of its creation – not only for the displaced Palestinians to whom that event was a disaster as unmitigated as it was undeserved, but also for the world community – were slow to become apparent. This slow rate of a growth in understanding served Israel well.

The actual circumstances of the United Nations Resolution on the partition of Palestine have been described. But the importance of that resolution to the Israelis' own view of their legal justification to occupy the land of Palestine is crucial, as important as the myth of their descent from earlier inhabitants of Palestine. The legal status of the UN resolution can be dealt with summarily.

The United Nations and the nations of the industrial West, notably Britain and America, have the principal credit for the presence of Israel amongst the community of nations. As such, their leaders have, though living in vastly different circumstances, an obligation to understand the processes to which, consciously or not, they gave countenance and which have been invoked to give Israel the appearance of a legal claim to existence. Thus there is an argument which says that the claim of the Jewish population of Israel to descent or inheritance from the tribes of Biblical times, and hence to the possession of the land of Palestine in right of that descent, is irrelevant since both their presence and the statehood of Israel are legalised by the United Nations' decision to partition Palestine in 1947. This argument, an entirely circular one, is dubious on several grounds.

First, as has been demonstrated, the United Nations had no legal or moral right whatsoever to partition Palestine without regard for the wishes of the majority of the indigenous population.

Second, Israel has taken to itself a larger territory than even the United Nations intended in the partition plan and thus has usurped the legal rights of possession of the inhabitants of those areas. Further, this illegal act has been compounded by permitting the establishment of permanent settlements in the territories which it has occupied since 1967, in direct contravention of international law.

Third, the argument that the United Nations decision superseded the Biblical claims of the Jewish population is vitiated by the fact that the member states of the United Nations Assembly, who voted for the partition of Palestine and hence the creation of the Jewish state, did so only because of the sustained campaigns of the Zionists who employed the argument of 'Biblical origins' as the fundamental basis for their claim to the rights of possession. This claim is repeated to this day by every Israeli politician who speaks of 'the homeland' or who claims, as so many do with such strident frequency, that their literal and direct ancestors were, once upon a time, driven from the land and that they have returned to claim their ancestral rights.

Finally, there is one consequence of the foundation of the Israeli state which is the logical outcome of the idea that Israel represents the Jewish homeland, in which an identifiable, historic Jewish entity existed and was capable of being reconstructed. This is the 'Law of Return', enshrined in the Israeli legal code, which expresses the absolute right of a Jew living outside Israel to 'return' and to establish residence in the country. If words mean anything at all, it is clear that the concept of the descent of the Jewish population of Israel from the tribes of Old Testament times is fundamental to their claim to possession of the land they now occupy. It is upon this principle that the existence of Israel is founded.

The 'Law of Return', a nakedly racialist concept, in that it differentiates between one people and others on what it asserts,

41

however speciously, as ethnic grounds, is an extraordinary document, its terms startling when enshrined in the laws of a modern state. It was intended principally to serve the interests of the European migrants and was not for the Jews of Oriental origin. However, as will be seen further in Chapter 9, it has been used as much to permit the return of a Yemeni farmer as a Hungarian banker. Its provisions are:

1 Every Jew has the right to immigrate to the country.
2 (a) Immigration shall be on the basis of immigration visas.
  (b) Immigrant visas shall be issued to any Jews expressing a desire to settle in Israel, except if the Minister of Immigration is satisfied that the applicant:
   (i) acts against the Jewish nation; or
   (ii) may threaten the public health or state security.
3 (a) A Jew who comes to Israel and after his arrival expresses a desire to settle there may, while in Israel, obtain an immigrant certificate.
  (b) The exceptions listed in Article 2 (b) shall apply also with respect to the issue of an immigrant certificate, but a person shall not be regarded as a threat to public health as a result of an illness that he contracts after his arrival in Israel.
4 Every Jew who migrated to the country before this law goes into effect, and every Jew who was born in the country either before or after the law is effective enjoys the same status as any person who migrated on the basis of this law.
5 The Minister of Immigration is delegated to enforce this law and he may enact regulations in connection with its implementation and for the issue of immigrant visas and immigrant certificates.

It is this law, perhaps more than any other, which demonstrates the essentially racialist thinking which lies behind so much of Israel's political character, for it confers on the Jews a special right to live in a particular state by virtue merely of the fact that they are Jews, no matter from what part of the world they may come. By perpetrating the idea of a prescriptive right for all Jews to Israeli *nationality*, the law is deeply offensive and it stands as a most cruel affront to the true indigenes of Palestine, of whatever religious denominations or of none. Its racialist character is clearly demonstrated by the repeated insistence of successive Israeli governments that the 'Law of Return' applies only to Jews, no matter their origins, and does not apply to Palestinians born on their ancestral land.

It is the historicity and validity of the fundamental Jewishness of that part of Palestine which is now Israel and the continued existence of the State of Israel as a specifically Jewish political entity which this study considers. Its principal conclusion is that the insistence on the Jewish character of Israel is nugatory, contradictory to the realities and dangerous to the security not only of the Middle East but of much of the world community.

For more than forty years now Israel has been wandering in a wilderness of its own making. The foundation of the Israeli state was a response to the distress of European Jews who themselves had been nurtured in the ideas of nineteenth-century nationalism. Inevitably, it must have seemed reasonable to them to seek a solution to their suffering at the hands of their fellow Europeans by establishing the sort of supremacist rule in Palestine which they had seen set up, with every evidence of success, by the imperial European powers across the world. To the simple political concept of colonialism – its simplicity demonstrated by the expression of the early Zionists' belief that the Palestinians would welcome them into their land, as the bringers of civilisation – was added the prescriptive rights of habitation in Palestine conveyed to them by their assumption of the myths of the tribes of pre- and post-Exilic times in Palestine. This absorption of the myths of another people in another age had the effect of making the Jews of Europe partners with the very imperial powers whose nationalist and expansionist policies they envied so much and absorbed so readily. Because they shared many of the same myths which the imperial powers had taken to themselves they found a sympathetic audience for their proposals, an audience already predisposed to them by its own self-interest.

The concept of nationalism and the promotion of Zionism were the twin manifestations on which the sufferings of the Palestinian people, the least culpable of victims, were to be based in the times to come. The singular misfortune of Israel itself was that the state was founded just as the tide of colonialism was beginning to roll back, leaving Israel isolated and vulnerable, a fossilised example of the imperial dream. Israel as a Zionist entity in the Middle East, asserting the 'rights' of a settler people over the rights of the indigenes, is as unnatural a political construct as the white supremacist regime in South Africa, with which it has sustained so close a relationship, thus demonstrating the sinister logic of like attracting like. Interestingly, it would seem that South Africa, so long the bastion of the resistance to political change, will be the first to accept policies with regard to the indigenous population, unthinkable only a short while ago.

Of course, for many Jews leaving Europe in the wake both of Russian pogroms and the Nazi persecutions, Israel *was* a haven, a refuge most earnestly sought. In the early days of the fulfilment of the Zionist plan there was neither the time nor the inclination to think much about the Palestinians or their supposed rights. Prophecy and politics, always a heady combination, came together to produce a warrant for the new state's existence, around which were constellated the pride and yearnings of a community which history, for whatever reason, had not treated kindly. That this community itself soon became in turn the oppressor is a tragic, but, to the historian, not an unfamiliar irony.

The world has moved on over the forty years of Israel's existence, lost in its wilderness. The convulsions which have come about in the aftermath of the realignment of Russian policy, the moving closer together of the two hitherto antagonistic super-powers, will make it increasingly difficult for Israel to sustain her special influence with the United States, an influence which ultimately is corrupting both.

However, there may be one ray of hopeful light in what is otherwise a very sombre landscape. Contrary to appearance and to much accepted belief, the rise to the majority in Israel by the Jews of Oriental origin (see Chapter 9) may, in the medium or longer term at least, be an occasion for optimism. Such optimism reflects the hope that the Orientals, largely uninfluenced by Zionism and with little cause to love their Ashkenazi neighbours, will find it easier to come to an understanding with the Arab Palestinians, with whom they have far more in common than they have differences. And there is another group within the heart of Israeli society on which some hope may also be placed. This is represented by the increasingly numerous and articulate voices within the Ashkenazi community itself, especially amongst younger people born in Israel. These are the ones who have to bear the brunt of the decisions of the ageing men who rule the state, to contain, with more or less brutality depending upon the presence or absence of international television cameras, the frustrations and anger of the Palestinians.

Both Israelis and Palestinians of goodwill can surely recognise in each other that they are the victims of the same delusions which have marked the years of Israel's existence. Both peoples have suffered from the corruption of those ideals which may with honour be ascribed to the Jewish people throughout their history.

For this is the other dismal tragedy of the existence of Israel: it is not only the Palestinians who suffer by its continued presence, but it is also the Jewish heritage in the larger world which is tarnished by Israel's perversity. A state which employs phosphorus bombs against school children and the old, and exploding dogs (sent into Palestinian camps and emplacements) against the indigenous population from which they have taken the land is no longer the people of Gamaliel, Maimonides, Einstein and Freud. This is warfare waged with the imaginative monstrousness of booby-trapped babies in Vietnam.

It is perhaps the Jewish misfortune that their own view of their history is essentially collectivist. It may be that this is the reason why they have tended often to favour collectivist solutions to social and political issues, why, for example, they have been inclined to support European revolutionary and nihilist movements, though it is a circumstance hardly to be wondered at when their treatment at the hands of their fellow Europeans is recalled. In this collectivist view of the world and of their place in it, much of the essential character of the Jews, viewed as an historical phenomenon, may be understood. It is unfortunate, to say the least, that Zionism misled the Jewish spirit into perverse and uncharacteristic pathways by seeking to impose an outdated nationalism on its essentially collectivist identity. In this lies the inherent contradiction of Israel's position in the community of nations today.

Since the end of the ancient world Judaism has strained against both Christianity and Islam, which are at once its offspring and its competitors. In the high days of Jewish cultural flowering – in, for example, the engagingly decadent days of Mediterranean Hellenism – Judaism represented a subtle, yet superior, set of beliefs and canons of behaviour which exercised a great appeal to a world grown weary of a multiplicity of gods and competing cults, with the corresponding lack of certainty which such chaotic polytheism induced. The onset of two rival monotheistic faiths, the later of which, Islam, is in a very real sense the fulfilment of the Mosaic tradition, has been both baffling and dismaying for Jewish religious belief. That belief, corrupted by the tergiversations of the politicians, has been turned in our time into a capacity for mischief and for the exploitation of a people even more defenceless than were the Jews themselves, when they had to bear the persecutions of the Christians and the Muslims' contempt.

3

EXORCISING EUROPE'S DEMONS – ZIONISM AND RACE

The acceptance of the State of Israel by the international community was, in reality, the response to a peculiarly European problem: the centuries of persecution meted out to the Jews of Europe, culminating in the atrocities of the Nazi regime and of its adherents and supporters in those European states which fell under Nazi domination. The nature of Europe's responsibility in this issue is what makes the question of Israel's continued existence in the form in which it was founded so profoundly important to the world as a whole.

The European persecution of the Jews in the twentieth century marked the recurrence of a psychopathological condition of formidable proportions and profound depth. The presence of substantial Jewish communities in most European countries had been a factor in those countries' social and economic fabric for upwards of a thousand years, in some cases for longer still. As, sadly, is the common experience of many minorities, particularly those which manifest very distinct characteristics and possess an evident and definable 'differentness', the Jewish communities had lived through a diverse history and a varied experience amongst Christian nations; at times they were courted and favoured, at other times persecuted and repressed. Many of the most penetrating and persistent aspects of Jewish culture, including both the sense of separateness from the generality of Christendom and the identity between one Jewish community with another regardless of the frontiers of national states, stem from this period and from this experience. Equally certainly the deep-seated Jewish sense of insecurity has its origins in the generally beastly manner in which Europe treated them.

The ability to sustain a distinct and coherent culture, strongly identified with religious practice and organisation, together with the universal need for members of a minority always to strive harder to achieve status and recognition, became distinguishing marks of the Jewish communities of Europe. Many rulers of European states, notably in medieval times, found Jews to be valuable servants, not least because of their ability to transcend frontiers, which enabled them to move assets across political boundaries. In this practice they succeeded to the experience – and to some of the power – gained by the great monastic orders of knighthood in later medieval times who had, surprisingly perhaps to those who do not know their history, in effect invented the European banking system. This ability to conduct their affairs trans-nationally undoubtedly gave rise to the idea of the existence of a Jewish international network, which, in the sense proposed, did actually exist, and an international Jewish conspiracy, which patently did not. The Jews were often, at a somewhat humbler level, identified with activities such as money-lending and debt-collection, which inevitably made them feared and disliked by the peasants and townsfolk alike among whom they lived, worked and often flourished considerably.

To this distrust of their place in society by those amongst whom they lived, was added a sense, often cautiously expressed, but none the less entirely real, of superiority on the part of the Jews themselves. Such a tendency often goes with high achievers from minorities as – the consequence both of precept and of tradition – they are convinced of their rightful primacy over the more powerful society which they see around them and among whom they are obliged to exist with deference. This sense of exclusive, superior identity over those whom they see asserting their dominance and demanding respect and sub-mission often manifests itself as arrogance – or so it is easily described by those who feel threatened by its expression. The interaction of such conflicting ideas and emotions inevitably, and on occasion after occasion, produced violent and unmistakeably profoundly neurotic confrontations between Jewish communi-ties and the Christians amongst whom they lived in Europe.

In later medieval times and subsequently, after the dispersion of the Jews from Spain and Portugal in which they had survived, ironically, as remnants of Muslim rule over the Iberian penin-sula, a considerable fraction of what then represented Jewry was obliged to live in other Christian lands, particularly in western, central and later in eastern Europe. This happened at a time when European culture and its religious beliefs were exerting an increasingly powerful influence throughout a world which was becoming larger through trade and conquest, and richer in resources and opportunity. Christians customarily stigmatised the Jews as the 'murderers of Christ'; as Jewish populations spread, so did the hatred which their alleged 'murder' of Christ invoked. In the Middle Ages the hatred engendered by this accusation was enough to foment frequent outbreaks of mindless violence against the Jews in many cities of Europe. In the cities, they lived in what came to be called 'ghettoes' (after an area of Venice which was once marked out for their occupation), sometimes in squalor, sometimes in conditions of sumptuousness and luxury, the latter making their periodic persecution still more welcome and profitable.

The mendicant orders of Christendom, the monks who subsisted on the charity of the communities in which they lived, especially the Franciscans and the Dominicans, were tireless in a particularly merciless harrying of the Jews.[1] This was pursued with such relentless vehemence and to such a degree that the conclusion is inescapable that such persecution was pathological in origin; the unnatural character of monastic life clearly induced fantasies of a sort which could only be released or assuaged by the infliction of pain on an easily identifiable 'enemy'. To the Jews' supposed responsibility for the killing of Christ were added various mythical elements, of which the most notorious was the accusation of child- (specifically boy-) murder, to provide innocent blood, it was averred by their monkish hunters, for various of their nameless rituals. These patently hysterical manifestations of the instinct to exploit brutally a minority's vulnerability were sadly not infrequent.

Nor, in fairness, were such outbreaks of cruelty directed only towards the Jews. Thus in the earliest days of Christian political domination in the East, the Gnostics were ruthlessly perscuted. Later, Christian heretics like the Cathars, the Albigensians, the Knights Templar, and dissenting groups such as the Anabaptists, were all hounded and abused by the orthodox authorities in much the same way.[2] But the Jews represented a constant factor, a sort of benchmark in European psychopathology, the marking out and persecution of a safe target for what was, unmistakably, sheer sadistic exploitation. Throughout much of the history of

European states, as much in their own continent as when far removed from their homelands, one of the most potent aspects of the European psyche seems to have been the need to dominate and humiliate. The treatment of minorities is one aspect of this psychosis, as is the practice of slavery as conducted by the European nations.

It is sadly all too easy to set down the record of Christian persecutions against the Jews and other minorities. Christianity is essentially conformist, insisting, like Islam, on the primacy of its revelation. However, it must be understood in terms of its own time. Prior to the Reformation, tolerance of differing systems of belief was simply not a choice open to Christian rulers or the societies they governed. Those that might exercise some degree or toleration, as some of the principalities in southern France attempted to do, were themselves swept away. Tolerance was sinful: the acceptance of heretics or infidels within a Christian society was unreservedly to be condemned. In this respect, Islam was the more tolerant of the two societies, permitting the existence of both Judaism and Christianity, though under severe constraints.

Only in recent years has it become possible to apply something like objective standards to the examination of some of these issues. In the decades after the end of the Second World War, coinciding as they did with the emergence of the State of Israel on to the world stage, the memory of the persecution of the Jews under the Nazi ideologies was simply too fresh. Now, however, some scholars are beginning to question received opinion and to look anew at some of the more entrenched positions which have been erected to protect, amongst other considerations, Europe's own view of itself.[3]

It has been argued, persuasively, that the cultural history of Europe has been distorted since the end of the eighteenth century by the suppression by European scholars of the Egyptian and Phoenician roots of European culture. This has come about because scholars of the post-Enlightenment rejected as unacceptable the idea that Greece owed its civilisation, in large part at least, to colonies of Egyptian and Phoenician migrants which were established in Greece. This notion, indeed, was entirely in keeping with the Greeks' own idea about the origins of their society but, to the increasingly racialist minds of the nineteenth century the idea that the supposedly pristine culture of Europe, born in the pure light of Greece, was received from African (Egyptian) and semitic (Phoenician) sources was unacceptable. Europe was set upon marked nationalistic and, later, imperial perceptions which eventually were to lead to an aggressive racism. Thus it is suggested that as a result of the influence of powerful and often dominant academics, especially in Classical studies, in France, Germany and, to a lesser degree, Britain, the Egyptian and Phoenician roots were thrust down and only the bright flowering of classical Greece was allowed to flourish, apparently bursting out fully formed, like Athena from the head of Zeus.

The term 'semitic' here is used in its proper linguistic sense. Phoenician was a branch of the great Canaanite language group which formed one of the principal streams of Western semitic. However the argument also employs the term 'anti-semitic' in its applied (and, in this writer's view, incorrect) meaning of being antagonistic to the Jews or to assumed 'semitic' influences stemming from or identified with, Jewishness.

The author of this study observes: 'anti-semitism can be seen as a luxury, to be indulged in only when there are no outside enemies.'[4] Certainly the history of the Jews in Europe would suggest that their periodic persecution is a need which wells up from some particularly black depth of the European psyche. This need now finds itself confronting a phenomenon with which it has not previously had to deal, a spectrum of assertions from Jews themselves. The foundation of the State of Israel has produced one notable by-product: the natural assertiveness of a repressed minority like the Jews has been able to express itself in a range of responses which extend from simple pride, through assertions of superiority over other communities, to the full racist baying of a Kahane, or Begin when at his least guarded.

Jewish communities both within and outside Israel have become quick to condemn anything which they see as an attack on their status as Jews, which, in the way of politics, has become identified with the nationality so readily conferred by the State of Israel.

It has become correspondingly less rewarding for those groups in Western societies to whom the Jews, when they were cowed and vulnerable, would represent a natural target, to attack an enemy who may respond. Better by far to turn such attentions to blacks, Asians or any other minority which lacks

51

the incentive to resist conferred by a powerful state which, if it is unloved, is respected.

The turmoil which has followed the collapse of the Soviet system, the emergence of the independent republics and the reunification of the two Germanies has demonstrated, if demonstration were needed, how close to the surface in the European psyche is the need to find and persecute minorities. As this is written, the Bosnian Muslims represent an immediate reference; so too do the Russians in Estonia and the Albanians in Greece. The harassing of the new European immigrants in what was East Germany is matched by the rejection by their cousins in the western part of the country of migrants of impeccable German ancestry. At a still more mindless level, demonstrations in Poland have rekindled that country's deep-seated hatred of Jews; in Russia too the economic ills of the country are ascribed to the Jews, as once they were in the days of the Tsars.

In Europe the need to find an enemy from the east seems to be strong: 'the semites' provided a convenient focus for the expression of what has come to be termed 'race-hatred'.[5] The Jews having been largely off-limits as targets since the end of the Second World War, the Russians and their satellites provided some alternative sport, though it was one more easily indulged in by states than by individuals, in the nature of things. But now even that degree of eastern menace has disappeared.

The old stereotypes die hard however. The new anti-semitism is directed against the Arabs who are now portrayed with all the physical and moral disabilities which were once the delight of anti-Jewish propagandists. The Arab ('Arab' and 'Muslim' are of course terms which are interchangeable) is shown to be gross, hook-nosed, black-haired, rapacious, cruel, exploitative. He is monstrously rich, his wealth undeserved and unearned; he is the cause of many of the industrial world's misfortunes by reason of his grasp of a vital resource, oil.

All of these stereotypes could be duplicated (with 'banking' substituted for 'oil') in anti-Jewish tracts at the end of the last century (when such libels were particularly popular) or in the 1930s when Nazi propaganda picked up the anti-capitalist diatribes which had focussed on Jews as one of the unmistakable causes of Europe's and America's economic distress.

The constant pursuit of the Jews undoubtedly went deep into the European consciousness. It was a monstrous growth which, if it sometimes lay dormant, could quickly and on almost any occasion, be called into dreadful life. It gave Jew-baiting a particular place in the perversions peculiar to the European and Christian mind. But European persecution of the Jews was, in part at least, the consequence of the Judaic roots of Western religious culture. Christianity became, par excellence, the religion of Europe, but its roots were quite obviously extra-European. The violent reaction against Jews and Judaism which Europe periodically manifested can be seen as an attempt to reject, or to escape from, this aspect of its own cultural past.

All peoples are the products and the prisoners of their own prevailing myths. The nature of myth is closely identified with the nature of language on which it relies for verbal expression, though the origins of myth lie in the collective unconscious of the people. Myth and language are closely intertwined: linguistically, Judaism may be said to be semitic in the sense that it originated in the region from which semitic-speakers came, just as Islam, which originated in the same region, may also be said to be semitic. As such Judaism was a form of belief which does not easily or naturally root itself in a Europe which had its own indigenous myths. This corpus of myth was suppressed but periodically surged to the surface again in, amongst other forms, a virulent rejection of the Judaistic heritage and the consequent destruction of the most readily accessible vessels of Judaism on which it could lay hands.

Indeed the persecution of the Jews by Europeans in the Ages of Faith and subsequently, whenever such persecutions have been grounded on the story of the Jews' rejection of Christ and their alleged acceptance of a blood-guilt for his death, must surely be recognised not only as a disgraceful episode in the history of the entire continent, but as absurd. The overwhelming majority of Jews thus persecuted have no lineal connection whatsoever (or, for those of Oriental origin, only of the most tenuous sort) with the population of Palestine at the time of Christ's death in Jerusalem in the early decades of the present era. That so many of the Jews thus persecuted cannot with accuracy be called semites at all – as will be demonstrated later – makes their tragedy the more ironic, but none the less terrible.

The worst excesses of the European persecution of the Jews, at least until the nineteenth century, were particularly the inspiration of Rome. The Catholic church was unrelenting in its hunting of the Jews, as much for financial gain – since the sequestration of Jewish assets was as welcome to ecclesiastical coffers as to royal treasuries – as it was a consequence of religious fervour. The position of the Jews in Europe began to change significantly after the Reformation. With increased access to the contents of the Bible, then generally translated into European vernacular languages for the first time, the relationship between Christianity and its Jewish heritage became more explicit, even to the simple. Fundamentalist groups began to preach the absolute truth of the books of the Old Testament as vigorously as they promoted their displacement by the Gospels of the new dispensation. As, very slowly, literacy spread throughout Europe, so did this awareness of the heritage of the Hebrew Testament. Its character was also promoted by the work of the painters and, to a lesser degree, of sculptors who found in the dramatic and often bloody epics which the Bible recounted, more rewarding subjects for their art, to counterbalance the often blander anecdotes of the Gospel story.

By the seventeenth century Jewish communities were deeply embedded in most western European cities and in many eastern ones as well. They were well positioned to take advantage, for themselves and for the societies amongst which they lived, of the opening up of trade routes internationally and of the beginnings of industrialisation; they were amongst the first true capitalists. More significantly too, at this time, the learned, intellectually venturesome Jew began to be a familiar figure in the rapidly flowering cultural life of many European cities.

The contributions of Jews to the European intellectual revolution did not, however, do much in the long term for the position of Jews in European society, certainly not for the poor or disadvantaged amongst them. There was considerable pressure on them in most European cities to assimilate, to be absorbed into the mainstream of financial, commercial and social life. Assimilated indeed many Jews were, but enough remained as an identifiable group to provoke, often, intense and contradictory emotions in the minds and hearts of the peoples amongst whom they lived; admiration, envy, contempt, affection, fear were all mixed up into one confused and neurotic amalgam.

The combination of the Enlightenment and the spread both of nationalism and of industrialisation in the eighteenth and nineteenth centuries contributed important strands to the fabric of the Jewish presence in Europe. Jews had always been in the forefront of free-thinking movements; they responded with ready enthusiasm to the new atmosphere which the scientific mood of the eighteenth century encouraged. Their apparently congenital entrepreneurial ability and their skill at leaping frontiers placed them well to take advantage of the opportunities offered by the growth of manufactories and the constant need of Europe's developing industrial economies for new sources of capital.

At the level of ordinary social intercourse, of the relationship of Jewish communities and of individual Jews with the societies in which they lived, their experience varied widely. In Britain, after their formal expulsion in 1290 and the seemingly inevitable bouts of medieval persecution, the Jews had been cautiously welcomed back from the seventeenth century onwards. Jewish communities in England became rich and were respected; many Jews became totally assimilated and penetrated the highest levels of the aristocracy. By the mid-nineteenth century Jews were able to become Members of Parliament, relieved of the necessity of taking a Christian form of oath. A few decades later a Jew, admittedly one who had been baptised in a fit of pique by his free-thinking father, became first the Leader of the Conservative Party and later perhaps the most enduringly influential and innovative Prime Minister of the century.

At this time it is possible to detect in English religious and intellectual circles what has been termed (inaccurately in the view of this study, in at least one respect) 'philo-semitism'. Certainly in the nineteenth century there was an enthusiasm for Jewish history and for the Jewish roots of Christianity which was quite unprecedented. Common offshoots of this enthusiasm manifested themselves in a typically English form of mild eccentricity by the British Israelites, for example, who were disposed to prove that the ancient Britons were the remnants of one or more of the Lost Tribes of Israel, whose identity and fate intrigued and perplexed many a learned divine. Such manifestations may well be dismissed as nothing more than examples of the improbabilities which the human intellect will accept as reality but for the fact that the enthusiasm for the Jewish faith out of which they grew played a part in conditioning public and political opinion to an acceptance of the Biblical claim to Palestine when the early Zionists came to make it.

It is certainly true that, especially in Britain, the nineteenth century enthusiasm for the newly minted practice of archaeology found one of its most responsive audiences amongst those who had been educated in what came to be identified as 'Biblical archaeology' and even more so by those divines who had, as it were, a vested interest in it; the place of archaeology in this record is further and specifically examined in Chapter 6. This, whatever its later pretensions, was originally concerned with proving the historicity of the Christian Bible and, hence, of those parts which were derived from the Jewish traditions of the Old Testament. With the concern to prove the historic reality of episodes related in the Old Testament there followed, inevitably, the acceptance of the role played by the Jews (by whatever name they might for the while be called) in those episodes. Thus the close identity of Christianity and Jewish 'history' was assured. It did not occur to many to enquire whether those generally rather strange and perplexing people who lived usually in somewhat enclosed communities in European cities were Jews in the same sense that the people of the Biblical stories were Jews.

In any event, when the founders of Zionism came upon the political and other circles of influence whom it was necessary for them to persuade of the rightness of their cause, they found the entire generation psychologically and culturally prepared to accept, at their own valuation, their claims to the inheritance of the Biblical covenant with the Almighty. If it had not happened it would be difficult to invent so improbable an outcome.

In France the Revolution had opened the ranks of both government and army to Jews. There had long been powerful communities resident in French cities, especially in the south; their earlier history had, however, been no more fortunate than that of their co-religionists in other European cities. In the waves of persecution which were periodically directed by the Papacy and the royal authority of France against Christian heretics, Jews were as often the victims, slaughtered by Christian knights or burned in what were literally holocausts of innocents. The Jews were expelled from France by that sinister monarch, Phillippe le Bel;[6] they returned after they were driven out of Spain and Portugal at the beginning of the sixteenth century. But, although anti-Jewish feeling ran deep in France and could readily be called up to fuel a controversy like that which overwhelmed the unfortunate Dreyfus, French Jews in the nineteenth century were generally well regarded and well respected.

The German and Austro-Hungarian Empires, despite occasional manifestations of ethnic or social prejudice which, as in other parts of Europe, did not operate exclusively against Jews, were broadly welcoming to them. In Germany in particular the Jews were powerful, rich and numerous. German Jews played leading parts in all aspects of the flowering of German culture and society in the imperial period which led up to the Great War, in which many Jewish officers discharged their duties with distinction and courage.

The Jews of Germany came to be deeply influenced by the new concepts of nationalism to which the creation of the German Empire in the latter part of the nineteenth century gave a special focus. This intense sense of nationality was to have a considerable influence on the development of Zionism, which also began to appear as a political concept towards the end of the century.

It was in Russian lands that the most unremitting policy of persecution was directed against Jewish communities. In an empire in which the majority of the population lived in conditions of privation and squalor it was always useful for the authorities to have a distinctive minority which could be held responsible for the larger misfortunes or whose tormenting distracted from the miserable conditions of the majority. It was in Eastern Europe that the seeds which would one day grow into the State of Israel were planted and ripened.

As Europe became more prosperous, so did the prosperity of many of the continent's Jewish communities increase. This produced the result, perhaps inevitably, that such mounting prosperity fuelled a degree of envy which became increasingly virulent. The expressions of envy often stemmed most aggressively from the newly implanted urban proletariats, which saw some Jews growing rich whilst the urban poor grew demonstrably poorer. The stereotype of the newly rich Jew, living ostentatiously and flaunting his wealth, became another occasion for hatred, contempt and, frequently, for physical attack.

By the latter part of the nineteenth century it could truly be said that in the minds of many Jews and non-Jews alike there existed a 'Jewish problem' in Europe. The rising tide of nationalism added to a popular identification of the problem by the existence, real or mythical, of interconnecting networks of Jewish banking and commercial interests which, as in the past, were presumed to transcend frontiers and national, that is to say non-Jewish, interests.

The rise of the United States, to which Jews were among the first immigrants and against whose commercial influence the Americans' initial attempts at discrimination foundered, gave further support to the concept of nationhood, even if the nation in question was itself a transplant and a mixture of all the races on earth. With the European enthusiasm for nationalism coming still more powerfully into play it is not to be wondered that some Jews, though initially only a very small number, began themselves to manifest a desire for nationhood.

It is at this point that it is appropriate to comment on the part that language has played in this issue. The concept of nationalism presupposes the existence of a nation; a nation is often identified as being synonymous with the term 'race'. This is clearly not so, for the two terms in fact have no direct correspondence.

It will be stated here, with some emphasis, that by no known definition of the terms other than the purely poetic, can the Jews be termed either a nation or a race. Judaism is a canon of religious belief and social practice; the two are as closely linked as they are in that daughter of Judaism, Islam. The practice of Judaism, and the exclusiveness which was always a part of its most cogent appeal, led to the development of a distinct and identifiable persona amongst the peoples, of all races, character and appearance, who shared the beliefs and followed the social behaviour which went with them.

The Jews have in common the membership of a religious and social group: they are a sect, a community. In this, they are surely analogous to the Shia in Islam or, indeed, to Muslims as a whole. By the same token it is as unrealistic to describe the Jews as a 'race', as it would be to apply this term to the generality of Christians or Muslims. There is no Muslim, no Christian race; there is, equally certainly, no Jewish race.

Jews are to be found amongst all nations and most races. Many are Europeans, others Arabs, Chinese, Slavs, Indians. It has been observed (see below) that physiologically Jewish communities bear more resemblance to the populations amongst whom they live than to other Jewish communities living in other areas. There is no 'typical Jew', no 'Jewish type' and certainly no Jewish race.

Since the Israeli claim to Palestine rests, in large degree, on the acceptance of the idea of the special nature of the Jewish people, entitling them to a permanent, politically definable sovereign state in which to live, merely in consequence of their claiming Jewishness, it is pertinent to examine some of the other evidence for and against the recognition of the Jews as a distinct people, other than as a consequence of religious affiliation. It will be necessary to consider some of the works which contribute to the understanding – or the further confusion – of the situation. It will also be appropriate to consider the findings of a survey of the historical and scientific evidence for regarding the Jews as a race or a nation. Since the claim to Palestine was originally expressed in terms of a 'national home' for the Jews, such considerations need to be faced here.

There seems to have been a belief, and one that has been long held, that the Jews are in some substantive, definable way different from the peoples amongst whom they have lived; such an idea seems to have exercised the minds of Jews as much as it clearly has those of non-Jews. The latter, especially in the Christian states of Europe, expressed their apprehensions and their uncertainties about the Jews by persecution, contempt, exploitation, fear; they sustained the fact of separateness by means of legal and social pressures. The Jews, at least until modern times, have contributed to the sense of difference by dress, food, social and religious practices, endogamous marriage customs (though these have never been wholly inflexible) and by the simple expedient of insisting on their separateness, their difference from non-Jews. The long-running dispute in orthodox religious circles on what constitutes a Jew (a dispute which seems, to a non-Jew, often to be pursued with both extraordinary vigour and remarkable venom) demonstrates what appears to be a profoundly inward-looking concern. Even in sophisticated Western societies Jewish humour, values, avocations and the sense of community with other Jewish communities all reinforce the idea of Jews being in some way 'different' from the majority amongst whom they live. Yet the reality is that in essential details Jews are indistinguishable from their neighbours.

None the less, it is Jewish differentness (however that may, for the occasion, be defined) which, in a political dimension, gave birth to the idea of the 'national home' and eventually to the idea of the Jewish state. These two concepts need to be examined in the context of the presumed need to provide a social and political structure within which the Jews might feel secure and, with the expression of this need, to determine whether there are any objective ways of establishing the nature of Jewishness (other than by the assertion of its existence) which would permit the application of ideas of nationality or nationhood to the Jews, in any meaningful sense, in terms of modern politics. Such considerations are relevant to the larger theme of this book in so far as, if it were to be established that the Jews were indeed a nation, then it might be argued that they should be entitled to live as a nation, to identify with a 'homeland'. For such a development to be acceptable would require a series of quite specific criteria and qualifications.

It has already been observed that the Jews do not constitute a race. This, admittedly, is a difficult term to define precisely. A working definition might proceed on the lines that a race, like a species in the larger animal kingdom, is a numerically significant body of individuals who possess certain permanent and recognisable physical characteristics in common, and who will be linked by blood or lineal descent from a common ancestral stock. Such a definition has all sorts of flaws in it and exceptions which have to be made to it, all of which probably demonstrate the fragility of the concept of race as anything other than a term of general and superficial, if convenient, distinction between human groups. It is a concept which certainly has very little ground in scientifically verifiable reality. Race clearly cannot mean a community which exists only by shared religious perception, whose members are drawn from a melange of national and ethnic origins, many of whom will have been introduced to the community by means other than lineal descent from identifiable ancestors and who have no common language or linguistic roots in common.

The suggestion that Jews are members of one race has been examined extensively over the past century and more. The most accessible summary of the current position, based on a close and detailed examination of the available data drawn from a very diverse range of reference, is *The Myth of the Jewish Race* by Patai and Patai.[7]

60

As one of the authors identifies his own Jewish (Ashkenazi) origins, the title of the work is clearly not intended to be provocative. The title does, however, at an early stage declare its authors' position clearly: that there is no Jewish race, when a definition of that term is sought by the application of scientific or historical criteria.

Briefly stated, *The Myth of the Jewish Race* reviews the known history of the Jews from Biblical times onwards. It points to the constant infusion of different stocks into established Jewish communities over the centuries and to the effect of institutional or social influences such as conversion (forced or otherwise), mixed marriages, and even rape as factors constantly varying the genetic composition of any given Jewish community. It pays special attention to the effects of the various waves of proselytism which swept over Jewish communities in late antiquity and in early Christian times. The Khazars (of whom more later) have their place in the story, as do the complicated movements of the converted pre-Islamic Arabian tribes and the expulsion of those tribes which would not renounce Judaism when the Prophet broadcast his revelation to the peoples of the peninsula.

The question of whether or not the Jews constitute a race is, on the one hand, a consequence of their own search for a sort of communal identity and, on the other, the perceptions of non-Jews towards them. This need for an identity seems to be particularly strongly entrenched in the Jewish psyche, despite the evident apprehension by many Jews of their 'otherness' from those amongst whom they have lived, in the Biblical phrase as 'strangers and sojourners'. This evident need manifests itself in the issue of what actually constitutes Jewishness, ranging from the one extreme of 'a Jew is whoever thinks that he is a Jew' to the rigidly orthodox view that Jewishness can only be conferred by birth from a Jewish woman, who must herself therefore be of unassailably Jewish stock.

The Patais avoid the question, a difficult one in all conscience, of the origins of the people with whom the God of the Old Testament was said to have covenanted. However, this issue is of some importance since it is relevant to any claim which Jews living today might have a descent from the tribes whose exploits are recorded in the books of the Old Testament and in the Talmud. Since the tribes from whom modern Jews claim descent would have been genetically indistinguishable from the other peoples of the Levant in the late second to mid-first millennium, this diffidence perhaps is not to be wondered at.

The Patais trace the history of the Jews from the mid-first millennium. They are here on secure scholarly ground since it is only possible to speak with certainty of the Jews as a distinct group from post-Exilic times onwards. As part of the process of the dilution of whatever was the original stock from which the Jews of late antiquity might be said to descend, they cite the category of 'God Fearers', believers who did not accede wholly to Jewish practice or custom and who did not constitute members of Jewish communities but who, none the less, were accepted as proper partners for orthodox Jews in marriage or concubinage. In later centuries they also point to the admittedly disputed 'droit du seigneur' in European lands for the further dilution of Jewish genes. Similarly the often induced, if not actually forcible, conversion of the slaves of the more prosperous Jewish households in Muslim as well as in Christian lands, a well documented and frequently indulged practice, diffused the original genetic pool still more.

The evidence of the effect of widespread activity by Jewish missionaries in Arabia in pre-Islamic times will be further described later. At this point, it may be said that, so effective was Jewish proselytising that, for example, the Kingdom of Himyar, one of the most important of the South Arabian kingdoms in early Christian pre-Islamic times, became wholly Judaised as a result of a decision by the King of Himyar to accept the teachings of itinerant Jewish missionaries.[8] When the Jewish clans in Arabia at the time of the Prophet were offered the choice of expulsion or conversion, those who did not convert migrated out of Arabia and so added their 'Arabian' genes to the communities established around the shores of the Mediterranean, amongst whom they settled and by whom they were absorbed.

In this context it is pertinent to note that members of the later Jewish communities to survive in the Arabian peninsula, notably those in the Yemen (some of whom still live there, despite substantial migrations to Israel since the 1950s) are, genetically, indistinguishable from their Arab neighbours. This has been so despite, in the case of the Yemeni communities, their relative isolation over the last several hundred years.

The situation of the Jews of North Africa, one of the most

considerable and influential of the communities and established at least since Roman times and probably for longer still, is revealing. The inhabitants of North Africa, for whatever reason, responded keenly to Jewish missionary zeal in late antiquity; it seems probable that the Berbers in particular warmed to Judaism and provided a considerable element in the composition of the communities in the area. In all the great cities strung out along the southern Mediterranean littoral, Jewish communities were numerous, powerful, rich and highly cultured. From this rich stratum the later communities in Muslim lands and in Europe were to draw abundantly.

The Patais consider the evidence for the existence of a recognisable 'Jewish mind', though they accept that such a concept is difficult to quantify. They consider whether the Jews, when judged by acceptable psychological and anthropological criteria, can be shown as being of a different or a higher quality of intellectual ability than non-Jews. Their conclusion, based on a summary of rather disparate evidence, is that 'there is a higher percentage of individuals with a high general intelligence among Jews than among non-Jews'. They suggest that in scholarly pursuits Jews are 'over-represented' when compared with other groups.

They are emphatic that any differences which may be detected between Jews and non-Jews in these respects are the consequences of environmental factors. They propose that the most influential of these is the isolation or separation of Jewish communities living amongst non-Jews, the concentration of their energies on scholarly and intellectual pursuits, and the need to excel.

It will be understood that the Patais' evidence is drawn almost wholly from Ashkenazi cases and sources. The validity of their judgement may be confirmed by this very fact: the generally more tolerant – or indifferent – attitude of Muslim societies which will be described later, and the Islamic respect for learning, did not put the same pressure on the Oriental Jews to excel, or require them to concentrate themselves as was the case with Western or European communities. The search for intellectual excellence is not of itself of significance in Oriental Jewish communities.

The Myth of the Jewish Race is a thorough and careful study: it considers the evidence whether certain individuals or groups can be said to 'look Jewish' and dismisses the idea for the illusion that the evidence so clearly shows it to be. In this respect, as in others, the Patais' most frequently quoted conclusion, namely that the Jews tend to demonstrate the characteristics of the communities amongst whom they live to a degree greater than they show similarity with other Jewish groups, is borne out.

The most compelling aspect of the Patais' study, however, lies in their examination of clinical and genetic evidence which can be called to determine whether there are significant common factors linking the members of Jewish communities and differentiating them from other, non-Jewish communities.

They review those morphological traits of Jewish individuals which can be analysed: height, hair and eye colour, shape and size of nose, cephalic index, hand-clasping and arm-folding, fingerprint patterns, tooth morphology. From most of these factors the authors conclude that 'the evidence shows such variability that ... they refute the hypothesis of Jewish racial unity.' However, they do discern some evidence from fingerprint analysis which would suggest that 'some relatedness amongst such widely separated Jewish groups as those from Germany, Turkey, Morocco and Yemen.' They consider that the pattern found in all these groups is suggestive of a Mediterranean origin.

Many of the most telling of the Patais' observations are to be found in the study of genetic indices of Jewish populations. Such studies are still comparatively undeveloped: as the Patais point out, only a very small sample has so far been made of the 10,000 to 50,000 genes which all human beings possess. They point out, too, that apparent similarities in gene frequencies amongst disparate populations may reflect factors such as natural selection as much as any others, including a putative common or related origin.

The examination of blood group genes, red cell and serum proteins, all factors which are capable of identification and analysis, suggest an affinity between Jewish populations and Mediterranean groups. This is, of course, in accordance with the evidence of history, bearing in mind the rapid and extensive spread of Judaism as a result of population drift, conversion and social integration which have taken place around the Mediterranean's shores throughout Jewish history. Most particularly this process occurred during late antiquity, when the population base for the later communities in North Africa and Europe was laid down. But the evidence for a Mediterranean-linked association for modern Jewish populations does not, in itself, provide any grounds for speaking of a Jewish race nor indeed for regarding the Jews as a people any more homogeneous than any other. It assuredly does not provide any scientific authority for a claim of descent from groups living in the Levant in Biblical times.

The incidence of particular diseases among specific population groups can provide much relevant genetic information and help to identify associations or connections between one group and another. Such conditions as Tay-Sachs Disease, a recessive inherited condition which results in accumulations of fatty substances in the brain and is almost entirely confined to Ashkenazi Jews, as are Gaucher's Disease, Niemann Pick Disease, Hunter's Disease, Familial Dysantonomia, Bloom's Syndrome, Crohn's Disease (though non-Jews too suffer from this condition), and a variety of other conditions have been thought to be found especially amongst Western Jewish populations. The significant incidence of such conditions has been confirmed amongst widely disparate Jewish groups and it is notable that no one condition can be said to be characteristic of Jews in particular. Unlike the situation which pertains amongst the Ashkenazi communities, which have, inevitably, been much more extensively studied, no one disease (with the partial exception of Familial Mediterranean Fever) can be observed throughout either the Sephardi community or the Orientals as a whole. Thus few conclusions of real substance can be drawn from this evidence, other than the apparent lack of any correspondence in such conditions between the Ashkenazi and non-Ashkenazi communities.

There can be little doubt that the authors of *The Myth of the Jewish Race* have proved their case, that to speak of a Jewish race cannot be supported by the available evidence; where the term or its analogues have been used in the past the context is suspect, disparaging and frequently racialist. Certainly the genetic evidence studied gives no substance to the view that the Jews are an homogeneous ethnic group; they are, it may be said, as diverse as the rest of us.

As an aside it may be remarked that it is significant that

C. G. Jung, that most perceptive of the pioneers of analytical psychology, came to the same conclusion about the Jews in Europe and the general similarities which they demonstrated to the populations amongst which they lived (or, as I would prefer to put it, of which they were a part). In *Mind and Earth* (first published as *Mensche und Erde* in 1927) Jung wrote of the influence of what we might today call the environment on peoples living in a particular place at a particular time:

> We can observe in the Jews of the various European countries marked differences which can only be explained by the peculiarities of the people they live amongst. It is not difficult to tell a Spanish Jew from a North African Jew, a German Jew from a Russian Jew. One can even distinguish the various types of Russian Jews, the Polish from the North Russian and Cossack type. In spite of the similarity of race there are pronounced differences whose cause is obscure. It is extremely hard to define these differences exactly, though a student of human nature feels them at once.[9]

Though Jung speaks here of 'race', his understanding of the essential common identity of Jews with the populations among whom they live is striking. This insight of Jung's is part of the same sequence of penetrations into the human psyche which he made at this time, including what can only be called his precognition of the coming of National Socialism in Germany when he spoke of 'the blond beast', which he saw struggling to liberate itself in the psyche of many of his German patients and analysands, and of which he wrote in 1918.[10]

An inevitable consequence of the diversity of the characteristics of Jewish populations is that the Jews cannot be said to have any racial or ethnic connection with Palestine. But even if it could be proved conclusively that all or even the majority of all Jews living today were the direct lineal descendants of the ancient inhabitants of Palestine, this would give them no moral or legal right to 'return'. If such arguments were valid then the Celts could insist on their right of return to the Danube basin from whence, it is generally considered, Celtic speakers originated and from where they dispersed westwards to settle in Germany, France and the British Isles. Only history can confer the rights to nationhood.

But of course no direct descent can be established for the Jews any more than it could be for the Celts – though the survival of Celtic languages into modern times would give them something of an advantage, perhaps. The Jewish claim to Palestine rests only on the fact of possession: whether it is authorised by the myth of the covenant must depend on each individual's point of view. It was religious conditioning which prepared the European powers – or more precisely, the British in the first instance – to accept the idea of a 'national home'. A nation must be bound by common language, laws, customs, government and history. A nation may, of course, be formed out of the fusion of disparate peoples, as happened with the United States or, indeed, as is in the process of happening with the Jews now living in Israel. But the Jews from Europe, the actual founders of the Israeli state, did not possess the common elements to constitute nationhood, as a matter of political right, as was the case, for example, with the Dutch or as is clearly the case with the Irish.

The point can, perhaps, be made more tellingly by identifying some of the groups in the Near and Middle East who are at present deprived of nationhood yet who demonstrably fulfil the criteria for constituting a nation. Thus the Kurds have a distinct and well recorded history, speak their own language, live in a structured society and merely have the misfortune that their traditional lands are located within the frontiers of four modern states. The Armenians, similarly, are a people of the most distinct character, again with their own language, customs and hierarchies long established. The Palestinians, though they share in the culture and history of the larger Arab world, are clearly, by all recognisable criteria, a nation. The Jews, as Jews, patently are not.

The concept of a 'home' or 'homeland', too, is highly tendentious, suggesting as it does the place of origin of a particular people or community. To have any valid claim to possession of a particular territory a bloodline is surely necessary; in the United States an Apache will not be well received if he claims possession of the tribal lands of the Mohawk. It is simply not acceptable to rest such claims on make-believe. It may be understandable for a person of Scottish ancestry living in Australia to nurture some notion of Scotland as 'home'. But, as all jurists would surely agree, such fancies do not constitute rights nor, in such a case, the title to Scottish nationality – if indeed there were to be such a legal concept.

This excursion into the semantics of 'race', 'nation' and 'home' is prompted by the broad-based and objective nature of the evidence presented by the authors of *The Myth of the Jewish Race*. They do not of course concern themselves with the definitions of such terms for, with the exception of the first of them, they are not immediately relevant to their thesis. But they do allow themselves one curious indulgence, which sits oddly with the rest of their study. This is a chapter dealing with what they term 'The Latest Libel: the Jew as Racist'. In the chapters of their book relating to the history of the Jew in Europe they record the appearance of the 'blood libel', the peculiarly Christian calumny that the Jews abducted children and others to extract their blood for use in some unspeakable ritual practice.

The 'Latest Libel', however, is slightly different. This appears to be a response to the condemnation of Zionism as 'a form of racism', contained in a resolution passed by that ill-omened body, the General Assembly of the United Nations. Understandably Zionists, Israelis and many Jews who are neither, display anger and profess bafflement when this accusation is advanced. The Resolution in question, UN Resolution 3379 (XXX) 10 November 1975, proposed that 'Zionism is a form of racism and racial discrimination'. Its terms were based on and indeed repeated the definition contained in Resolution 1904 (XVIII) of 20 November 1963 which defined racial discrimination as 'any distinction, exclusion, restriction, or preference based on race, colour, descent, or national or ethnic origin.'

Israel supported the 1963 Resolution; the Resolution of 1975 was deeply mortifying to it. The Patais advance the rather curious view that, as they have proved conclusively that the Jews do not constitute a race, the Jews cannot therefore be accused of racism. Of course it is not the Jews or Judaism which are thus accused, though doubtless as strong a case could be made for Jews to be convicted of racism as may be done for any other group. The Old Testament, if taken literally, would certainly appear to be fiercely disparaging about the nature and character of people other than those chosen by the Bible's principal, capricious divinity – and even they do not escape from some fairly contumelious comment.

But the fact is that Zionism *is* racist, certainly in the terms of the United Nations 1963 Resolution. The Law of Return which grants any Jew of any national or ethnic origins the right of Israeli citizenship whilst excluding Palestinian Arabs from returning to what, in reality, is *their* homeland stands clearly within the Resolution's terms. The continued exclusion of the Palestinians from their homeland and the repeated cases of expulsion of Arabs emphasise the point. The essentially racist character of Zionism, as defined by the United Nations at a time when the Third World countries had not achieved the numerical or political influence which they hold today, and which at the time was not directed specifically against Israel, has now been assumed by Israel as state policy, despite the universal belief of Jews that they, of all people, should not be condemned as racists.

The United States and her allies were unstinting in their persistent pressure on the United Nations to rescind the 1971 resolution. This was duly accomplished to Israel's evident satisfaction and relief. But the rescinding of the resolution does nothing to change the condition which first gave rise to it. Zionism is patently and explicitly racist and Israel, in adopting Zionism as its basic tenet, is committed to a racist policy. The withdrawal of a United Nations resolution which proclaims that fact can no more change the nature of Israel than the passing of the resolution originally made Zionism racist.

4

LANGUAGE, PROPAGANDA AND ZIONISM

The curious uses to which language can be subjected have made discussion of the confrontation of the Arabs and the Israelis especially fraught: the terms which are used with greater or lesser precision in discussing the land of Palestine and its present dilemma have moved into Humpty Dumpty's world, of meaning precisely whatever the propagandist chooses they shall mean. First Palestine itself: this term is generally accepted as describing the historical and geographical entity which was the area of the British Mandate and which had previously been administered by the Ottoman Empire. It comprised, latterly, the districts or administrative units of Acre, Nablus and Jerusalem: the last, however, because of its religious significance, enjoyed a special status and was linked directly to Constantinople. Palestine, in the Ottoman period, was generally ruled from the governate of Damascus. Reaching back into earlier historical times, it had been ruled by a succession of peoples or powers: the Canaanites, Philistines, Israelites, Assyrians, Babylonians, Persians, Greeks, Romans, Byzantines, the Muslim empires, the Christians (briefly), the Turks, and the British (more briefly still). Despite this diversity of overlords, its people were, like most other peoples of the Levant and the Fertile Crescent, peasants and small townsfolk and as such, largely as unchanging in composition as in the character of their lives.

These were the Palestinians, the people who had lived continuously in the land, generation after generation, whether Muslim, Christian or Jewish by religious affiliation. Until the proclamation of the State of Israel, the term 'Palestinian' was clearly understood, whether employed adjectivally as in 'Palestinian village' or 'a Palestinian woman' or nominally, as 'the

70

Palestinians'. It is important, in passing, to note that 'Palestinian' does not imply only Muslim associations: although the majority of the indigenous population of Palestine is now Muslim, there has always been a sizeable number of equally indigenous Christians and, before Israel's creation, a tiny residual Jewish community, mainly confined to Jerusalem.

The words associated with the Jewish element in the population of Israel and beyond it are more complex and certainly more contentious than those which apply to the Palestinians themselves. Since they are associated with the Jewish character of Israel they carry with them all the overtones which they have acquired outside Israel, in the centuries before its conception and in lands far distant from the eastern Mediterranean.

The three most frequently recurring terms employed in the context of Palestine politics and Israel are *Jew*, *Semite* and *Zionist* and their cognates. They are three singularly difficult terms to define since each has many layers of meaning. This does not, however, generally prevent everyone who uses them from being quite confident that they know what they mean and that those who read or hear them will understand what the originator intended them to understand. It is the Humpty Dumpty school of linguistics which determines such attitudes.

The term 'Jew' is meaningful when it is used to denote the membership of a community with shared cultural and, though no longer essentially, religious characteristics, customs and beliefs. In antiquity the people who inhabited the towns and villages of the Middle East, specifically those of the Arabian peninsula and the desert regions extending into the lands known today as Syria, Jordan and Iraq, together with parts of the north and west of Saudi Arabia, were bound together by common customs and related languages. Some may have been nomadic: by no means all of them were nomads and it should be remembered that nomadism is often a later refinement of living in desert lands and not a primitive stage on the progress to a settled way of life. By the beginnings of the first millennium BC it is possible to put names to some of the languages of the Arabian peninsula and its peripheral regions, and to the peoples who spoke them. The first reference to the Arabs occurs in an inscription of Shalmaneser III, composed after the battle of Qargan in 852 BC.[1] The first definite reference to the Jews is less sure, but it is certainly somewhat later; the term really has no

71

meaning until after the Persian period. There is, incidentally, no historical or archaeological evidence for the presence of the Hebrews, or of any group that can, with reasonable certainty, be identified with them, in Egypt at the time of the events leading up to what the Bible has recorded as the Exodus (see also Chapter 6).

What is indisputable is that by the middle of the first millennium (*circa* 500 BC) the members of the particular linguistic group which was later to be called the Jews, speaking a dialect of the ancestral Canaanite language which had, in all probability originated in the region of what is today north-west Saudi Arabia, Jordan and southern Syria, manifested the most remarkable poetic and editorial sensibility, producing in the process a singularly splendid canon of myth and tribal lore. This rich expression of the people's poetic energy was drawn from their own cultural background and that of many of their neighbours, including some who did not belong to their family of languages but with whom they were or had once been in contact, either directly or others of whom they had no surviving memory. Of these the Sumerians were amongst the most powerful of such influences.

The Sumerians, the first urban civilisation known to history, lived in the southern region of what is today Iraq; they were amongst the most creative of ancient peoples. Amongst other innovations of profound influence, without which the world today would be an entirely different place, the Sumerians invented writing, first as a system of accountancy, later in a flexible form which allowed for, and indeed encouraged, literary expression. They were inveterate storytellers and, in the manner of all humanity, speculated about their conditions and their place in the order of the universe. They invented a rich theogany and a diverse, if rather unappealing, collection of divinities. They disappeared from the historical record at the end of the third millennium BC, though their language continued in a limited and fossilised form to survive in ritual usage.[2]

In this it was a precedent for what was, some fifteen hundred years later, to happen to Hebrew. The speakers of that language, however, even in the days when it flourished as a living tongue, recalled little of the Sumerians' existence, though they were to derive some of their most compelling myths from them and from their Babylonian and Assyrian successors – the latter semitic speakers all of them, unlike the Sumerians whose language is unlike any others, living or dead. From this medley of cultural experience was produced a corpus of myth and poetry which has profoundly enriched humanity: that such is the case may be ascribed by the devout to its divine inspiration, by the sceptical to the vagaries of historical chance and poetic imagination. From the middle of the first millennium BC, especially after the Babylonian exile, the Jews become a definable, discernible group, living amongst other Near Eastern people. What these people, at this time, had in common was a shared semitic root to the languages which they spoke.[3]

It was remarked earlier that it is apparently difficult, in the contemporary world, to define precisely what is meant by the term 'Jew'. In antiquity, after the Babylonian captivity, the definition seems to have been relatively clear, meaning a member of one of the communities which followed the teachings of the rabbis who looked to the temple as the fount of their beliefs, which were also to be enshrined in the books of the Torah. In later times, partly because of the widespread practice of proselytisation, this comparatively well defined character of the Jews became blurred, to the extent that, not altogether frivolously, it was said that a Jew is whoever considers himself to be a Jew. Whilst the most orthodox rabbinical circles will today insist that Jewishness is inherent in descent from an acknowledged Jewish mother, the view of Jewishness as something like a form of self-expression demolished any exclusive quality which might have been thought to attach itself to Jewishness, certainly in any genetic or linear sense. However the *claim* of Jewishness is apparently sufficient to give title to Israeli nationality.

It is informative, in this context, to consider the equally uncertain application of the term 'Arab' to so many otherwise disparate peoples. It is clear that when Arabs use the term they use it in a generally cultural sense: an Arab is one who speaks Arabic and whose culture is derived from the shared experience of generations of Arabic speakers. Thus Berbers, Africans, Hamito-Semites and Levantines can all be classed as 'Arabs' but the term does not imply any distinct or specific racial affiliations, however the term 'race' may be defined. The inhabitants of the Arabian peninsula, the northern Arabian and Syro-Arabian deserts are probably the only people who can properly be called

Arabians, just as they are probably the only true semites, using that term in its proper, if narrow, linguistic sense.

One of the more important societies which developed in the Near East in the last centuries of the ancient world was that of the Nabataeans, who lived in what is now north-west Saudi Arabia and in Jordan, where their capital, Petra, survives as one of the wonders descending from the ancient world. The Nabataeans were ancestral to the modern Arabs and they spoke a language which is akin to Arabic. They developed a prosperous and extremely viable state with a dynasty of kings who treated with Rome on something approaching terms of equality. They were, interestingly enough, expert in irrigation and achieved a considerable reputation for 'turning the desert green'. They were eventually subsumed into the Roman Empire, their kingdom forming the province of Arabia Petraea.

The Nabataeans flourished at a time of great prosperity for the Jewish communities in the Levant and around the Mediterranean. Nabataean prosperity was based on the control of most of the caravan routes bringing spices and incense up, out of Arabia, to the Roman world. It is clear from many records of the time that the Arab Nabataeans and the Jewish communities who were their neighbours lived amicably together, considering each other to be of the same people, merely with differing religious observances. The Jews' general adoption of Aramaic as their spoken language, with its close affinity to Nabataean, obviously assisted their friendly and peaceable relationship.

This introduces, in its proper context, the second term considered here, which is used even more indiscriminately. 'Semite' and its cognates, especially its antithesis, 'anti-semite', cannot with honesty or accuracy be given a racial connotation: once again, it must be said, there is no semitic race. *Semite* and *semitic* refer specifically and solely to a linguistic division. Semitic languages are those which had their roots originally in the northern, perhaps specifically the north-western, quadrant of the Arabian peninsula and the desert regions which run northwards from it. Today the only true semitic language surviving in common currency is Arabic: Amharic, the principal language of Ethiopia, is closely akin to semitic tongues in its origins, but it is not a semitic language. In ancient times a rich variety of semitic languages flourished in the Near East, but these became subsumed into various well defined groups, of which Arabic is today the only living survivor. Hebrew, as it is spoken today as the official language of Israel, is a largely artificial construct, so much so that no one now is sure how Hebrew was pronounced in ancient times. Of this, more will be said.

If a generalised observation about the historical character of the speakers of semitic languages is sought it could be said that they have been especially identified with the waging of war, often of a particularly bloodthirsty sort, against their neighbours. The books of the Old Testament are an unremitting record of dire and savage attacks being launched by the semitic speakers whose wars it particularly celebrates, usually at the behest of their stern and unforgiving divinity. But they were by no means the first people speaking a semitic language who wreaked havoc on the lands around them. It can be argued that the gentle and creative Sumerians who spoke a non-semitic language and whose disputes, conducted on the scale of minute sorties of one little city state against another, were restricted to themselves, were eventually subsumed into a semitic-speaking flood which, over the centuries, poured out of the deserts.

The Akkadians and their successors the Babylonians and the Assyrians were all semitic speakers. The Akkadians created the first empire (under Sargon I) and obliterated their opponents in Mesopotamia and further away still in campaigns of conquest.[4] Sargon's proclamations are ripe examples of the sort of political bombast and vituperative denigration of his enemies which is not unknown today. The Babylonians and the Assyrians were even more aggressive, the latter especially so, for they have left behind a visual record of their rule of subject peoples – impalement, burning at the stake, the cutting off of limbs – which would fuel the fantasies of a thousand concentration camp commanders. Yet it is as absurd to attribute culpability to a linguistic group who lived in the Middle East centuries ago as it would be – perhaps – to condemn the speakers of English for the crimes of the slave trade.

It is manifestly meaningless to attempt to equate *semite* exclusively with *Jewish*: the two terms in no sense mean the same thing. It may be said, with tolerable accuracy, that the only true semites are the Arabs of the Arabian peninsula and other peripheral lands since they alone speak a semite language as their mother tongue. In summary, to be anti-semitic today can only mean, ludicrously, to be hostile to the Arabic language or, more sinisterly, to those who speak it.

The third term in general currency is 'Zionist'. This has, in the context of Israel as it is constituted today, a purely political significance and meaning. However, 'Zion' was one of the expressions which, in Jewish religious belief, meant the supreme community of Judaism: in this context its closest analogue is probably 'Jewry', but that term has none of the historic and emotional associations that 'Zion' conveys. It was adopted, in a brilliant propaganda stroke, as the term around which the various disparate groups of Jewish activists in the latter part of the last century could rally in the campaign to secure a homeland for the Jews. With the adoption of Zionism as the focus of the general propaganda armoury of the activists, came a convergence with the idea of the 'Return', an ancient Jewish aspiration related to the Dispersion, around which the early Zionists found that they could assemble their extremely diverse constituency. Zionism became the political movement which campaigned for the creation of a Jewish homeland, later for the return of all Jews to the land of Israel, to Zion. Zionism is often used in much the same sense as *Arabism* is employed, to denote the common sense of identity of all Arabic speakers regardless of nationality (or religious affiliation), or *negritude*, to express the sense of identity of peoples of African descent.

It is important to understand that there are two distinct concepts of 'Zion'. One is the political movement which promotes a programme demanding the patriation of all Jews in the world to the State of Israel. Zionism is a particularly ruthless creed, materialistic, humanist and, in the form which it assumed at the beginning of the present century, resolutely socialistic. It is an expression of belief in the exclusive nature of Jews and of Judaism and of the special status which should be accorded to them. Nowhere is this concept more evident than in the relationship between the Jews and the Palestinians. It is clear, from the time of the earliest expressions of Zionist aspirations to the latest declarations by the leaders of modern Israel such as Begin and Shamir, that Zionism has no place for the indigenous people of Palestine, whose only role is to act as the 'hewers of wood and drawers of water'[5] for the Jewish immigrants. The Arabs are seen as a kind of sub-Man or *'untermensch'*, a term whose nature is demonstrated by its use by the Nazis to categorise the Slavs and, sometimes, the Jews themselves. Shamir, when the Prime Minister of Israel, described the Arabs as 'grasshoppers compared to us', an expression which hardly conveys a sense of partnership and goodwill, by those that he at least clearly conceives as the ruling Jewish elite, towards a subject people. But it is inescapable, after even a reasonably objective consideration of Zionist pronouncements from the earliest days to the present, that the Jews are to be seen as a *'volk'*, a people of special qualities, needs and rights.

Within this context it must be recognised that Zionism is to be deplored for precisely the same reasons that Nazism was recognised as evil and Marxism, at least in the political systems which it inspired, is evil. Nazism exalted the interests of a *'volk'* above all others, particularly above those of allegedly lesser peoples; Marxism exalted the interests of a class. Zionism exists in the same dismal swampland of politics as the others; it too exalts the interests of a particular people above all others, despising the indigenes of the land which its followers have appropriated.

But *Zion*, as a religious concept, is entirely different from the political expression which has adopted it. It is closely connected with the role of the Messiah, the promised Redeemer, in Jewish religious lore; hence, in orthodox belief, the yearning for the realisation of 'Zion' on earth is not to be achieved, except at the end of days, when the Messiah returns to lead God's people home. It is very significant that the most orthodox rabbinical authorities are implacably opposed to the existence of the Zionist state, rejecting absolutely Israel the political entity, with armies, a foreign policy and the presumption to interfere in religious affairs. Worse still, in the minds of the most orthodox, the state presumes to enact what it chooses to call laws, when all law has been laid down by Divine intervention in the form of the Books of the Torah. Whilst they often present a grotesque picture of mindless bigotry, the extreme orthodox are, in the minds of many, closer to the nature of Judaism than the sleek European propagandists and the gunmen of Mossad who so often appeared to be the most typical servants of the Israeli state.

Thus the two Zions, the secular, political Zion and the Zion of religious tradition, have nothing whatsoever to do with each other. Indeed, they are in a very real sense mutually exclusive.

It is a tribute to the political skills of the Zionists that they have succeeded in blurring this distinction, at least to all except those to whom it is a matter of the most profound religious belief.

To the observer it would appear that there is a formidable barrier between political Zionism and the most deep-seated religious traditions of the Jewish people. From the earliest traditions, through the work of the editors of the Old Testament, and from the evidence of the great commentators of late antiquity and the Middle Ages, it is clear that the idea of a Jewish state as a political entity, was to be emphatically rejected by the Jewish community as a whole. Even when suffering under a tyrannous ruler it were better, according to this view, that God's people should suffer, rather than forsake their ancient heritage as the Chosen. As such, earthly or human institutions were of no account, for God alone had determined the only form of government proper for the Jews, enshrined forever in the Torah, the Books of the Law. To attempt to confine this god-given law within the bounds of a human state or the laws of man was ultimately and irrevocably blasphemous.[6] The nature of Jewish fundamentalism, in this respect, is well covered by the startling arrogance of the expression of belief by Agudah, the movement created by the Orthodox Sages, representing the most unbending interpretation of the Torah: 'The world was created for the sake of Israel. ... This means that the *raison d'être* of the world is the establishment of the regime of the Torah in the Land of Israel.'[7] This comment, which may strike the dispassionate observer as both elitist and exalted, does not, it should be observed, countenance the establishment of the State of Israel as it exists today but as a community governed solely by the Torah and, naturally enough, those religious scholars who believe that they alone can interpret it.

But the Zionists of the latter part of the nineteenth and the first half of the twentieth centuries were unaware of or, more likely, indifferent to the mutterings of religious scholars. Secular men living in a secular world, they were able very easily to conceal the real nature of historical Jewishness even from their constituents. They were able to present them with a prospectus for political identity, in direct opposition to the essential character of the myths which underlay their inherited culture and which they had acquired rather than inherited from the Jews of antiquity.

Those who seized on the ancient identification of the idealised land of Israel as 'Zion' were, from the outset, the most committed protagonists of the Jewish settlement of Palestine and the creation of the Jewish state. From this brilliant conflation, Theodore Herzl, the notably secular-minded founder of political Zionism at the end of the last century, and his followers promoted a political movement for the Zionisation (or Judaisation) of Palestine. Israel was brought into existence as a consequence of intense, constantly sustained pressure in Britain, the United States and, to a lesser degree, in European countries, as a response to the peculiarly European problem of the persecution of the Jews.

It is one of the ironies of history that European civilisation, which has in so many respects raised the spirit of man to heights previously unimagined, has also, in the name of its civilising mission and its predominant religious faith, perpetrated more acts of aggression and cruelty against other peoples than any other in history. The deliberate isolation and persecution of minorities, of those who dissent against the prevailing orthodoxy of the ruling establishment, has repeatedly shown itself as a characteristic of European history over the past thousand years and more. It is a sad and dismal record and there is no doubt that some of its blackest pages are those which reveal the frequency with which the Jews have been the target for this particular aberration. It must be said that Zionism is essentially the product of the European persecution of the Jews.

Zionism as a political belief, once articulated, quickly woke a response amongst European Jews and those who were sympathetic to them, as an answer to their centuries-long record of suffering at the hands of their tormentors. Though political Zionism originated in Germany and despite the fact that many of its earliest protagonists came from the German Empire, it early on drew its most devoted adherents from Russian lands. Jews had been permitted to settle only comparatively late in lands controlled by the Tsarist administration. None the less a particularly virulent form of anti-Jewishness manifested itself there, frequently expressed in the pogroms which were directed against Jewish communities. In western and southern Russia, in Poland and in Lithuania the lives of the Jews were desperate. Russian Jews tended to be amongst the most disadvantaged of all Jewish communities, living the lives of the poorest peasants, barely surviving at subsistence level, or in equally miserable conditions in the cities and small towns. They had few if any of the sometimes equivocal advantages enjoyed by their fellow-Jews in western countries; it is in consequence greatly to their credit that they kept their enthusiasm for learning and for the pursuit of personal excellence and advancement which to this day typifies so many of the members of the Jewish communities which descend from them.

The Ottoman Empire, the most powerful and militant polity in the Islamic world, was especially welcoming to the Jews.[8] When the Jewish communities of Spain and Portugal were expelled, the most powerful Muslim state in the world offered them haven and security. In the eighteenth century, when the Jews of Eastern Europe found the burden of Christian rule intolerable, they were encouraged to move to the east and to settle themselves in the cities of the Empire. The Sultan, on several recorded occasions, intervened with European princes asking for toleration for the Jews, established Jewish communities in the Ottoman cities, and sent emissaries to the west to promote Jewish migration not to Palestine but to the prosperous and highly civilised cities of the Ottoman Caliphate.

This concern for the protection of the Jews and the status which Jewish communities enjoyed in Ottoman lands gives a special point and poignancy to the entirely false assertion, common in Israel today, that the Jews of the Orient and the Muslims have always hated and feared each other and that the Jews were constantly marked out for persecution by Muslim rulers. The life of minorities in Muslim lands was often far from paradisal, except in comparison with life in Christian lands. But the treatment of Jews in Ottoman lands was regarded by Jews themselves throughout those vast domains as infinitely superior to that experienced under a Christian dispensation, as many distinguished Jewish sources of the time testify.[9]

By the end of the eighteenth century some further migration of Jews from eastern Europe took place, first towards the west, accelerating as countries as distant as Britain and America welcomed them. At the same time a trickle of religious Jews began to make their way towards Palestine, to swell the microscipic community which had lived there since Crusader times, and no doubt from earlier times still.

By the end of the nineteenth century the Jews, predominantly from eastern Europe who had migrated westwards and who formed the basis of Jewish communities in Western Europe, had achieved considerable prosperity and influence. Because many of them were high achievers they were to be found in positions when they were able to influence policy and opinion in many Western countries, to a degree which far outweighed their numbers in the societies in which they lived. They were accepted in those societies, with all the reservations of course that any secure and established elite directs towards the advance of newcomers. But accepted they generally were and their power, political and financial, grew prodigiously, not least in the minds of those who remained their enemies. When Zionism appeared as a distinct political doctrine it elicited a series of responses in Europe which were rooted in the acceptance of Judaism as ancestral to Christianity and, equally, the rejection of the Jews as an alien implant in the European body politic.

The history of Zionism has been written exhaustively by its supporters and opponents alike. The product of a dynamic, wholly secularised German Jew, Theodore Herzl, Zionism was from its earliest days identified as a movement of unmistakably European character, growing out of the concepts of nationalism which emerged so powerfully in the eighteenth and nineteenth centuries. Its objective was to obtain a secure country in which Jews could live safely, free from the knout and cossack charge.

Herzl conceived the idea of a 'Judenstaat', the Jewish state.[10] In proposing a separate political identity for the Jews, Herzl was vigorously opposed by virtually the whole of the Jewish establishment in European countries. The leaders of European Jewry saw their hard-won achievements of respect and acceptance in the societies of which, increasingly, they considered themselves to be a part, set at naught by an irresponsible and capricious nationalism, which the more traditional of them recognised to be at odds with the essential character of Jewish history.

At this time Zionism had not focussed on Palestine as the land which it sought to plant itself; East Africa, Madagascar and Australia were proposed as possible sites for settlement. But once the idea of a Palestinian location had been expressed it was eagerly accepted by the Zionists themselves as the most obvious locus for their ambitions. Palestine became a metaphor for the sense of national identity which Zionism fostered. Later,

Zionism was taken up enthusiastically by politicians in Europe such as Churchill, who saw advantage in the espousal of the cause. Indeed, in fairness to Churchill, support for Zionism seems to have been one of the very few policies which he maintained consistently throughout his peculiarly feckless political career, which was otherwise devoted to tacking in whichever direction the political wind seemed for the moment to be blowing, in the hope that it might somehow bring him the office and political influence which eluded him for most of his lifetime. But in his adherance to the advancement of Zionist interests he was by no means typical, either of his time or of his contemporaries. Gradually, however, Zionism began to make notable inroads into Western policy and to increase significantly the number of its adherents in Western lands.

The campaign for the establishment of a Jewish state in Palestine was conducted mainly in the drawing rooms of the politically powerful, the offices of ministers who might be persuaded to support the cause, and in the sanctums of bankers and businessmen who were coming more and more to dominate the politics as much as they did the economies of the West. Nobody at this point considered it worth consulting the Palestinians. They were, in the first place, a subject people of the Ottoman Empire – which was not an institution much disposed to canvass the opinions of its subjects – and later, after the Great War, of the British Empire, as holders of the Mandate awarded to it by the Powers at the Peace Conference held in 1919. Of course, some Palestinian notables, alarmed at the evident increase in Jewish immigration, protested vigorously, but their complaints went largely unheard. Trouble between the two communities was inevitable; the British tried, feebly, to pacify both sides and succeeded in satisfying neither.

But before the Mandate was committed to Britain an episode occurred which has become fundamental to the creation of the Jewish state. The Balfour Declaration stands high in the lists of political actions whose influence endured long after the immediate situation they were intended to confront. It was released in the form of a letter to Lord Rothschild, a keen supporter of the Zionist cause, from the Foreign Secretary of the day, Arthur Balfour. Though it has been quoted on countless occasions it must have its place here too, since it is one of the fundamental pieces in the game which was ultimately to result in the creation of Israel. The Declaration stated:

> His Majesty's Government view with favour the establishment in Palestine of a national home for the Jewish people and will use their best endeavours to facilitate the achievement of this object, it being clearly understood that nothing should be done which may prejudice the civil and religious rights of existing non-Jewish communities in Palestine or the rights and political status enjoyed by Jews in any other country.[11]

Few such brief and relatively bland statements have left such political havoc in their wake. The intention of the British government of the day, hard-pressed and at a dangerous point in the war with the Central Powers, was to mobilise Jewish support in Britain and more particularly in America, where it was actually inclined to favour Germany and its allies, to the Allied cause.[12] The motivation was neither particularly idealistic nor high-minded; rather it was an example of the baleful consequences of the short-term expedient so readily adopted by politicians at all times. It has, however, been employed ruthlessly, by Zionist and Israeli politicians in turn, to justify both the prospect and the existence of Israel as a sovereign Jewish state. That there is nothing whatsoever in the Declaration that admits of the interpretation that a sovereign state, let alone a specifically sectarian one, was intended by those who drafted it or by its signatory, has counted for nothing: the Balfour Declaration, with the equally illusory vote of the United Nations General Assembly which is alleged to have conferred legal status on Israel, have stood as the two great foundations on which the political status of Israel has been raised.

Not the least of the ironies of the situation surrounding the creation of the State of Israel is the fact that Arthur Balfour, who has from time to time assumed heroic proportions in Zionist myth-making, was resolutely anti-Jewish. He made clear his distaste for Jews and Jewry in conversation with Chaim Weizmann, who was to become the first president of Israel. In a particularly surreal episode Balfour recalled to Weizmann a conversation which he had held with, of all sympathetic listeners, Cosima Wagner, in the devoutly anti-Jewish stronghold of Bayreuth.[13]

Despite the expression of hope regarding the treatment of non-Jewish communities which is enshrined in the Declaration, it is clear that the early Zionists gave little attention to the Muslim and Christian Arabs of Palestine, as little attention, indeed, as they gave to the Oriental Jews living in the Middle East from early times. The Arabs, if they were considered at all, were seen as a convenient (and cheap) labour-force, waiting patiently for the coming of the Zionist settlers. It was confidently averred that once the Arabs saw that the Jewish presence in their land was there to stay and they observed the superior technology which the immigrants would bring with them, any opposition from them could be expected to wither away. Remarkably, this idea, so remote from reality, seems to have been believed by Jews and non-Jews alike. In essential terms, from the outset there never was any place for the Arabs in the Zionist vision of the Jewish state, nor, if the matter is viewed objectively, could there be. The Zionists, from the beginning, recognised that they would be considered as interlopers who would have to justify their continued presence in the country by coercion, not by persuasion.

The introduction of large groups of alien, European Jewish immigrants into Palestine disturbed disastrously the balance between the various communities which had lived together for centuries. The destabilisation which the growing number of immigrants wrought in Palestine before 1948 was to be repeated a hundredfold by the presence of Israel as a political factor in the Middle East, from the moment of its foundation in 1948 to the present day.

Another of the documents essential to an understanding of the origins and character of the state of Israel is often referred to, but less frequently are its terms described or its provisions considered. The language of the Mandate, under which Britain was appointed to govern Palestine is, by any standard, remarkable. Taken in the context of its time and the distrust and dislike in which the generality of the Jewish people were held, it is quite extraordinary; it reads today as though it were dictated solely by Jewish interests. Its purport is unmistakable; the Jewish nature of Palestine is conceded, as is the wholly spurious 'historical link' between Palestine and the Jews of Europe. The terms of the Mandate should have alerted all to the inevitability of Jewish supremacy being accepted in Palestine by the Powers;

indeed, many Arabs recognised it so, but were powerless to influence the course of events.

The Mandate (see Appendix 1 for the full text of this remarkable document) reiterates the pious but, as it was to be, worthless expression of the Balfour Declaration, some parts of which are clearly subsumed within it, requiring the rights of non-Jewish communities in Palestine to be respected. It then speaks of 'reconstructing their [the Jews'] national home in that country'. This clearly anticipates, by invoking a specious historical precedent, the creation of a Jewish political entity. The Mandate has as one of its principal objectives the creation in Palestine of such 'political, administrative and economic conditions as will secure the establishment of the Jewish national home'. More extraordinary still, an 'appropriate Jewish Agency' was to be recognised as the proper organ of 'advising and co-operating with the Administration of Palestine'. This turned out to be the Zionist Organisation, though in 1922 when the Mandate was promulgated, it was representative of only a tiny fraction of the opinion of world Jewry. Jewish immigration was to be facilitated and a nationality law, perhaps the most extraordinary of all the Mandate's provisions, was to be framed to 'facilitate the acquisition of Palestinian citizenship by Jews'. The Zionist Organisation was to be assisted in the development of land and services. It is little to be wondered at that many Arabs, the Palestinians included, see the Mandate as further evidence of long-planned policy to appropriate their land.

From this time onwards, it must have been clear to any alert observer that the future of the Palestinians had been lost. The terms of the Mandate are prolix, but there is little doubt that the British government foresaw the prospect of a federal structure, or something very like it, determining the political future of Palestine. However, its reference to 'a Jewish National Home' repeated the ambiguity of the Balfour Declaration in its most important respect. To the Zionists the idea of 'sharing' the Promised Land was entirely unacceptable. Their policy was simply to possess it all.

The situation in Palestine deteriorated markedly during the years between the wars. Little notice was taken by the European powers or by America of reports of the persecution of the Jews by the Nazis in Germany; Jews themselves, understandably, turned to the idea of Palestine as a refuge from an increasingly dreadful reality. The British prevaricated and the Palestinians were outraged but largely impotent; no one came out of those years with credit or the significant achievement of their aims.

But the years immediately before the war were important in the history of the Zionist movement. Though immigration was restrained by the British authorities, thousands of European Jews did move to Palestine. Many were earnestly socialist in their political orientation, which was to colour the politics of the early years of the Israeli state. From their number were created the kibbutz movement and the collectivist agricultural and small-scale industrial projects which grew up in and around the kibbutzim.

The part played by the various Zionist organisations during the rise of Nazism in Germany and its by-products in other European countries has been extensively studied but little reported.[14] This is no doubt because it is largely discreditable to the Zionist establishment, for it is to be found frequently displaying a preparedness to come to terms with the Nazis which is distasteful and frightening by turns. At one point Zionist organisations were negotiating with the Nazis to promote the export of German products to facilitate the emigration of Jews to Palestine. At another, the Zionists tried to negate the efforts of the Jewish anti-Nazi travel boycott, which they saw as likely to prejudice their negotiations with the Nazi authorities. The practice of negotiating with a mortal enemy recurs throughout the history of Zionism and Israel, even to the present day when controversy can surround a play which relates to the efforts of a Hungarian Jewish leader, Rezso Kasztner to enable a group of Jews, including members of his own family, to escape in return for payment to the Nazi authorities, or the part which Israel played in the Iran-Contra affair.[15]

Throughout the period immediately before the outbreak of the Second World War, the Zionist groups played a devious and complex game which resonated long afterward into the years when Israel had been created as an independent state. There was a substantial constituency amongst the Jews of eastern Europe who were drawn to fascism in organisational party terms and in the promotion of an exclusivist 'volkisch' mentality in ideology as well. This was especially true in Poland. One of the most important influences to emerge from Polish Zionism was that of the sinister figure of Vladimir Ze'ev Jabotinsky, who is identified with Revisionism, a particularly absolutist form of Zionism which was unashamedly nationalistic and racist.[16] Early on Jabotinsky had compromised himself with Petliura, a fervently fascist politician who, like many of his sort, saw the acceptance of Palestine as a 'dumping ground' for Europe's Jews and hence as a solution to Europe's 'Jewish question'. Later Jabotinsky became the leader of the Bitai movement, a fascist group which even adopted the Nazis' brown shirts as its uniform. Out of this unsavoury amalgam eventually emerged Jabotinsky's spiritual and political successor, Menachem Begin, and the Herut Party, one of the principal components of the modern Likud grouping in Israel today. Bitai was – and remains, in its present vestigial form, its principal body having been absorbed into the mainstream of Israeli politics – unreservedly fascist.

So bizarre and complex were the machinations of the Zionist groups pre-war, so obsessionally fixed were they on the seizure of Palestine by whatever means, that reason seems sometimes to have deserted their leaders. Thus they are to be found at one point receiving the good wishes of Heydrich, the unspeakable SS man who later became 'Protector of Czech lands' ('Our good wishes, together with our official good will, go with them,' he observed, of the migrants to Palestine),[17] and in an even more chillingly weird episode Eichmann visited Palestine with the encouragement of Haganah, the terrorist group whose leadership was later to provide the nucleus of the Israeli army and the security forces.[18] Eichmann's mission involved a visit to a kibbutz, which impressed him greatly. His contact in Palestine was a virulent Zionist, Polke, who at one time offered the services of the Haganah to provide intelligence about the activities of Muslim leaders to the Nazis. It is difficult to offer a meaningful comment on such sinister, if maniacal, politicking; however, in these episodes are the seeds of Israel's readiness to compromise herself with her overt enemies or with the enemies of her friends, if such a course of action, even if judged in the shortest of terms, is seen to advance her aims or policies.

Developments equally sinister for the Palestinians followed the migration of the Jews from Europe. These were the practices attending the acquisition of land by Jewish settlers, promoted principally through the medium of the Jewish Agency by means which were frequently suspect or downright illegal.[19] Large tracts of land had been acquired by various Jewish individuals and charities, principally from absentee Christian landlords, from early in the present century. As many of the Arab villagers had lived on the land from time beyond memory, there were few land records. The Ottomans, in any case, had not favoured such proofs of ownership by people who were often regarded as little more than serfs. This was to prove of great advantage to the Israeli state's programme of land acquisition, often by compulsory land purchases of extreme legal dubiety, since the state could, with impunity, dispute the Arabs' legal title to lands in which they lived. The dispossession of the Arabs of their land has always followed the course of Israeli development in Israel itself and, later, in the Occupied Territories. The groundwork for this policy was laid down in the pre-war period.

The Second World War saw the frenzy of Nazi persecution turned against the Jews. Quite apart from what was happening in Germany itself, even more frightening evidence of decades of envy and dislike of the Jewish communities which had been planted in Western Europe manifested itself in those countries which fell under German hegemony, in persecutions of the Jews in countries where otherwise they had appeared to be tolerated. But the European enthusiasm for the persecution of minorities was still very much alive in France, in Czechoslovakia, Yugoslavia, Austria, Hungary and Rumania. In many cases it seemed as though the servants of the Nazis in these countries sought to outdo the ferocity of their masters in eliminating Jewish communities.

Even in wartime the role of some of the Zionist leaders at this time, in what has been revealed about their dealings with the Nazi leadership, was clearly equivocal, to say the least. The part played by Lehi (Lochamaei Herut Yisrael), which later was to become better known as the Stern Gang, was particularly reprehensible, but it must be said that, not for the first or last time in the history of the Zionist right wing, like was calling to like.[20] It is clear that a deal was proposed with the Nazi authorities and Jewish leaders whereby a million Jews would be permitted to emigrate to America. The United States agreed, but the Zionist leadership opposed the idea vehemently, insisting that no deal should be done which did not allow migration to Palestine. To have agreed to the proposal for migration to America would, they realised, have destroyed the idea of Palestine as the only proper home for the Jews, to be secure from whatever menace; equally they knew that for the British government, as the holder of the Mandate, to agree to such a proposal would be unthinkable. Thus a million Jews were consigned to the gas chambers and the gallows to satisfy the political imperatives of their self-appointed saviours; such was the outstanding achievement of the Jewish Agency, the Zionist body which was, in the fullness of time, to become the nucleus of the government of the Jewish state.[21]

During the war the Zionist leadership, by this time well organised, well financed and politically extremely sophisticated, let no occasion pass for the advancement of their cause, pressing for the translation of the equivocal statements of the Balfour Declaration into full-blown recognition of a Jewish national state in Palestine. They badgered Churchill – despite his open commitment to their cause – and the other allied leaders without cease, indifferent to any interests other than their own and dismissive of any action which did not, in their view, contribute directly to the Zionisation of Palestine, which had to have the primacy over any other issue. Their pressure on the American administration, which, under Roosevelt's resolutely anti-British leadership, was disposed to stand aside in the conflict with the Axis powers, seeing it as an essentially European matter, was probably one of the most decisive in bringing that reluctant ally to the side of Britain and the handful of other countries which stood against Germany and her allies. Their motivation, however, was clear: an Allied victory was essential to the realisation of the Zionists' plans.

In the immediate aftermath of the war Britain, exhausted and bankrupt (the latter state produced largely as a result of the greed and suspicion of its American ally), found itself still the unhappy holder of the Palestinian Mandate. The Zionists renewed their campaign with still greater violence; under their dispensation the deliberate use of terror tactics directly against innocent urban populations was introduced to the modern world for the first time. To the Zionists' dismay, however, the British seemed again to prevaricate and to show reluctance, particularly as expressed in the policies of the Foreign Secretary Ernest Bevin, to hand over full and unrestricted power to them.[22] Terrorism escalated into a frightful campaign of bombing and mayhem, characteristically directed towards the softest of targets, notably civilian groups. The campaign, which has been well documented, was unleashed in Palestinian towns and villages by groups led by men like Menachem Begin and Yitzhak Shamir; that both of these were to become Prime Ministers of Israel after statehood was achieved was a measure of the erosion which Jewish values and ideals had suffered as a consequence of Israel's creation.[23]

The tactic of employing terror against civilian targets was invoked by the leadership of the Zionist gangs quite specifically and ruthlessly. In the light of the rejection of such practices by all decent people, their leaders have tried to justify their campaigns as being directed primarily against a colonial occupying power. But this argument is specious, since the victims, carefully targeted, were as often as not harmless civilians. This was calculated policy: by inspiring terror amongst civilian populations the Zionist leadership sought to achieve several quite specific objectives: the harassment of an occupying power which lacked the will to retaliate in like measure; the intimidation of Arab populations in areas coveted by the settlers who, it was anticipated, would eventually migrate into Palestine; and the coercion of any Jewish groups who might, on humanitarian or political grounds, propose a dialogue with the Arab inhabitants or promote a policy of something less than absolute Jewish domination. It was a policy which, many years later, would have been recognised by Lebanese civilian populations, after Israel's invasion of that unhappy land.

The campaign of terror executed by organisations like the Stern Gang and Irgun wreaked havoc in Palestine and demoralised the civilian and military establishments. Britain capitulated and surrendered the Mandate, returning it to the United Nations. Eventually the British withdrew, ignominiously. On the evidence of newsreels of the time the only creatures to regret their departure were some sad and bereft dogs who may be seen wistfully watching the troop ships depart, standing on the quayside as their one-time friends sailed westwards into the sunset.

5

PROPAGANDA, HISTORY AND THE POWER OF MYTH

The language of propaganda and polemic has its own rules. Orwellian 'newspeak' has become a commonplace reality. For the whole of the post-war period words have been used by politicians to mean the exact opposite of their literal meaning: 'democracy' has signified oppression, 'freedom' enslavement, 'liberty' the loss of all rights for the individual. The history of Israel has been the occasion for many other examples of the torturing of language to make words mean whatever their user chooses they shall mean.

It will have been apparent how dangerously prejudiced the several terms most commonly employed in the polemics of Israel and the Palestinians have become; equally, it must be clear how very distinct they are, each from the other. If the prefix 'anti–' is placed against any of them, then a quite different series of values emerges. Thus, to be 'anti-Jew' or 'anti-Jewish' would imply an antipathy to and a rejection of the culture and perhaps the religious beliefs of the Jewish community; it could also imply a dislike of Jews as a distinct social group, or as individuals. As such, it may well be that there are people who may be so described; there are, without doubt, people who are anti-Catholic, anti-Protestant, or probably, for that matter, anti-Primitive Methodist. There certainly are plenty of people who are anti-Muslim or anti-Arab.

It is surely unacceptable to identify the term 'Jew' with 'Israel', as many of the protagonists of the Jewish state find it necessary to do. To be 'anti-Israeli' cannot, by any stretch of the most febrile imagination, be represented as the same condition as

91

being 'anti-Jewish', no matter how hard Israel's propagandists try to make it so.

Of course popular usage, that licence for all manner of language debasement, must be taken into account, but in reality 'anti-semite', though it has acquired the status of a convenient jargon, is really equally devoid of any meaning; it could just conceivably, be applied to certain Sumerian commentators living in southern Iraq in the third millennium BC, who had a marked dislike of Semitic-speaking desert people whom they categorised as 'those who know not grain'. In more recent times it is one of the many triumphs of Israeli propaganda that 'anti-Zionist' has been equated with 'anti-semite' which in turn has been manipulated to mean anti-Jewish. Opposition to the Israeli state or to the policies and actions of the Israeli government is instantly condemned as 'anti-semitic'. This device has become one of the classic response mechanisms of all Israeli propagandists. Thus a retiring Israeli Ambassador to London, speaking of the criticism of his government's policies over the Israeli invasion of Lebanon which he encountered when he arrived to take up his appointment, was quoted[1] as saying: 'Some newspapers were guilty of obscene exaggeration about civilian casualties. They even talked of "genocide". To me, a Jew, this was monstrous. It was, I am afraid, anti-semitism.' This observation, it should be remembered, was in the context of Israel's policies in Lebanon which including standing back as the Maronite Phalange were unleashed on the Palestinians in the Sabra and Chatila refugee camps, an episode which must stand high in the annals of contemporary infamy.

The antics which words are made to go through are a tribute both to the persistence and the skill of Israeli propagandists. Thus all Palestinians are 'terrorists'; indiscriminate bombing by the Israeli forces or their Christian surrogates is conducted with 'surgical precision', no matter that the outcome may be the destruction of civilian hospitals and schools and the slaughter of those inside them. An Israeli who commits acts of murder against Arabs is 'deranged'; an Arab who attacks Israeli targets is a terrorist *and* a murderer.

The saddest aspect of all this is not the damage done to language, which has borne a great deal of abuse and perversion in its time and will doubtless undergo much more before the race of men is ended. But the fact that so many otherwise respectable Western journals accepted the Israeli vocabulary must give all decent people cause for sadness.

It would of course be naive in the extreme to pretend that the Palestinians have always conducted themselves with restraint, with sensitive consideration for the feelings of others or with a perpetual sense of the supreme importance of truth. But the incitement to violence which has so often characterised the public attitudes of parties to the conflict has not always been of their making. The deaths of children, the destruction of the family homes of the old, the seizure of property and all the myriad wrongs which they have suffered would surely make a more placid people rebel. Yet the Palestinians have been vilified and presented as objects of hatred and contempt, as much as were their persecutors in the evil years before and during the Second World War.

The success with which the Israeli political hierarchy has been able to equate 'Palestinian' with 'terrorist' is one of the most cruel twists of this sorry tale. Whilst it might be said with truth that there are several individuals in the upper levels of the Israeli establishment who are peculiarly well qualified to recognise a terrorist when they see one, in the case of the Palestinians the term is harsh and unjust. The Palestinians are a dispossessed people, ignored for most of their lifetime by the state which has taken their land and by the rest of the world; they were, not so long ago, a simple people, living quiet lives in their ancestral towns and villages. From these they were driven by harsh invaders; whole generations of Palestinian children have in consequence grown to adulthood in the foetid horror of the refugee camps, nurtured on hate. It ill becomes the Israelis to speak of such as terrorists, when they have been given no choice but to try to recover their land by the only means which it seems their enemies will understand.

But, whatever may be the turns and twists of Israel's and Zionists' propaganda since the foundation of the Israeli state, it suited the Western powers to represent Israel as their one ally in the Middle East on whom, on the basis of dependence and self-interest, it was believed they could rely, at whatever cost. To sustain this policy it has been expedient to accept the Biblical fable that the land at the eastern end of the Mediterranean was given to a Chosen people by the God of the Old Testament, a divinity that the Christian world acknowledges as does Islam.

93

This coincidence of a shared divinity is a consequence of what is surely one of the more far-reaching elements of chance in history. This common inheritance of a particular fable, not in itself very different from a hundred similar fables and aetiological myths in other cultures around the world, has been employed to justify the Jewish seizure and subsequent rule of much of the land of Palestine. It matters nothing that the majority of those Jews who founded the State of Israel were humanists, agnostic, even atheistic almost to a man – what else indeed could they be given the intellectual climate of European Jewry throughout the nineteenth century and for much of the eighteenth? But without the fables the people of Brunei or the Congo have as solid a claim to Palestine as do the people of Poland, Lithuania or Central Asia.

The inherent fallacies in the attempt to bring the arguments of history to the support of Israel's claim to Palestine can best be demonstrated by a recourse to history itself. This may be accomplished by examining how the Europeans, in seeking a solution to the problems of their own treatment of the Jews, transferred the problem to another, already largely disadvantaged, people at the eastern end of the Mediterranean.

The fundamental issue on which the Jewish population of Eastern Europe based their claim to Palestine was that they were the descendants of the land's original inhabitants who had been promised it by God, had been dispossessed and were reclaiming their homeland from later invaders, the Palestinian Arabs. The fable of the covenant between the Jewish people of antiquity and their tribal divinity was invoked to emphasise the sacred nature of the claim. This claim was one which would be acknowledged by most Europeans raised in a nominally Christian society, whose own religious beliefs were drawn in large part from the same Biblical contexts as those of the Jews.

In reality, the people who lived in Palestine in the early years of this century were, most of them, descendants of those who had lived there since the very earliest times. This was true regardless of their religious affiliation; whether they might be Muslim, Christian or Jewish (other than those who settled there in the eighteenth and nineteenth centuries), these were the aboriginal inhabitants of Palestine.

It is reasonable to make some allowance for the effect of population movements, wars, invasions and migrations. But these probably did very little to alter the essential composition and character of the population of Palestine over the millennia. In general, the people of Palestine were as much autochthonous as, say, the French; they were as much the descendants of people living in the same land two or three thousand years earlier as the Germans might claim to be descended from the tribes who were so troublesome to the Romans.

In late antiquity there were, indeed, considerable population movements in and around the eastern Mediterranean. Not the least of these was the result of a characteristically brutal Roman solution to the continued troublesome character of the Jewish Palestinians living in and around Jerusalem. A series of relatively small-scale but none the less tiresome revolts encouraged the Romans to destroy much of Jerusalem and to drive out its population. The remaining population, left undisturbed by the Romans, living on the land as their ancestors had done for long ages, continued to eke out a modest existence and were of concern to few, other than the occasional pilgrim or the itinerant and adventurous scholar. Thus the situation remained until the Crusades. During the eighteenth century there was a trickle of migrants into Palestine, drawn from Middle Eastern communities and some, though very few, from eastern Europe. By the beginning of the nineteenth century the Jews in Palestine numbered 8,000. By 1880, they had increased to 20,000. At the time of the Balfour Declaration the Jews represented less than 10 per cent of the total population of Palestine.[2] In 1922, according to official figures, the Jewish population was 84,000 out of a total of 750,000 inhabitants.[3]

In the 20s and 30s of the present century the rate of immigration by Jews into Palestine increased. By 1931 the total population had risen to over 1,000,000: the Jews now accounted for more than 170,000. By 1946, immediately before the British surrender of the Mandate and the United Nations plan to partition Palestine, the total population was estimated as being just under 2,000,000 and the Jewish component had risen to over 600,000.[4]

Despite the rise in the number of Jewish immigrants the overwhelming majority of the inhabitants of Palestine were the indigenes, the Muslim and Christian families who had lived there for as long as people had been living in the lands of the Levant.

The ancestors of all the indigenous inhabitants of Palestine were members of what were originally amorphous tribal federations which swirled around the peripheries of the great seminal civilisations of Egypt, the Levant and Mesopotamia. Most of these peoples came up from, or out of, the Syro-Arabian desert regions. Their movements – and their menace – are variously and spasmodically recorded in Egyptian and Mesopotamian texts from the middle of the third millennium onwards; they were of course present in the region from much earlier times still.

There is no certainty about the names which these ill-defined groups bore in the earliest times that they manifested themselves. Much of the coastal area they then inhabited was known as 'Canaan'. The language which they spoke was Canaanite; they were known as a distinct people in the eighteenth century BC.[5] At this point the only meaningful distinctions that can be made between the various groups are linguistic.

Disraeli's dictum, 'All is race: there is no other truth', a thought expressed through his character Sidonia, a sort of super-Jew and an unabashed projection of the author himself in his novel, *Tancred*,[6] is bad anthropology and worse politics. The only intelligible distinctions that can be made between peoples, whether of the same, related or different 'races', are cultural and even these must be heavily qualified. Of all cultural factors the most significant is language. Although inevitably the lines often become very blurred – and it is especially difficult to determine the nature and relationships of many ancient languages – language does provide one of the very few reliable criteria in determining a people's cultural character and affiliations over long stretches of time.

In the record of the civilisations of the ancient Near East there are certain great linguistic families which profoundly influenced the course of human history and the development of the sort of society which has descended to the world of the present; indeed, many of the influences which were present in the seminal cultures of the Near East are still at work today. In the Nile Valley a predominantly African linguistic stream became fused with influences from the desert peoples, who pressed on the Valley from both east and west. In Mesopotamia, the languages which had developed in the deserts and in the oases, from northern Syria to the borders of Iran, became dominant and eliminated the strange, non-semitic, apparently *sui generis* language of the Sumerians.

The important family of languages which had their origin in the Syro-Arabian deserts are classified as semitic. It cannot be stated too often, nor too emphatically, that semitic is purely to be understood as a linguistic term; it is in no way descriptive of race nor can it properly be applied to any group which does not speak a semitic language as its mother tongue. The majority of Jews living today are not semites and they are not native semitic speakers.

The State of Israel is thus seen to be founded on a basis of fable. The claim advanced by the Zionists and later by many believing Jews to the land of Palestine is based on the story of a covenant between the members of congeries of nomadic tribes and settled peoples living on the fringes of Syro-Arabian deserts in the first millennium BC with a tribal divinity, a conflation of many competing divinities, known to posterity as Jehovah, Yahweh or, more poetically, as the Most High. The history of these peoples, and of their tricky and often malevolent divinity, is set out in what Christians call the Old Testament.

The relationships of the Hebrews (the name by which the people who claim the early books of the Bible as a record of their early history are generally called) with other contemporary peoples of the Near and Middle East have been extensively studied, often with confused and contradictory results. It is difficult, to say the least, to identify with any assurance any of the many linguistic or tribal groups which existed in the area with the Hebrews until well into the first millennium BC, at which time the Arabs are also first mentioned as an identifiable entity. Without doubt, all of the groups which ranged round this region were related, possessing many similar social customs, religious practices and beliefs, as well as strong linguistic affiliations.

Judaism, as a canon of belief surviving today, can undoubtedly trace its descent back to the beliefs which were common to many of these desert peoples. As a theological system it is essentially post-Exilic in its exegesis: the term *Jew* is only relevant after the Exile.[7] To attempt to identify the modern Israelis with the Israelites of the time of the Kingship, for example, is, in historical terms, wholly untenable. The Hebrew speakers of the early centuries of the first millennium BC were, in essential terms, no different from the other semitic-speaking tribes who occupied parts of the northern reaches of the Syro-Arabian deserts and settled in its towns and cities. They were not even monotheistic but, like their cousins with whom they shared the desert oases and coastal towns, worshipped many gods. It took a long time for Jahweh to assert his primacy, though for long afterwards he (or, more properly perhaps, his adherents and promoters) remained apprehensive about the power of his rivals to appeal to his followers.

The 'Hebrew' tribes were distinct in some of their cultural refinements; their gift for poetic expression (and, in later days, their good fortune in acquiring translators of the quality of the editors of the King James recension of the Bible) ensured their immortality. Archaeology has not been generous with hard evidence from sites that can with confidence be ascribed to places named in the Bible before the Exile; the history of Jewish government in the lands which they were later to claim as the homeland of the Jews is in fact very slight. The supremacy of rulers – whether kings or others – who can with certainty be called Jewish lasted some three hundred years, less, as has been remarked, than the period during which the Romans ruled Britain. In the sixth century BC much of the Hebrew population of Palestine, together with other inhabitants, were transferred to the east. After the Babylonian captivity many remnants of the communities migrated south, whilst others remained in the east and seeded the historic Jewish populations of Mesopotamia. Still others drifted down to the Mediterranean where they joined existing Jewish communities, which had long thrived in the coastal cities on both sides of the Middle Sea as well as at its eastern extremity. (See also Chapter 6 for further evidence on this issue.)

Culturally, Israel today has an essentially eastern European identity and character. This indeed has always been its strength and its pride. Even at the level of popular culture, Israel is European; every song and every dance proclaims the Polish or Russian origins of Israel. From the outset Israel has sought to be treated as a European enclave in the eastern Mediterranean. Its membership of the European Broadcasting Union is but one, if trivial, example of its insistence on its European character: even at the level of the absurd, Israel's contributions to the annual Eurovision Song Contest demonstrated its concern to miss no opportunity to continue its identification with the continent from which Zionism sprang. It is in Europe and not at all in the Middle East that the historic origins of Israel must be sought.

The great majority of European Jews have no trace of neareastern, pre-Exilic (or for that matter post-Exilic) Palestinian blood in their veins. The Jews who have lived in Europe since the sixteenth century have often been called Ashkenazim, a term which originated amongst the Jews of Spain (and hence from those originating mainly from North Africa) who moved on to Eastern Europe when they were expelled from Spain by the Most Catholic Sovereigns of that cruel land in 1493; their cousins in Portugal followed them in 1497. They met and merged with the small communities, mostly Mediterranean in origin, which had moved into the increasingly prosperous cities of post-Reformation Europe; they also encountered the survivors of one of the more bizarre but enduring and influential political decisions ever made on the continent: that which introduced to history the communities of Jews who lived on the periphery of the Byzantine Empire. The strange, unlikely people who were at the centre of this most significant expansion of Jewish communities in Eastern Europe, were the Khazars.

It has been said that most European Jews living today are descended from this improbable little nation.[8] This may indeed be something of an exaggeration, but it probably contains more truth than fantasy. The Khazars were one of the Turkic tribes which, moving westwards as a consequence of what are still largely undefined pressures in inner Asia, began to settle round the northern edges of the Byzantine Empire, in the middle of the first millennium AD. Their arrival was provoked by circumstances similar to those which later produced the Mongol invasions. The Khazars first appear to have settled in southern Russia, in the region between the Caucasus, the Don and the Volga; there they began to shed their nomadic character and to acquire the trappings of statehood.

The Khazars, having settled, prospered. As a result they became of interest both to the Byzantine and the Muslim Empires, for they soon found themselves in uneasy communication with each of the great powers of the day. Both powers exerted pressure on the pagan Khazars to accept their version of the true faith, orthodox Christianity on the one hand, Islam on the other. The Khazars, evidently an intelligent people, were anxious to keep their options open and it seemed to them that it did not in any case take the judgement of a political genius to realise that the acceptance by them of one of the two great religious orthodoxies would immediately alienate the other. The Khazars were thus obliged to seek an original solution to their dilemma: the solution they found was remarkable – they Judaised, that is to say, they declared themselves Jews and in doing so hoped to ward off the attentions of both their mighty suitors.

The Khazars went about their search for an acceptable identity and a respectable religious allegiance methodically, at least according to the version set down in the so-called Khazar Correspondence. It is reported that to the Muslim envoys who sought to convert them to Islam, they put the question 'Which faith do you respect the more, Judaism or Christianity?' The Muslims without hesitation answered 'Judaism'. To the Byzantine divines, who were promoting the attractions of orthodoxy, they presented a similar enquiry, 'Which faith do you respect the more, Judaism or Islam?' The Christians with one voice averred, 'Judaism'. Thus the choice was made and the Khazars became Jews. If nothing else, it is a pleasant story.

They were a numerous, intelligent and industrious people, farmers, artisans and merchants. They possessed many of the virtues associated both with high-achieving European Jews to this day and with the peasant communities of Eastern Europe, beloved of Jewish (and Israeli) folk myth. Their device of proclaiming Judaism as their state religion of course resulted in their being harried and persecuted by *both* their neighbours; such an outcome might perhaps have been predicted, suggesting that whatever may have been the Khazars' virtues, political acumen was not, after all, high amongst them. In time, the Khazars disappeared as a distinct entity, but by that time Judaism was firmly planted amongst a large number of peasants, smallholders and modest townsfolk living in southern Russia. Gradually some of their surplus populations drifted westwards, settling in most of the eastern European cities, though the original communities had tended always to be strongly peasant in character. They came to represent an important stratum in the lineage of the Ashkenazi Jews, having migrated into Poland, Lithuania and Hungary.

This significant influence of the Khazars on the ancestry of European Jews is now generally accepted by those historians who have considered the matter, though understandably their conclusions have not been welcomed by the Israeli establishment. To accept such a thesis would make still greater nonsense of the Israeli claim for the world's Jews to be descended from the pre-Exilic inhabitants of Palestine.

That complex polymath and publicist Arthur Koestler made the existence of the Khazars known to a wide non-professional public in *The Thirteenth Tribe.*[9] In this he summarised, as coolly and elegantly as he always developed a cogent argument, what to many of his readers must have been the distinctly surprising part played by the Khazars in the history of European Jewry. However, he did not, as indeed he was at pains to demonstrate, discover their history for himself. The study of the Khazars and of their contribution to the blood-stock of the Ashkenazim was a subject for nineteenth-century scholarship, when it was not in any sense considered controversial. For it is only when it comes into collision with Zionism, and by the very fact of its existence makes a nonsense of the Zionist concept of the 'return' to Israel, that it becomes a matter of controversy and not merely the stuff of a rather stolid scholarship. No nineteenth-century Jewish scholar who had considered the matter would have thought the Khazar contribution to his ancestry doubtful, and certainly not one to be concealed.[10]

Moreover, Israeli scholars have not attempted to counter the argument seriously, preferring simply to dismiss it, denying the existence of the evidence which supports it as they do so, and presenting instead the equation 'Israelis = Jews = Israelites = Jews = Israelis'. Thus presented, however, that equation may seem lacking somewhat in absolute credibility, yet it represents an expression of the fable which lies at the core of Israel's claim to historical succession in Palestine.

Even the evidence of language testifies against the Israeli claim to the land of Palestine, on the grounds of history. Today Hebrew is the official language of the State of Israel; but Hebrew, as it is written and spoken today, is an artificial construct, the product of the laboratory and the study rather than a genuine ethnological linguistic survival. Much of its vocalisation was in fact deduced from a study of spoken Arabic which, unlike Hebrew, remained in current usage.

Hebrew is inextricably identified with the people of the Old Testament (it is, strictly speaking, a Canaanite dialect) and, by extension and in the past often with pejorative overtones, with the Jews as a distinct group. It is commonly represented as unique evidence of that elusive quality, 'Jewishness', and as a witness to the specific quality of the Jewish heritage. But the Jews had not employed Hebrew as a spoken language for more than 2,500 years before the creation of the State of Israel.

It was a brilliant stroke of policy to make Hebrew the official language of the new Israeli state; it was a policy not, however, achieved easily or without considerable opposition from the earliest Zionist councils. Many of the first Zionists, prgamatists to a man, saw the imposition of Hebrew as an absurd, archaising and retrogressive step; they would have preferred German or Yiddish to become the common language of any Jewish state that might be brought into being. In fact, modern Hebrew is a thoroughly unnatural construct which has had to be learned by every immigrant, as well as by many of those Jews who were living in Palestine before the creation of the state. The language of western Jewry, of the Ashkenazim, was Yiddish, a Low German dialect which is part of the Germanic branch of the Indo-European family of languages. The European Jews have never spoken Hebrew conversationally, holding that it would be considered blasphemous to do so since Hebrew was reserved for prayer and study; it was the language of God and hence appropriate only when addressed to Him. The rejection of the idea that Hebrew can be employed as a popular tongue is one of the distinguishing marks of the ultra-orthodox in Israel to this day.

There is another branch of the international Jewish community, the Oriental Jews or Sephardim, of whom there will be much more to say in Chapter 8. At this point it should be observed that those Jews who lived in Arab lands (including Palestine) have always spoken Arabic as their mother tongue, just as those who lived in Spain, Portugal and Italy as well as those smaller communities in other countries round the world spoke the dominant language of the peoples amongst whom they lived. The Sephardim of the Iberian peninsula and the Latin lands of Europe did also develop their equivalents of Yiddish, of which the most important was Ladino, but it was no more directly related to Hebrew than was Yiddish.

Hebrew of course remained one of the principal liturgical languages, the language of Torah and the rituals of the synagogue; it was not in fact the only language of the liturgy as Aramaic, the *lingua franca* of late antiquity in the near East, also survived in legal texts and in some aspects of ritual. Hebrew was also an important though by no means the only language of Jewish scholarship, in much the same way as Latin and Greek were the languages of European scholarship, until their primacy was eroded by the Reformation. Thus the Spaniard Solomon ibn Verga wrote in Hebrew;[11] indeed such Spanish commentaries, though written in a Muslim land, did much to preserve Hebrew as a language in scholarly usage. Maimonides,[12] on the other hand, one of the great Jewish scholars of the Middle Ages of whom most educated people will have heard, wrote in Arabic, even on the most sacred and abstruse topics.

But even in a scholarly or ritual context the method of pronouncing Hebrew had been forgotten, after the dispersion to, and the return from, Babylon. Hebrew, in common with semitic languages, does not write its vowels; thus its transmission as a spoken language can only be effected by oral example and tradition. The same is true of Arabic, the only living semitic language.

The form of spoken Hebrew which Israel has invented would be meaningless to a member of a Hebrew-speaking tribe of, let us say, the seventh century BC, which is approximately the last time that the language was in general, vernacular use. Even by the time of Christ, Hebrew as a spoken language had virtually disappeared. The earliest followers of Christ, though all of them were Jews, spoke Aramaic, one of the languages most extensively spoken throughout the Near East at the end of the first millennium BC.

Aramaic is one of the linguistic streams ancestral to Arabic, which has replaced it as the language generally spoken throughout the region. The Muslim conquests of the seventh century onwards exported Arabic to North Africa and eastwards to the borders of Iran. In the heartland of Arabia and the Syro-Arabian deserts, including Palestine, Aramaic had evolved into Arabic by Prophetic times and was spoken by the vast majority of the population of the region, regardless of their religious affiliations; at this time there were substantial Christian populations in

Arabia and the surrounding lands, as well as sizeable Jewish communities.[13]

There were some exceptions to this general principle of the dominance of Arabic in the Arabian peninsula and adjacent lands, but these were usually found amongst very small and isolated communities like the Samaritans, the Christian Assyrians, and the mountain people of southern Oman who retained their traditional languages, at least in the security of their own families. But even that was not the case with Hebrew, to any comparable extent. Aramaic itself evolved in much later times into a specialised juridical and liturgical usage, which from the middle of the first millennium joined the catalogue of the other languages most generally employed by Jews up to the end of the Middle Ages and which included Hebrew, Chaldaean, Greek and Arabic; of these, the two most influential languages were Aramaic and its descendent, Arabic, though Greek, the inheritance of the period of the most vivid flowering of Jewish culture in Hellenistic times, was also an important factor in the moulding of Jewish cultural and philosophical concepts.

The only common language spoken by the majority of the Jews who were the founders of the State of Israel was Yiddish. It is no more directly related to Hebrew than is Welsh or Hungarian. It is not, however, a modern fabrication. It has as respectable an ancestry as most European languages, with Old Yiddish being spoken AD c.1250-c.1500, making its development, in chronological terms, comparable with that of modern English. The extent to which Yiddish was spoken throughout the Western Jewish communities was an important factor in providing their common cultural experience. Much of Israeli culture today derives directly as well as indirectly from this inheritance of a common linguistic background. It is this consideration, more than any other, which determines the essentially European nature of Israeli society.

The seeds of Zionism were destined, from the outset, to fall on fertile ground in the Europe from which it sprang. Myth is a powerful force in the hands of determined and skilled polemicists, and the manipulation of myth was to become one of the hallmarks of the Zionist politician or propagandist. It was not only the myths associated with the idea of a 'return' to a land with which they had no historic connection whatsoever, which were to be used skilfully to bolster the Zionist case;

another sort of myth was to be brought into service to promote their cause, immediately creating a powerful response amongst influential non-Jews whose support it was vital for them to enlist.

Although the founders of Zionism were, almost to a man (as indeed their successors have largely remained) resolutely non-religious, they were quick to call on the ancient scriptures, which they held in common with the Gentiles. Without this coincidence of a shared religious inheritance it is very doubtful indeed if Zionism would ever have been given serious attention by western interests; had the Balts, let us say, laid claim to Beijing on the ground of some common myth, such a claim would have been dismissed as preposterous. Equally, if the dominant religion of Europe had been rooted in the Mabinogion, the myths of the Welsh might today be perplexing the peace of the nations of a substantial part of the civilised world.

The fact that European Jews could point to the books of the Old Testament, on which much of Europe's religious faith was grounded, as the common heritage of Jew and Christian, strengthened the appeal and immediate impact of the Zionist cause immeasurably. This applied equally to the unlearned to whom the Bible was the revealed word of God and historically indisputable, as to the sophisticated who might dispute details of belief and interpretation, but who seem never to have paused to ask whether the Jews of Poland, for example, were the same people who had allegedly entered into a covenant with the Almighty for a lien on a land to which they now laid claim with an increasingly vociferous demand.

Many Europeans, even if their Christian faith was more nominal than real, found that these protestations of the workings of divine policy struck a chord, resonating deep in their consciousness; when those who discovered these echoes from the deepest levels of their infant beliefs were also policy-makers in their own countries, the coincidence was politically significant. The concept, 'a land without a people waiting for a people without a land'[14] (a slogan whose burnished professionalism typifies the quality of Zionist propaganda) created an immediate response and immense sympathy; that the concept was demonstrably false did not disturb anyone unduly at the time when it was vigorously promoted.

The impact of the fable of the covenant has been of significant influence, not only in the minds of Christians (or, more properly, in the minds of those brought up and educated in a Christian, western tradition) but also, most notably, in the minds of Arabs and not least in the minds of Muslims. This surprising victory of persuasion over both truth and self-interest has been one of the most significant victories in the psychological war which Israel has directed so skilfully and unremittingly against the Arab world since 1948.

Muslims accept the validity of most Jewish theological teaching, since in their view, like the Christians the Jews are people of the Book and reprehensible only in that they cling to an earlier, superseded revelation. The Muslim community is thus, as it were, programmed to accept the idea that Israeli migrants to the land of Palestine have the power of revelation on their side, though they would also argue that it is so only up to a point since, by their sinful intransigence, the Hebrews forfeited the divine mandate which once they had been given.

None the less, Muslims have been unreasoningly impressed by the Israelis' claim to be descended from the aboriginal inhabitants of Palestine. Sadly, this fiction has been given further substance by the wish of many Palestinian Muslims to be identified with the warriors, austere in character but sparse in numbers, who burst out of Arabia in the early years of Islam and who spread Muhammad's message to the Syro-Arabian deserts and far beyond. Thus many Muslim writers proposed that the Palestinians (or at least the Muslims amongst them) were the offspring of the armies which the Prophet's fervour brought up out of the peninsula; even to this day it is not unusual to hear a Palestinian talking of 'fourteen centuries of occupation' by *his* ancestors, thus immediately conceding much of the otherwise entirely implausible Zionist case. No doubt some of the original Muslims from Arabia did settle in the lusher, more kindly lands to the north, but if so, they were a very small component in the society which they conquered.

The belief in the widespread dispersion of legions of seventh-century Arabians, so clearly at odds with history, is also to be found in Egypt where the Christian Copts will assure any listener that *they* are the true descendants of the Egyptians of Pharaonic times, whilst the Muslim population is the product of the invaders who entered Egypt in the armies of Amr ibn As, who conquered the land from its Byzantine overlords in the name of Islam. The evident nonsensical nature of this idea, demonstrated by the overwhelming preponderance of Muslims in Egyptian society, has done nothing to diminish the enthusiasm with which the idea is still adhered to in some Coptic quarters.

Islam was spread, with remarkable swiftness, amongst the Christian and other communities – including the pagans and the Jews – who lived in Palestine at the time. Their experience in this respect was no different from that of the countless other peoples whom the Muslims encountered in their first outpouring. The Arabs' lack of understanding of this crucial phase of their own history and their acceptance, however qualified, of Jewish claims to Palestinian ancestry, has often blunted their response to the more extravagant claims which Zionism advanced. The Arabs have not helped their cause by referring, however jokingly, to 'our cousins', when speaking of the Israelis and of European Jews generally. They have been too ready to accept, as literal truth, the myth of the common fatherhood of Abraham for themselves and for a folk whose origins were lost in the mists of hither Asia at the time when Abraham might have been supposed to have lived. It is a tribute to the power of Israeli persuasion that so improbable an idea has gained such currency, among even their own most devoted enemies.

Muslim scholars, too, have not always helped the development of the historical background to the Israeli claim to Palestine by tending to dismiss pre-Islamic history as somehow less worthy of attention than the period following the Apostolate of Muhammad. The pre-Islamic period is, in Muslim parlance, 'The Age of Ignorance' and as such does not merit or reward the consideration of responsible scholars. In consequence the myth-makers have tended to have their own way with the version so eagerly seized on by the Zionists and their friends, becoming, in effect, canonical.

The idea that the Jews of Israel, without distinction including the Jews of European origin, and the Arabs, including the Palestinians, are genetically related is still perpetuated, not least by popular journalists. Thus *Time* magazine remarked, 'They [the Arabs and Jews] are technically cousins as their ancestors, Isaac and Ishmael, were half-brothers.'[15] The use of the word 'technically' is remarkable both in the attempt to confer a spurious scientific quality on the comment and in its sheer simplicity of mind. It is difficult to believe that the same journal would, for example, with equal solemnity have repeated some fiction of popular or pseudo-science (extraterrestrials at the Pyramids perhaps) or related an old wives' tale in commenting on medical practice. Yet it, and many others like it, will cheerfully give currency to such illiterate nonsense as the Isaac-Ishmael descent of two peoples, one indigenous to the Middle East and the other predominantly Eastern European, with much of its ancestry in hither Asia.

The idea of the common ancestry of Arabs and Jews has been promoted, quite cynically, by many Zionist propagandists, despite their general contempt for religion. To do so lends their case a certain fragile authority, notably amongst the credulous (and those who wish to be persuaded), the religious-minded and, most notably, amongst groups such as the fundamentalist Christian sects. By the Jews claiming a common ancestry with them, the Arabs have often been too timorous and too much influenced by their own tribal myths, to deny what is clearly, by any objective standard, a wholly insupportable fantasy, at all levels and on all grounds.

There is only one thing more remarkable than the propagation of the idea of the common ancestry of the Arabs and the Jews by otherwise sensible and educated people, and that is the acceptance of it by people equally sensible and educated. The myths attending the existence of Israel are a further testimony, if testimony were needed, of the credulity of humankind.

6

ARCHAEOLOGY AS
PROPAGANDA

There are few aspects of the conflict of the Palestinians and the Israelis which are likely to provoke laughter; a sardonic smile, possibly, may greet another diplomatic sally or some unusually extreme example of political posturing, but laughter must seem an inappropriate response to a confrontation which has brought so much suffering to so many innocent people. None the less there is one circumstance in which laughter, mocking and incredulous, is the only proper, the inevitable response. It is occasioned by the attempts of the Israeli authorities to exploit the blameless discipline of archaeology to give support to their claim to be the direct successors of the people who, according to the myths, entered into a covenant with their tribal divinity for the possession of the land, four thousand years ago.

That the European immigrants into Israel should rapidly develop an enthusiasm for archaeology in their new home was perhaps to be expected. Many Jewish scholars in the nineteenth century had been in the forefront of the newly fledged science of archaeology in France, Britain and Germany. Especially distinguished in linguistic studies, Jewish scholars made significant contributions to an awareness of the past which, during that century, became a preoccupation of many European societies. Their contribution was not principally, or even particularly, related to studies bearing on Jewish history, though of course there were important historians of Jewry and Judaism who were Jews; but men like Halévy and Weil made important contributions to Egyptology, Mesopotamian studies and the early history of Anatolia. Only Greece and Rome do not seem particularly to have attracted Jewish academics but their involvement in what was to become acknowledged as Oriental studies was great.

Palestine, in its capacity as the Jewish and Christian 'Holy Land', had of course been a focus for Jewish scholarship, but such scholarship was not especially partisan; if anything, it was notable for a rather rabbinical narrowness. It was when Zionism emerged as a political concept that even the relatively modest practice of archaeology was brought into its manipulative scope, along with other equally innocent academic disciplines, such as history, geography and linguistics.

In the latter part of the nineteenth century and persisting into the twentieth, the progress of Zionism was paralleled by and indeed was a spur for, the rise of Biblical archaeology. The anxiety to prove the historicity of the Bible had always been a powerful dynamic in some of the more fringe regions of Christian scholarship. Wiser theologians, especially those in the upper reaches of the Roman persuasion, were notably unenthusiastic about trying to apply the disciplines of historiography to so elusive, some would say chimerical, a set of co-ordinates as those which charted the course of the lives and actions of the leading figures recorded in the books of the Old Testament.

Roman reservations about searching for proveable fact in annals which so cheerfully conflated evident myth with possible historical record did not deter their Protestant colleagues, particularly those who had moved as far away from Rome as it was possible to do, from attempting to recover the original certainties of the revealed Word of God, before it had become overlaid with centuries of priestly accretions. The search for the truth of the Biblical record became a peculiarly Protestant bypath in the jungle of Christian scholarship.

There was, after all, a long-standing precedent for the interest of Protestant divines in searching for historical truth in the Bible. The researches of Archbishop Ussher, the incumbent of the see of Armagh in the seventeenth century, had led him to the conclusion that the world had been created on a Friday morning in October 4004BC. Based on this discovery, he proceeded to draw up a chronological table of the lifetimes of the Patriarchs and others featured in the Old Testament and of the events which the books described. Until well into the nineteenth century Archbishop Ussher's chronology was printed in English Bibles and inspired successive generations of scholars to confirm or amend this or that detail of the Archbishop's imaginative scholarship.

But it was not only the clergy of the Established English church who sought for confirmation for the basis of their beliefs in archaeology. There has always been a stratum of senior service officers who have been entrapped by a form of mysticism which expresses itself in an enthusiasm for Eastern religions and in the wilder shores of archaeology. Fawcett, hacking his way through the South American jungle in search of the heirs of Atlantis, is a good example of the type. Palestine saw others of the same sort, all of them steeped in the Bible from their infancy up and, as representatives of the imperial race, much inclined towards a sympathy for that other 'Chosen People' and the record of their supposed history. Gordon, Kitchener and Wingate are examples here – the last named, an eccentric but very courageous officer, being also a devout Zionist. It is significant that Jewish scholars, coming from a more sceptical cultural tradition, did not generally share in these esoteric levels of pseudo-scholarship.

The situation changed dramatically with the creation of the State of Israel. A number of the refugees from European persecution were historians and archaeologists; in any case, the Mandate, rather surprisingly, had included a provision (Clause 21) for the protection of Palestine's archaeological heritage, though at the same time it conferred an equal right on all member states of the League of Nations to conduct surveys and excavations in its territory. The Mandate government had however encouraged the formation of properly constituted professional bodies to oversee Palestine's archaeology. To these arrangements, vestigial though they were, Israel succeeded in 1948 and in their turn rapidly built up a much admired, highly proficient if somewhat isolated national archaeological service. At the same time a programme of museum building was put in train, both to preserve the archaeological remains and also to develop thematic museums whose content and presentation reflected some of the ideological preoccupations of the founders of the state.

Many of these, if somewhat predictable, are natural enough, given the strongly propagandistic character of Zionism and its by-products. The Herzl Museum is such a one; there are museums which perpetuate the history of Jewish persecutions in Russia, others which relate the story of the early settlers in Palestine, others still which commemorate the activities of Haganah (which some might fail to differentiate from urban terrorism) and, more creditably, the part played by the Jewish Brigade in two world wars. The equivocal career of Vladimir Jabotinsky also has its museum. There are several devoted to the persecution of the Jews by the Nazis; these sustain the Israeli identification of the 'Holocaust' as one of the principal reasons for the existence of the Jewish state.

Since 1948 archaeology in Israel has been required to fulfil a declared nationalistic purpose. It is used by the state to give a warrant to its own ideology and to its political assertions. In this practice Israel is no different from many newly emergent nations which have seen the exploitation of the findings of archaeology, and sometimes their specific orientation, as providing the swift achievement of a 'scientific' basis for their own view of the world and their place in it.

In the post-colonialist period (a clumsy phrase but one which acknowledges the political influences at work in the second half of the twentieth century) archaeology has frequently been called upon to contribute to, even to define, the national identity of a newly emerging state. Often the influence of the archaeologist has been wholly benign: the attribution of Great Zimbabwe, for example, to its African builders after decades of scholarly denial that 'savages' could have built so splendid a monument, is a case in point. Sometimes the results of the archaeologists' work, when it reaches the hands of the politician or the propagandist, is less happy. There were a number of Awful Warnings from Germany before the Second World War[1] and there have been later examples. Sometimes a view of the past gains credence which owes more to Disneyland than to the rigours of archaeology or of the historian, on whose work a 'reconstruction' will be based.

Archaeology is a powerful specific when administered outside its strictly academic boundaries. Most people respond to visions of the past, usually believing it to be a kinder, more generous or more leisurely time than the present. This view will eventually but inevitably lead to such past idiocies as the representations of a medieval England populated by merry Morris-dancing rustics. The sanitised recreations of north-country mill-life in the nineteenth century which have taken their place are hardly more acceptable.

The Israeli authorities early on realised the enthusiasm which can be generated amongst the public by a skilfully mounted and vigorously promoted view of antiquity. Israel's many museums, the result of private as well as public initiatives, were part of the process of binding the immigrants, especially the European immigrants, to their past, real in the case of those which recorded the persecutions of the nineteenth and twentieth centuries, imaginary in the representation of the supposed origins of 'the Jewish nation' in Palestine.

It must, in fairness, be acknowledged that this manipulation of the fruits of archaeology has not gone uncriticised by Israel's archaeologists. It has been acknowledged that there is 'discomfort felt by Israeli archaeologists in serving not only scholarly ends, but nationalistic purposes as well.'[2] The unease which this double commitment inevitably gives rise to, is evident from the comment of two Israeli archaeologists who otherwise are uncritical of the dualism: 'the religious impetus of both Christians and Jews on the one side and the national impetus of a young nation seeking for its origins on the other, give archaeology in Israel a special flavour. With these incentives Israel's archaeologists try to develop in their own way objective, scientific research.'[3]

Even non-Jewish archaeologists working in Israel in the earlier, heady days when it seemed that Israel could do no wrong shared the subjective character of much Israeli archaeology without qualms. This led them into the acceptance of a Biblically oriented view even of their own excavations. Thus W. F. Albright, one of the pioneers of twentieth-century Near Eastern archaeology, could offer such a comment as, 'From Abraham to modern times the Hebrews and their Israelite successors were essentially sedentary.'[4] (He is contrasting this state, not as one of idleness, but as compared with nomadism.) The redoubtable Dame Kathleen Kenyon, whose work at Jericho was of profound importance, could even give life to David, who never existed outside the pages of the Old Testament. Writing of Jerusalem she remarked, 'David certainly repaired the walls after capturing the city. *Of his repairs there is no definite evidence...*'[5] (my italics).

The extent to which Israel differs from other states in a similar stage of archaeological development is that it has quite blatantly

113

massaged the evidence which archaeology has produced, or, in Israel's case more particularly has *failed* to produce, to bolster its occupation of the land of Palestine. It has been noted already that from the earliest days of its existence Israel mobilised public interest in the past, to begin erecting a structure which would support the idea of a Jewish continuity of government in Palestine. This was intended to lend credence to the idea that the European Jewish immigrants making up the bulk of the population were, in some way, returning to the land of their ancestors.

There is probably no land in the world which has been as exhaustively surveyed and of which so many archaeological sites have been excavated as is the case of Israel. With something like a century of often fractious and frenetic survey by Christian investigators seeking to prove the historicity of the Bible and to locate its sites in a contemporary gazetteer, Israel inherited an immense amount of information on the land's past, to which its subsequent efforts added very substantially. Israel is a small country and much of it is desert: a century and a half of archaeological effort represents a formidable corpus of work. But the truth is that the efforts of Israeli archaeologists and their European and American colleagues have produced *nothing* of proven archaeological value in substantiating the claim which Israel makes to the antiquity of a Jewish presence in Palestine.

So absolute a rejection of what is still a generally perceived situation, namely, that there has been 'from time immemorial'[6] a Jewish presence in Palestine, no doubt needs further examination. It will not be too challenging to provide a critique of the history of Palestine and of the contribution of archaeology to demonstrate that, far from historical studies lending support to this contention, the evidence clearly shows that what has so long been accepted is yet another myth attached to the land of Palestine. Certainly there is no evidence to link, in any proveable, material sense, the people of Israel with the Early and Middle Bronze Ages, when the events chronicled in the first books of the Bible are supposed to have taken place.

There is simply no archaeological evidence to support the existence of David or Solomon;[7] the levels of Jerusalem, probably the most ardently excavated city in the world, which date from the supposed time of their kingship have revealed nothing of them. The area of the city which is described as 'the City of David' is named thus by the archaeologists (in this case, a hundred years or so ago) using the term which is quoted in the Biblical record as David's own, for the part of the city which he was believed to have founded.

The circularity of this example is fairly typical of what happens when believers, of whatever description, are seeking evidence to support their beliefs, proceeding from a preconception to a confirmation. Time and again when reading current descriptions of Late Bronze Age sites in Israel, for example, we will encounter comments like the following describing the sacking of Jerusalem by the tribe of Judah: 'If we assume that there were two waves of Israelite tribes in the thirteenth century BC ... we can draw the following picture: while in the first wave the King of Jerusalem was defeated but his city was not taken, in the second wave the tribe of Judah succeeded in destroying the city. *Unfortunately the archaeological evidence is too meagre to substantiate or disprove this*'[8] (my italics). Archaeologists, if they are wise, avoid making assumptions; they proceed from evidence to the postulation of a thesis.

Again, from the same source: '*It can be assumed* [my italics] that David took Jerusalem early in his reign.'[9] Since there is no evidence even of his existence, any such assumption is, to say the least, bold. Again: '*David seems to have transferred* [my italics] his seat from Hebron to the new capital at Jerusalem some seven years after he had conquered the stronghold of Zion.'[10].

Frequently commentators seeking to link the Biblical record with the results of excavations simply conflate the two, using descriptions contained in the Biblical texts to fill out the poor and fragmentary remains in the ground, which can be ascribed to the period of which it is assumed the Biblical account deals. What was thought to have been a wall built by David in Jerusalem was found to overlie seventh-century levels; it proved to have been built during the time of the Hasmoneans in the second century BC. The oldest surviving building in Jerusalem, the Phasael Tower and built by Herod, dates from 30BC.[11]

None of this would be of any great importance, for all archaeologists are fallible and must be allowed to change or qualify their findings as new evidence appears. But in the case of the political use made of archaeology in Israel, it cannot be dismissed so lightly. Either deliberate falsehoods are perpetuated – that, for example, archaeology has proved the existence of the great archetypal figures of which the Bible speaks – or assumptions are made which are entirely unsupported by material evidence, which yet is alleged to substantiate them.

Occasionally the truth manages to shine through these often tendentious reports. Then, commenting on the Israelite period (1200–586BC), one of the crucial periods on which Israeli state propaganda dwells exhaustively, the editors of *The Museums of Israel* write: '. . . a complete lack of remains; indeed all the Israel Museum can show of that period is a huge photo of Mount Sinai.'[12] *The Encyclopaedia of Archaeological Excavations in the Holy Land*, reviewing the history of excavation in Jerusalem, writes: 'Jerusalem archaeological finds and epigraphic and historical evidence do not provide a well-founded basis for constructing the development and history of Jerusalem from its founding to the establishment as the royal city of the Israelite Kingdom.'[13]

The embarrassment which this lack of evidence occasions, despite the immense efforts to recover it, sometimes prompts flights of something approaching whimsy. Thus, again from *The Museums of Israel*: '. . . Abraham and his offspring coming from Ur in Southern Mesopotamia to dwell in the southern part of the country. While the family tomb is purchased for perpetuity near Hebron they, like their own God, *have remained aloof from any tangible and material proof* [my italics], though, living forever in the words of the first book of the Bible.'[14] It is possible to admire the ingenuity of this passage whilst marvelling at its combination of the disingenuous and the cheeky.

In fact, again, there is no historical evidence whatever for Abraham and his family, nor is there any evidence of a semitic migration out of southern Mesopotamia at the beginning of the second millennium. The 'family tomb' at Hebron is surrounded by a wall of Herodian (first century BC) times; a tradition, said to go back no further than the time of the second temple (post-sixth century BC), identifies it as the burial place of Abraham and his successors.[15] There is not a whit of archaeological evidence to support the suggestion in reality.

There is no archaeological evidence for the existence of Moses, none for the captivity in Egypt, none for the Exodus. The momentous events described in the books of the Old Testament have left no trace in the annals of other peoples of the ancient Near East.[16] The extensive textual material derived from other cultures, many of them vastly more ancient than any texts from or relating to Israel, have been mined to find any references which can be paralleled with others in the Bible. The fact that, on one hand, they are often entirely unrelated or, on the other, that – as is the case with some of the great myths like the Flood story – the Biblical recensions are obviously derived from the earlier texts, does not inhibit their adoption to 'prove' the priority, or at least the equal authority, of the Biblical texts.

An example of the readiness of some Israeli scholars and the Israeli authorities in general to grasp at any ancient straw which might float by was demonstrated by the case of the vast archive of tablets excavated at Tel Mardikh, the site of the ancient capital city of Ebla. This large site in Syria was the centre of an important trading empire, flourishing in the mid-third to early second millennium.[17] Many of the thousands of baked clay tablets recovered from the site, of which a substantial proportion is still untranslated, are records of trade and traders. Great excitement was created by the early deciphered texts, a number of which spoke of individuals with names which were evidently related to such familiar names as Abraham and David. This was at once proclaimed as certain evidence of the antiquity of the Jewish presence in the Levant.

In fact, of course, it was nothing of the sort. The names in the Elba archives are drawn from the common linguistic stock of the time and the region. The names which were hailed as Jewish, appearing some two thousand years before it is even possible to speak of the Jews, were simply examples of common semitic names, which have continued in use amongst the Arabs of the region to the present day.

Israel's archaeology was given its peculiarly nationalistic character by the chance that in the early years of the state's existence two particularly charismatic military leaders, who emerged from the various conflicts with the Arabs, were much involved with archaeology. One, Yigael Yadin, was a professional archaeologist, and the son of another, E. Sukenik, one of the first Jewish archaeologists to work in Palestine; the other, Moshe Dayan, was an enthusiastic collector of antiquities, who was not too careful of the provenance of some of his acquisitions. This fact was particularly revealed by his activities after the 1967 occupation of the Sinai peninsula by Israel's forces.

Yadin was the more influential figure of the two. His sense of occasion and of the applications of propaganda in the service of the state were well developed. When the Dead Sea Scrolls were discovered, a discovery made public virtually at the moment of Israel's independence, Yadin hailed it as 'miraculous'.[18] That subsequent research has shown the scrolls to have little bearing on the development even of rabbinical Judaism did not signify.

However, Yadin was especially associated with the excavation of the fortress at Masada.[19] This remote and bleak rock platform in the mountains of the Dead Sea region was the setting for a stand by the Zealots, a fanatical sect which appeared in Palestine in late antiquity, against the Roman administration in the country. In AD 66 the Zealots and their women and children were besieged by the Romans. Rather than surrender the Zealot leaders ordered the killing of the women and children and ultimately of all the men in the fortress, rather than submit to Roman control.

The massacre at Masada has entered Israeli mythology as demonstrating the resolve of a group of Jewish political activists not to submit to foreign domination. The parallels to be drawn with the activities of Haganah and the Stern Gang (Lehi) were not lost on Israel's publicists. Masada has been described as 'a symbol of Jewish courage and a monument to great national figures'.[20]

In fact the events at Masada were simply another unhappy entry in the boundless annals of religious fanaticism. It is to be doubted if the women and children were consulted about their fate, any more than were the unfortunates who died in the Jonestown massacre in the forests of Guyana. But it was grist to the mill of those who sought to harness the findings of archaeology to the justification of a policy of exploitation two thousand years later.

It is unrewarding, to say the least, to try to apply the techniques of archaeology to the uncovering of myth. Myth and the archetypal figures which it engenders lie in the depths of the unconscious, collective or individual. They will not be found by the most diligent excavators, though traces of their influence may certainly be discovered in the works of men. They are, after all, simply immortal shadows.

None of these comments should be seen either as an attempt to denigrate one of the principal streams which contribute to the concept of monotheism, which has had so profound if so

118

equivocal an influence on the world, nor to belittle the genuine achievements of Israel's archaeology. The nature of the monotheistic canon of belief will, if it is of true substance, not be diminished either by the misapplication of historical and archaeological processes, nor, for that matter, by what I write. The Bible, after all, is about the relationships of God and humanity. These can, in the nature of things, hardly be susceptible to literal proof.

The achievements of Israeli archaeologists and of the many foreign teams who have been working in Israel since the creation of the state are, by any standards, impressive. That they have not produced the evidence which the Israeli authorities hoped for is neither the fault of archaeology nor of the archaeologists; it was not there to find. The corpus of knowledge has been greatly enlarged, however, and the archaeology which it has revealed is really the archaeology of Palestine.

Thus, an outstanding addition to the understanding of the origins of modern humanity has come out of Israel in recent years. Evidence of an exceptionally early form of *Homo sapiens sapiens* has been identified, from the Qafzeh cave in Lower Galilee, dating from 90–100,000 years before the present.[21] This is very much earlier than any previous specimens of the species of fully modern man. Previously, the earliest were thought to be those found at Cro-Magnon in south-western France, the name of which was to describe the first known examples of modern man; these remains have generally been dated to around 40,000 years before the present. In consequence the evidence recovered from Qafzeh is of great importance in extending the time-scale of the appearance of the direct ancestors of all the world's contemporary populations of *Homo sapiens sapiens*. It raises again the possibility, though it does not resolve it, that the Upper Palaeolithic populations of south-western Europe derived from the Near East. This would probably account for the morphological similarities between the European Upper Palaeolithic people and the Natufian of the Levant, many tens of thousands of years later.[22]

Israeli archaeology has done much to clarify the transition from Upper Palaeolithic populations of south-western Europe and their successors in the Levant and the Near East, who were ancestral to the first agriculturalists in northern Iraq and Iran. Of these groups, the Natufians, first identified in the uplands behind the coastal plains of Palestine, are amongst the most significant. One of the most arresting discoveries of this period was the burial at Ain Mallaha of a man of high status, perhaps a chief or, allowing for the inadequacies of the term, a shaman.[23] He was buried with a beaded circlet on his head, extensive grave goods and, close to his skeletal hand, a baton or mace. He was lying on his back, his head supported on stones so that, it appeared, he could look forever towards Mount Hermon. Israeli archaeology has been particularly fortunate in the remarkable quantity of material which has been recovered from the somewhat later periods, though still very early in historical terms, running back into the fourth millennium BC. Another important discovery of Israeli archaeology was the extraordinary Nahal Mishmar treasure excavated from a Judaean cave.[24] This consists of a hoard of over 600 finely made copper artefacts; it is entirely unprecedented. For once it is probably fair to describe the pieces as 'ritual objects'; they include maces, animal figurines and a number of what are always described as 'crowns' but which obviously are something else, for they would only fit the head of a very small king; what they might in reality be is not at all evident. The hoard is dated to the end of the fourth and the beginning of the third millennium BC.

Throughout this period of immense expansion of human settlements and human culture Palestine shared in the advances and the vicissitudes of the region of which it was a part. In the ancient Near East, from about 10,000 years ago our species underwent a series of social transformations and developments which were entirely unlike any experienced by any other animal species. The processes which brought these changes about are but dimly understood; it is clear, however, that the human psyche underwent developments as profound as those which manifested themselves in social change and material and techno- logical advance.

It is of course perfectly acceptable to attribute all such changes and advances to the intervention of a supreme directing intelli- gence if one chooses to do so. However, this is essentially a response coming out of the human psyche and must be treated as such and identified for what it is: one of the great myths by which *Homo sapiens sapiens* has always needed to live. It is unwise even to ignore myth or to underestimate its influence; it is equally unwise to set the whole course of one's life by its precepts or admonitions or to seek for its physical reality, worse still to try to force one's own interpretation of the myth on others.

All over Palestine is to be found evidence of the wide-ranging contact which the people who lived in the land sustained throughout their long history. The Israelite influence was not particularly long-lived though it was of immense and enduring importance, an importance which is vastly greater in lands far distant from Palestine than ever it was within it. Palestine's archaeology is as rich as any in the lands which march with it. It must, however, be seen in this context and it should not be taken over by a group of settlers who claim non-existent rights to the past.

It is to the present point that archaeological discoveries of equal weight, and from similar periods, have been made in Israel's close neighbour, Jordan; hardly surprising, since historically Jordan is part of Palestine, too. The remarkable sculptures from Ain Ghazal,[25] some of the earliest known to archaeology, are evidence of a well developed cultic and social structure in the eighth millennium. Equally extraordinary, though somewhat later in date, are the excavations conducted at the site of Jawa in north-east Jordan[26] where an early (fourth millennium) settlement established in the most inhospitable conditions has been identified. These Jordanian discoveries – and there are many others – are as much triumphs of Palestine archaeology as are those made in what is today the state of Israel.

It is only in very recent times that it has been possible to question, even to deny, the received wisdom of the past in regard to the stories, for example, which inform the three great monotheistic religions. Until the nineteenth century the power of state Christianity, particularly Protestantism, prevented all but the most courageous – or foolhardy – from questioning the historical paradigms which, it was believed, underlay the revealed truth of Christianity. In more recent times the political influence exercised by Zionism and its supporters has led to the acceptance of a situation in one branch of academic studies which would be unthinkable elsewhere; the exclusion of scholarly analysis and dispute in common to both cases.

This situation is changing, however. Although the questioning of the literal truths of the Biblical stories goes back to the last century, it is only since the liberating influence of some branches of analytical psychology has left the consulting room and penetrated the historian's – and particularly the political historian's – library that a more objective approach, freed from the necessity of proving a preordained set of convictions, has begun to take hold. Now, at an increasing rate, studies of impeccable academic antecedants are appearing which present these archaic texts for what they are, literary productions of great power but only of marginal historical reliability.[27]

One of the most remarkable of these recent studies, and certainly one of the most contentious is the series of books written by Professor Kamal Salibi, a distinguished Lebanese historian of considerable academic qualification. His thesis indeed far transcends a restructuring of the historical identity of the principal characters who appear in the books of the Old Testament, though this is an incidental outcome of his examination of the ancient texts. His principal concern, however, is to advance the theory that the landscape in which the Old Testament stories are set is not Palestine but Western Arabia.[28] It requires little imagination to understand the fury with which Dr Salibi's books were received, for it is difficult to imagine any theory at once which challenges so many entrenched power centres and preconceptions in one sweep – Biblical scholars, linguists, Jewish and Arab political interests, and successive generations of believers who have found consolation in the tales of humankind's redemption anticipated in and ultimately brought to realisation in the land of Palestine.

Salibi's argument is based principally on an exhaustive analysis of the toponyms of the Old Testament.[29] A command of the languages which contribute to the place names as much as to the proper names of the personalities who allegedly existed in the places named, gives Salibi great authority in analysing their inner meaning, a necessary process in the examination of any semitic language, ancient or, as in the case of Arabic, modern.

In essence, Salibi (a Christian Arab) like many historians before him, was conscious of the exceptional difficulty of matching the historical landscape of the Bible to the topography of Palestine. Time and again distances or the relationships of natural features to each other simply do not fit. This discrepancy has indeed been recognised in the past but has usually been glossed over. Salibi, for the first time, lays the topography of the Bible lands, as described in the Old Testament, over the map of Western Arabia (specifically the region which comprises the Asir and the southern Hijaz). The correspondence between the two which he achieves is remarkable and, judged purely in terms of its argument and the marshalling of the various elements of his case, compelling. Salibi enters even more controversial areas when he finds, on the basis of ancient, pre-Islamic Arabian parallels, the presence of virtually all the principal actors in the Bible stories in the gods and goddess of the hills, valleys, small towns, rivers and woodland areas of ancient Arabia.

The implication of Salibi's work are, of course, immense. Not only does it call for a complete re-appraisal of the religious beliefs of a substantial proportion of the world's population over the past two thousand years, it also has implications of the most profound condition for the question of Palestine today. If the true heartland of 'the Bible People' is Arabia then the Jewish claim to Palestine falls in ruins to the ground. Salibi is principally concerned with what, in Biblical terms, is the pre-Exilic period. He acknowledges that at some time, after the Exile, there was a migration or re-settling of people who previously had lived in Western Arabia, in Palestine. But the *religious* basis of the Jewish claim to Palestine which, as we have seen, lies at the root of the Zionist and Israel claim to legitimacy for their occupation of the land, depends upon the covenant between the congeries of semitic-speaking tribes, from which the claim is alleged to descend, and their tribal divinity, who 'promised' the land to them long before the historical fact of the Exile. If, however, the land is not in Palestine at all, but in Arabia, then where, it may reasonably be asked, are we?

Whether or not one accepts Salibi's argument (and though several scholars have roundly dismissed them, none, so far, appears actually to have refuted them), they open up a new area of linguistic analysis which obviously demands much further consideration. If the Patriarchs, heroes, Judges, Kings, and all the rest of the cast of the Old Testament stand revealed as divinities growing out of a small and in archaeological terms, unexplored area of western Arabia, then nothing will ever be quite the same again.

It would be foolish to deny that ancient texts have an historical value. They can provide a useful underlying structure to historical analyses and set up valuable markers which can assist in charting the perceived high points of a people's experience, as much as the psychological imperatives of the past of which they form a part. They must, however, be allowed to exist within their own dimension; they should not be required to fulfil a purpose for which they were never intended and which they can never accommodate.

The historical questions which the Bible leaves unanswered are not the only ones which ancient texts present to their readers today. For several centuries scholars have been baffled by Homer's descriptions of the Trojan War. Still today there is a wide gap between Homer's poetic insights into the nature of the protagonists in the story and of the warring factions involved, and the evidence of archaeology on the plain of the Scamander. But no one could insist today that Homer's contribution to the cultural inheritance of Europe is primarily historical or is in any way diminished because Priam's city is not the largest or richest level of the site at Hissarlik.[30]

The Epic of Gilgamesh, the oldest and one of the greatest literary epics, first written down in the third millennium BC (hence, upwards of two thousand years before the majority of the books of the Old Testament) tells the story of the lifetime of an historical King of Uruk in southern Mesopotamia who reigned in the first quarter of the third millennium.[31] It relates his partnership with his friend Enkidu, an entirely mythical projection of the wild man from the steppe who becomes Gilgamesh's alter ego. Together they go on a quest to the Cedar Mountain, to the edge of Ocean, and then to the Land of the Living. All of these locations had their equivalent in antiquity: the Cedar Mountain of Lebanon, the edge of Ocean, probably in the Arabian Gulf, and the Land of the Living, one of the names by which the mystical Land of Dilmun was known and which had its terrestrial reality in the Arabian Gulf islands. Any attempt, however, to chart Gilgamesh's journey on the basis of these correspondences and to search for archaeological evidence of his presence in them would be likely to prove, very quickly, a most discouraging enterprise.

If, without undue immodesty, I may quote myself,[32] I have suggested that the Pyramid Texts, the most ancient of all surviving religious documents in the history of the world, may contain elements of an Egyptian collective memory of a land far to the east, with which they had some connection in late prehistoric times. The Pyramid Texts are an extraordinary collection of spells, incantation, prayers, hymns and dialogues, some of which clearly reach back into predynastic times, inscribed on the interior walls of the royal pyramids of the Sixth Dynasty. The Texts give quite clear indications of location, climatic conditions and topography, if anyone chooses to read them that way. It would, however, be a very brave archaeologist who would set out to prove the Texts' historicity or to search for their existence in a terrestrial dimension.

Herein lies the problem. Neither Homer, the Epic of Gilgamesh nor the Pyramid Texts has been taken into the canon of revealed religion. It is only the fact initially of Christian apologists feeling the need to underwrite the revealed truth of the messages conveyed in the Old Testament by providing them with a structure of historical reality, that has produced the really quite extraordinary situation that nineteenth- and twentieth-century political activists have been enabled to base their claim to the land of Palestine.

The truth of Scripture, from whatever culture it derives, is essentially a matter of faith. It cannot, ever, be subject to material proof; archaeology can tell us much about the past but it cannot invent it, nor can it achieve or create physical remains which are not there. Miracles are the province of the enthusiasm of divines, not of the archaeologist's trowel.

There is a pleasing irony in the fact that whilst the Israeli state has been consolidating its hold on Palestine, in the process exploiting the outside world's predisposition to accept its status as *the* Holy Land, the repository of the religious aspirations of Jews, Christians and, to a lesser degree, Muslims (for Jerusalem is only the *third* most holy shrine in Islam), there was emerging from the mists of deepest antiquity a contender for the position of Holy Land, older than Palestine's and far more mysterious.

It has been known for more than a century that the editors of the books of the Old Testament borrowed many of the stories from much earlier, mostly Mesopotamian originals. These prototypical renderings of familiar myths were derived from Sumerian (hence, non-semitic) and Akkadian and Babylonian sources (both semitic languages). The borrowing was probably not deliberate or conscious but merely the absorption of common

125

elements in the folklore of peoples living in proximity with each other, by a process of cultural osmosis. One of the most ancient legends, first expressed by the Sumerians in an attempt to explain the organisation of the world around them and the part played by the gods in its creation, told of a distant land, 'the Place of the Rising Sun', 'the Land of the Living', 'the Blessed Land', where creation began, when the world was young and innocent.

Whilst the similarities are not absolute there is little doubt that the myth of the garden in which the first humans walked with God was derived from this source. The land was called 'Dilmun'.[33] In the late fourth millennium down to the middle of the third, it was located in eastern Arabia. Then its centre shifted to the island of Bahrain in the Arabian Gulf. There great temples, vast fields of well constructed grave mounds, and cities trading with the whole of the known world have been excavated since the early 1950s.

The laughter of the gods, wherever they may be, can sometimes be heard, very clearly.

If, in an ideal world perhaps, it were ever possible to achieve the sort of federal structure for a future state of Palestine which this book envisages, then the creation of a Palestinian archaeological service might provide the opportunity for the establishment of a working level of co-operation between the principal communities, in uncovering their country's past. Muslims, generally, have been less aware of the value of archaeology than have those nurtured in a Christian or Jewish cultural tradition. This is principally the result in the past of ideological constraints; these have not, however, prevented the growth of an important generation of Arab archaeologists in the North African countries and in the Levantine states such as Syria and Lebanon. Jordan, too, has a well qualified and highly experienced corps of archaeological specialists in all the disciplines appropriate to desert environments. With their Israeli colleagues the Jordanians would ensure the creation of a balanced and highly skilled antiquities service. It is perhaps merely sentimental to think that, at some distant point in the future, the archaeologists of Palestine, regardless of their religious allegiances, may work together to uncover the past of this disputed part of the ancient world.

7

THE POLITICAL REALITY

The belief that Israel is a special kind of state[1] and its Jewish citizens a special sort of people has bedevilled the search for a solution to the crisis which Israel's continued refusal to conform to acceptable patterns of behaviour presents to the world. From the outset the arrogance of Israel has been a formidable barrier to any sort of understanding with the Arab states. Israel was the haven for which European Jews had yearned; that it occupied land which was the birthright of another, disorganised, largely friendless and unlettered people mattered not at all. 'There is no such thing as Palestinians', as Mrs Meir, a Prime Minister of Israel, was later to remark, 'they do not exist'.[2] Such offensive nonsense is like the remark quoted earlier, of another Prime Minister, Yitzhak Shamir, whose principal role in the creation of the Israeli state was as a leader of the murderous Stern Gang responsible for the killing of the United Nations negotiator Count Bernadotte, of Lord Moyne and of others less distinguished, when he was moved to say, with a fine sense of near-Biblical rhetoric, 'From this mountain top and from the vantage point of history I say that these people [the Palestinians] are like grasshoppers compared to us.'[3] The Israeli establishment seems to be much given to contemptuous dismissal of the Palestinians in entomological terms. Thus General Raphael Eitan, the one-time Israeli Chief of Staff, speaking contemptuously of the Arabs, said, 'When we have settled the land all the Arabs will be able to do about it will be to scurry around like drugged cockroaches in a bottle.'[4]

It is difficult indeed to argue with such posturings; all these comments, however, demonstrate that contempt which has become the hallmark of so many of Israel's leaders when they are forced to consider the Palestinians not merely as 'terrorists' but as a people which they have greatly wronged. It is difficult not to see such remarks as nakedly racist.

To some degree, however, it is possible to understand the Israeli disregard for the Palestinians which still so evidently persists amongst the older generation of Israeli politicians. One of the more extraordinary aspects of the presence of the Israeli state in Palestine was that, for more than the first twenty years of its existence, Israel experienced very little effective opposition either from the Palestinians or from the Arab states as a whole. The wars of 1956[5] and 1967[6] provided opportunities for Israel to gain more territory and to reduce her vulnerability to the danger of any serious attack by the Arab states; the 1967 confrontation, a disaster of catastrophic proportions for the Arabs, increased Israel's sense of superiority which came to be expressed in an increasingly arrogant and dismissive attitude towards the Arabs. The Israelis did not apparently foresee the dangers which they were storing up for themselves by their occupation of lands on the west bank of the Jordan and in Gaza, which twenty years later would come back to haunt Israel like the Furies.

The Palestinians, in the early years of Israel's existence, were weak, disorganised and singularly ill-lead. Buffoons like Ahmed Shukairy strutted and postured before the Arab states, who despite whatever reservations they may have had felt the need to demonstrate some sort of solidarity with the Palestinians, and before world assemblies, which were as much embarrassed as they were bewildered by the hectic presentation of their case by the Israelis. To most Arabs the Israeli position was so self-evidently false that they could not conceive of any responsible politician or man of goodwill accepting it seriously. Gamal Abdul Nasser of Egypt, cast in the role of supreme villain by the Israelis who needed an enemy and who recognised a ready and initially simple-minded candidate in him, came to use the Palestinian case principally as a factor in his own increasingly complex politicking around the world. In the end he achieved very little for himself or for Egypt; for the Palestinians, he achieved virtually nothing. Israel, meanwhile, dominated the more influential outlets of world opinion and succeeded in presenting itself as the gallant little Europeanised state bravely resisting the monstrous onslaught of the entire Arab world.

Throughout this period Israel seemed to have had every opportunity, political or propagandistic, presented to her whilst her opponents were locked in internal dissension, ill-led and bemused by the attitude of the world powers to their misfortunes. Whenever Israeli brutality or repression became so obvious that it could not be denied or disregarded, some attempt might be made by a concerned politician or a representative of the international media who had not been wholly suborned (or, as was so often the case, simply charmed) by Israeli propagandists, to draw attention to the plight of the Palestinians. As though by some pre-arranged code such attempts would immediately be vitiated by some 'atrocity', the responsibility for which would inevitably be laid on the Palestinians. Sadly, they and their supporters were singularly slow in adapting themselves to the realities of politics and to their practice, even at a modestly sophisticated level.

For twenty years at least the Arab world was bedevilled by leaders like Nasser who, whatever good they achieved in making the Arabs a political force in the world, wasted years and hecatombs of men in the futile pursuit of political advantage and on the fantasy of unity, rooted in economies based on a discredited and bankrupt socialism. Throughout these lost decades Israel flourished prodigiously, her economy bolstered by colossal subventions from America and by a torrent of remittances from Jewry in Western lands. The Arabs were divided between the 'progressive' states which blundered down a socialist path and the 'moderate' or 'traditionalist' regimes which saw their interests as being closely identified with those of the industrialised West. The conservative states found themselves in the difficult position of being, effectively, clients of those Western states which had revealed themselves as most susceptible to the persuasion of Israeli trouble-making and influence-broking.

For years the Arab states distinguished themselves by ignominious squabbling, sometimes spilling over into direct and bloody confrontation. Palestine, if it was remembered at all, was treated as an afterthought or, more reprehensibly still, as a pawn in some other short-term policy. Occasionally some more visionary leader, like King Faisal of Saudi Arabia, drew attention to the rape of Palestine and to the dangers of the increasing Zionisation of Israel and the Occupied Territories, not only for the

129

Middle East, but for the world as a whole. His voice was ignored and, worse still, denigrated by some of those who should have been the Palestinians' protagonists.

The part played by the United States in this sorry record is hardly one of which that nation can be proud. The Zionists were of course right in directing their most intense efforts towards American centres of power in the period which immediately followed the end of the Second World War. Their plan for the settlement of Western-oriented, European-minded immigrants in so sensitive an area of the world met an immediate response from America which, in its near-pathological dislike of the British Empire and the whole colonialist phase of history, set out on the creation of a still greater, more dependent empire of which Israel soon became an essential part.

The creation of the State of Israel did not signal the decline in influence of the Zionist activists; far from it, indeed. Once Israel was a reality, her supporters turned their attention to the country that was host to the United Nations. Now the United States was to feel the full force of Zionist (soon *Israeli* would be a more honest term to employ) political and propagandistic activity. American foreign policy has, ever since, to a degree never experienced before in the history of supposedly mature states, been the prisoner of another country's demands, itself a tiny power, but one with an apparently limitless capacity for meddling. The manipulation by Israel of the important Jewish community in America has resulted in a corresponding manipulation of American policy.[7] America's humiliation has been complete; Israel has consistently abused the relationship which it has enjoyed with the United States by the actions of a large, active and ruthless Zionist lobby in America. As a consequence whatever has, in the immediate term, been determined as being in the best interests of the Zionist state has taken precedence over any considerations which American policy might otherwise advance in the interests of its own people, policy or economy.

It is difficult to establish which is the puppet and which the puppet-master in this curious embroglio of a super-power and a minute, sectarian, exclusivist and intensely militaristic state. Indeed when the histories of this period come to be written, that chapter which deals with the history of the State of Israel will present its authors with an impenetrable barrier of incredulity. First and foremost, of course, will be the evidence of the success of a tiny state foisting itself upon the world community on the basis of a tribal myth, whose roots lay in the second millennium BC, being employed to usurp the rights of another people in another world and time. But then the historians of the future, being people who doubtless will respect politics if they do not always acknowledge the power of myth, will be faced with a still greater improbability; Israel's achievement in directing a substantial part of the foreign and economic policies of the United States at a time when America was one of the world's two super-powers and immeasurably the stronger and more forceful of the two.

Yet the historians will have to acknowledge that the evidence is much as it appears to be: for decades the United States apparently allowed itself to be dominated by the declared self-interest of the State of Israel, seemingly without regard to its own interests or the interests of that part of the world of which it was the acknowledged leader. America presented nothing so much as the spectacle of some great pachyderm being led blindly to the edge of the abyss by a grinning and malevolent imp of discord.

Successive presidential candidates, of both the great parties, pledged themselves to the uncritical support of Israel in return for short-term political advantage and the infusion of substantial donations to their campaign funds. In return, Israel was allowed to pillage the land which it occupied in defiance of all international law and custom, to wage a cruel and repressive series of strikes against civilian populations, to destroy the Republic of Lebanon and, at the same time, to be the recipient of colossal grants of money and aid, drawn from the American taxpayer. Barely a word of protest was sounded in America and the Israelis continued on their way, blithely and cynically, without even an attempt at justification.

Since its inception Israel has received in US government grants and aid forty-three *billion* dollars ($43,000,000,000).[8] America has also, it is true, given much to the disadvantaged nations of the world but her generosity to others shrinks to insignificance when compared with what she has disgorged to Israel. How much greater would have been her destiny if she had employed some of the vast treasure that she wasted on Israel, to alleviate the distress of less fortunate but more honourable nations.

131

The colossal subventions which Israel has received are, of course, the source of the greening of the desert which was so powerful and so evocative an element in Israel's propagands in what might be called the 'middle period' of her history. The immense investment of money and technology which was poured into Israel would have made the landscape of the moon fertile and productive. The wonder has been that for all America's great generosity to Israel, its economy remains bankrupt and would collapse if – or perhaps when – ever this support is withdrawn.

The shame of the United States in mortgaging its great power to Israel was compounded – and indeed continues to be compounded – by the contemptuous and cynical manner in which Israel has behaved towards her benefactor. The support which America has given Israel has not prevented Israel from suborning American nationals to sell strategic secrets, nor from interfering in matters affecting the relations of America with other countries which Israel, mindful always only of her own interests as supreme above all others, judges to be unfavourable. In such circumstances Israel has not hesitated to employ the influence which she enjoys in the Congress to block policies which the American administration has itself previously determined to be in its nation's own best interests.

America has stood meekly by and seen Israel actively supporting the Iranians in the war with Iraq by the supply of material and weapons and the services of senior Israeli military strategists, though such support flouts the laws of the United States and, if undertaken by United States citizens, would result in their criminal prosecution. Israel was a principal instigator in the discreditable Iran-Contra episode, but the United States expressed only the mildest public rebuke. Israel has given much support to the extremist Iranian regime despite the humiliation meted out to the United States over the seizure of the US Embassy in Tehran and the unrestrained abuse directed against America by Iran's rulers. It now seems that nowhere in the world is safe from Israeli meddling. Whether it be the illegal export of weapons to South American drug cartels by the Israeli arms industry or the support of a cruel and discredited regime in Ethiopia by the loan of 'advisers' to an army which was engaged principally in the brutal repression of its own people, Israel is there.[9]

Thus, though originally America was responsible, partly in pursuit of what it saw as its own vital long-term interests, in the creation of Israel, United States policy has become the prisoner of Israel's single-minded selfishness. President Carter was a totally committed protagonist of the Israeli interest. His most unfortunate excursion into foreign policy resulted in the Camp David Accords.

President Sadat of Egypt, though a limited man, vain and capricious, dealt the Israelis a severe blow by his wholly unforeseen excursion to Jerusalem, which was to Israel as unexpected as it was unwelcome. Israel has always judged that it could not afford a reduction in the tension of the political situation in the Middle East. Reduced to its most simple terms, this has meant that it has never been able to contemplate a state of non-belligerency with the Arab states; all its international support has depended on being able to represent itself as beleaguered and perpetually endangered. For once Israel was hopelessly wrong-footed by Sadat's initiative. Menachem Begin, his face contorted into a rictus which the more kindly commentators interpreted as a smile, was obliged to participate in what came increasingly to be presented as an Israeli initiative for peace. The Arabs, and certainly not the Palestinians, gained nothing from it and when Israel had recovered from its first dismay it quickly assumed control of the Accords and has manipulated them ever since to its own advantage.

Israel's contempt for the peace process and its instigators was most dramatically revealed when the attack on Lebanon was launched, and thus precipitated the destruction of a little country which, if it was not without failings, yet demonstrated a degree of tolerance far removed from Israel's own vindictive assertiveness.

The Camp David Accords gave a most dangerous degree of encouragement to Israel in pursuing its militaristic objectives. The Accords resulted in the isolation of one of the principal protagonists on the Arab side, Egypt, for a very small price. Israel felt free to continue its illegal policy of implanting settlements on lands of which it is the Occupying Power and, as such, bound not to do so by explicit and unequivocal international law. Israel has chosen, once again, to act in flagrant and cynical disregard of international law and of the international community.

133

The close relationship which has persisted between Israel and the United States is now deeply harmful to the peoples of both countries. America has been induced to pour out great quantities of treasure, a policy which has resulted in the alienation, on an increasing scale, of a large part of international opinion. A more arrogant, less self-questioning state than America might dismiss such alienation as unimportant; the United States as the self-declared leader of the free nations of the world can hardly do so. For Israel's people, cut off from their original homelands in Europe and the Middle East, the consequences will be equally grave, perhaps, at an individual level, still more so. Israel's character as the Zionist state expresses their dilemma both as a symptom and as the root cause of the impending calamity of the Jewish people in Israel.

Whatever may have been the origins of Zionism as a plan to end the European persecutions of the Jewish people, it very rapidly changed into something much more sinister and malign, once the statehood of Israel seemed a realisable possibility. This indeed is Israel's tragedy: the drive which led to its creation may have been, in the hearts and minds of many of its early activists, a concept of the highest ideals, but because it ignored the rights and aspirations of the Palestinians, setting these at naught when compared with the need to assert the supremacy of the Jewish survivors of European persecutions, it contained the seeds of its own corruption.

A combination of factors contributed to this situation. The decline in such moral standards as the Zionists could claim accelerated in the aftermath of the Second World War and followed on the redistribution of political power, in particular from Europe to the United States. The policies of America were deeply influenced by anxieties induced by the dangers represented by the ambitions of Russia. The emergence of the Middle East as the reservoir of so much of the industrial world's oil reserves, and the appearance of a particularly sharply defined form of nationalism which carried disturbing overtones of Europe's millennium-long fears of Muslim conquest (an important element in the continent's collective psyche since the Crusades), all contributed to creating a political situation in which Israel could pursue her own interests virtually without hindrance. The presence of a Western-oriented, initially dependent state in the region clearly made convincing political sense to American policy-makers, and to some others of American's allies.

It would be simple-minded to argue that Israel has freely manipulated American policy in its own selfish interests in the post-war period without the ready acquiescence of America itself. Initially the support which America gave to Israel was as calculated as the support given to a dismal procession of petty dictatorships in Asia, Africa and South America, in pursuit of what she saw as the protection of her own most vital interests. In fairness, Israel is perhaps the only one of these American colonies which has actually survived and flourished, to a degree indeed which her mentor could neither have anticipated nor, in all probability, welcomed.

As the years have gone by, however, the relationship between the two has changed markedly. Because of the large Jewish community in America, with its very significant impact on the fortunes of both the great political parties, Israel has had the means of exercising a quite disproportionate influence on American policy. This influence has been far greater than that exerted by, for example, any of the South American republics or by Taiwan, South Korea or South Vietnam, even at the height of America's most intense commitment to the outfacing of communism in the Far East.

Israel has been able to repay some of her indebtedness to America by acting as a conduit for weapons and strategic equipment to countries or factions which it has suited America not to be seen to be supplying directly. This convenient posture by Israel, which has resulted in her identifying herself with some of the most deplorable regimes in the world, including South Africa and Iran, has had the effect of developing also a powerful arms industry in Israel itself, whose managers have come to exercise a more and more decisive influence on the policies of the state. The Israeli arms industry is now not only an important component in Israel's defensive and offensive strategies in the Middle East, but it has also become a most significant contributor to the otherwise extremely fragile Israeli economy. It makes a welcome and valuable contribution to the well paid employment of many people in Israel, including a large number of retired senior service officers, and to the earning of foreign currency, for which Israel has a desperate and near-insatiable need.

America's uncritical adherence to Israel's side in the face of intransigence and illegality, in countless votes at the United Nations, in a myriad of actions supporting Israel's coercion of the Palestinians, as readily as condoning its assaults on other states which it judges to be its enemies, has largely invalidated America's usefulness as a mediating force or as an agent for peace in the Middle East. It is now difficult to believe that America really has a major part to play in any future peace process.

The United States has had to pay a very high price for its friendship with this small, very dangerous country. Apart from the loss of political and moral influence which America has experienced, the United States defence (or, more precisely, arms) industry has repeatedly lost valuable orders because of the interference of Israel and its lobbyists in American affairs, whenever it seemed that Congress might authorise the sale of weapons or a defence system to a country which Israel judged to be inimical to its interests or security.

Increasingly Israel has become an aggressive militaristic state, her policies determined more by military imperatives and by the involvement of senior officers, transferred to civilian life, in the politics of the state.[10] Most of the really influential political figures in Israel today are senior service personnel in civilian clothing. Their presence in the cabinet room and in the higher echelons of the administration ensures the dominance of Israel's militaristic posture and of the military elite; indeed, it is difficult to imagine the situation ever changing in the present state of Israeli society.

The deep entrenchment of military imperatives and personnel in Israeli society, more than any other factor, reveals the hollowness of Israel's repeated insistence on its commitment to peace. Israel simply cannot afford peace; it cannot afford peace because it would at once forfeit the whole-hearted, most especially the financial and strategic, support of both the United States and of international Jewry, and the immense subventions to her treasury which both represent. Israel cannot afford peace because it would require the dismantling of the huge military machine which it has built up and of the arms industry which it supports. The dismantling of Israel's military capacity will be one of the most important and perhaps the most difficult of the steps

136

which must be taken if peace is to be brought to the Middle East.

To accept peace would also require the declaration of formally internationally recognised frontiers. This Israel has always most resolutely resisted, thus prompting the inevitable conclusion that she does not regard her present frontiers as final; the absence of recognised frontiers can only suggest a plan for future expansion of the state. This has been confirmed often enough by the substantial segment of the Israeli electorate which would seek to hold on to the Occupied Territories as much as it has been nourished by the various declarations regarding Eretz Israel, extending from the Nile to the Euphrates, which an earlier generation of Zionists tactlessly revealed as the real extent of Israel's territorial ambitions. The state which has always claimed a special moral status for its political stance has asserted, through the mouth of its sometime Prime Minister, that 'the frontier is where the Jews are, not where there is a line on the map'.[11]

This situation, however, changed once again with the events of August 1990 which led to the intervention of the United States and a group of her allies in the protection of the Arabian peninsula states. The invasion of Kuwait by Iraq in August 1990 and its aftermath will no doubt come to be seen as significant a watershed in the history of the Middle East as were the 1956 Suez crisis, the 1967 War between Israel and the Arab states, or the invasion of Lebanon in 1982. Each of these events, to mix metaphors, resulted in all the pieces being thrown up in the air, to form an entirely different pattern. This was the case with the Gulf crisis, but on a scale and with such implications for the future security of the region and the world which not even the most fevered political imagination could have envisaged.

The crisis in the Gulf changed radically the relationship of the United States with its clients, on both sides of the Israeli-Arab divide. When the communist states of Eastern Europe began, so spectacularly and unpredictably, to wither away, America was left with a very different-looking world over which to exercise its presumed hegemony. In the Middle East the radical Arab states no longer had the support, even at a political level, of Russia and its satellites, to allow them at least to dream of the prospect of a military confrontation with Israel.

The Jewish state, by the same token, was dramatically revealed as marginal to the United States' interest and to the future security of the region.

The invasion of Kuwait brought the issues which had been bedevilling the region and all those who were in any way concerned with it to the very top of the international agenda. More, the position in which America found itself meant that it should have been able to force all the parties to the Arab-Israeli conflict into facing the new realities of which the world post the Gulf war was suddenly seized.

The irony of the situation was, of course, that Saddam Hussein, whose blundering political ineptitude in the management of the Kuwait invasion was only matched by the deflation of his military posturing as soon as the Allies turned on the unfortunate Iraqi forces, had been the agent of such cataclysmic change. His belated and self-serving identification of the rights of the Palestinians with the prospects of negotiating the consequences of the invasion of Kuwait, forced the issue of Palestinian rights before the world when all the other factors in the crisis drove the Americans to act. Even the folly of the Palestinian political leadership in leaping into instant support of Saddam Hussein (rather than the measured, prevaricating and ambiguous response, which any sensible politician would have expressed) did not ultimately deny them their best opportunity for the judgement of their case that history had yet allowed them.

The Gulf war demonstrated that the centre of the world's interest in the Arabic-speaking world, the Middle East, or call it what you will, had shifted from the Eastern Mediterranean littoral south and eastwards to the Arabian peninsula. The centre is unlikely ever again to migrate northwards and so America could, for the first time, assume the dignity of the peace-broker without regard to the outraged squeals of its sometime client, or manipulating partner, the definition chosen depending upon individual taste. If an agreement, of substance and not merely of shadow, results from the PLO and the Israelis mutually recognising each other, it will be, in large part, the consequence of the dawning of the realities of politics on the United States and, however tearfully, on its Israeli client.

It was a feature of the Kuwait crisis that whenever a political choice was presented to the Iraqis, they invariably made the wrong one. The Palestinian leadership had long been skilled in this particular form of political ineptitude; now it became evident that the Israelis, too, when under intense political or diplomatic pressure, panicked and always chose the least desirable or the most damaging to their own interests of the alternatives which faced them. A particularly crass example of this ability to make unfortunate decisions in times of high crisis was the despatching of what were said to amount to *a thousand* AIPAC (American-Israel Political Action Committee) lobbyists to descend on the Congress in Washington.[12] Opponents of the way in which Israel had conducted its relations with the nation's principal legislative assembly had long deplored the arrogance of AIPAC and the Jewish-American lobby generally, which so evidently believed that they had the right to manipulate American policies and to channel rivers of American funds in the interests, not of the American people, but always in the interests of Israel. The power of AIPAC and its surrogates, a profoundly corrupting influence in American political society, received its most serious rebuff when the invasion of the thousand lobbyists collapsed in shaming exposure. This unfortunate episode was followed by another when in the aftermath of the American elections, the President of AIPAC[13] boasted of the influence which pro-Israeli groups had achieved in infiltrating the inner councils of the President-Elect. That the rejection of Israel's latest attempts to suborn centres of American political power was so swift, in this instance was the consequence of the long history of the betrayal of America's trust which had marked Israel's treatment of its closest friend and ally over many years past. It is an unappealing episode in a generally unhappy period of history; it is to be doubted if Israel can ever hope to restore its credibility, either in the United States or, for that matter, in the world at large.

Apart from the change which has come over the world's perception of Israel the most notable shift in the attitudes which the various partners to the dispute carry with them is that of Israel's perception of itself. One of the most enduring and successful of Israel's excursions into propaganda, especially since 1967, has been the promotion of the idea, which is deeply rooted in aspects of Zionism, that in some way Israel is a state committed to a rigorous morality to whom the normal criteria of judgements did not, in some way, apply. This is perhaps an inheritance from the idea, subscribed to in some mystical Jewish schools, that the Jews represent the conscience of humanity, through whose sufferings humankind will in some way be redeemed. This curious idea is closely linked to the exalted and transcendental view of themselves sustained by some Jewish fundamentalists. This view sees the Jews as being in some way qualitatively different from other and, it must be supposed, lesser peoples. A prominent authority has stated that God requires 'other normal nations' to abide by 'abstract codes' of justice and righteousness. Such laws, he states, do not apply to Jews.[14]

This highly coloured idea of the part which Israel and the Jewish people might be called upon to discharge in the interests of humanity at large can be accepted at the level of folklore, or the sort of relatively innocent assumptions of superiority which, sadly, all too many peoples have sustained despite all the evidence demonstrating how fragile are such pretensions. Israel's pretensions in this respect were only special in that a substantial fraction of the world, and that portion powerful in influence, was nurtured in the idea of the special nature of the Jewish people, according to the corpus of mystical legends to which they all subscribed.

This idea of special election has been irretrievably shattered by the events following the invasion of Lebanon and the *intifada*. Now, not only those who have, for whatever reason, opposed the expansionism of the Israeli state, but many, many Jews in Israel and abroad, have reacted with revulsion and the recognition that whatever ideals Zionism and Israel itself may once have represented have been discarded, soiled and devalued.

An unhappy consequence of this loss of moral standing, as a result of the practices of the Jewish state being exposed to the scrutiny of the world, has been the way in which Israel and many of its citizens have begun to manifest many of the characteristics which have become stereotypes of Jews and Jewishness. These are not the stereotypes of warmth, kindliness, intellect and a deep and abiding respect for human values – all of which can be adduced as characteristics of Jews in their most positive form – but rapaciousness, duplicity, treachery and an arrogant elitism which rides rough-shod over any who cross its path or oppose its aims. Since 1967 it has been only too easy to resort to the sort of criticism of Israel which prompts the cry of 'anti-semite' though, in truth, 'anti-Israeli' is what is meant.

Israel is thus one of the victims of the Gulf War. Her marginality, in any political or strategic sense, became clear in the confrontation with Iraq. Her frequently praised 'restraint' in not entering the conflict was the result of America's recognition of the dreadful consequence which would ensue, not least to the alliance, if Israel were allowed to participate. Now Israel has been left, a small economically unviable state in the eastern Mediterranean, subject to similar pressures and the same dangers of disintegration which threaten some of her immediate neighbours. Once Israel would have gained comfort from the rise of Islamic fundamentalism, the decline of communism and the effects of world recession on the Arab states around her. Now she can only reflect that she is perhaps the most vulnerable of all.

But it is not only the Israelis who have changed so significantly in the forty years of Israel's existence; the Arab population, too, has undergone a painful but crucial process of maturing. At the time of Israel's foundation, the vast preponderance of Arabs living in the Near and Middle East still consisted of peasants, small-town dwellers, nomads or semi-nomads. In Palestine itself the indigenous population was largely comprised of simple people, with the exception of a few leading families in the towns, some professionals, and the larger landowners. But now the Arab world, whether the rest of the world likes it or not, has emerged from five hundred years of slumber and is a force on the international stage. In part this is the result of the chance that Arab states control so much of the world's fossil hydro-carbons, in part also because of the extremely rapid industrial and commercial development which has taken place in some of the more important Arab states, particularly those in the Arabian peninsula and, though to a lesser extent, in North Africa. The change may be a consequence of the reinvigoration of Islam, or perhaps the emergence of Islam as a force of considerable significance is the result of the Arab world's reawakening. Some will see the appearance of a militant Islam as ominous. But, above all, the Arab world has changed as a consequence of the implantation of Israel in its midst.

The Arab states (more accurately, the Arabic-speaking states, stretching from Morocco to the Arabian Gulf) are undergoing their first period of growth and efflorescence since the high days of the Muslim Empires. By the year 2000 it is estimated that the population of the Arab states will be around the 400 million mark. This explosion of population will have a number of important consequences for Israel, and for Palestine.

This rate of growth will put considerable social and political pressures on the states of the Arab world and on the regimes which govern them. The economic prospects for countries such as Egypt and the Sudan are, in the view of some observers, abysmal; for Algeria they are discouraging, whilst a country such as Jordan can hardly hope to retain an independent economic existence.

As these countries move into an increasingly challenging period of their history, it will be more and more difficult for their rulers to resist pointing to the presence of Israel in their midst as the cause of their misfortunes. If this happens the level of confrontation between Israel and the Arab states will clearly rise to a hectic – perhaps fatal – level.

Such an outcome could be exceptionally dangerous for the Jewish population of Israel. It must now be clear that the United States, for so long Israel's generous and uncritical protector and universal provider, will not continue the same degree of support she has so unstintingly given over the years since Israel's foundation. Already signs ominous for the security of Israel are becoming apparent – an erosion of military and financial support and a reduction in the automatic level of political response, in the Congress and in international assemblies, which Israel has come to expect from America.

With this withdrawal of United States influence, leaving Israel catastrophically exposed, will coincide the inevitable collapse of Israel's economy. The world economy, and notably the economy of the Middle East, will be under increasing strains in the years to the end of the century and beyond; what funds Western industrial nations will have available for investment abroad will be directed to the reconstruction of the economies of Eastern Europe. The reduction of tension between East and West is already resulting in the reduction of defence expenditure; Israel's own arms industry, one of the most important components in her economy, will suffer accordingly. This will doubtless, in the short term at least, prompt Israel to further excursions into the deplorable world of the hire of mercenaries and the arming of drug cartels.

The events which took place in the Gulf when Iraq invaded Kuwait, and the response of the industrialised nations of the world to them, presented Israel with another foretaste of what the future may hold. It may be that America responded with

142

such vigour to the Iraqi threat in part at least because of Saddam's threats against Israel in the weeks immediately prior to his invasion of Kuwait. If this is so then it may be the last occasion when American policy is so influenced by its concern for Israel's security. Israel can do nothing to protect America's or the West's vital oil supplies. Her value, in the days when Arab nationalism seemed to real force to be reckoned with, was in providing a counter to demagogues like Nasser or to the threat of maverick states like Syria, supported by a Russian government which was content to allow *its* surrogates to keep the Middle Eastern pot boiling, just as America (and, to a lesser extent, some of the European states) allowed Israel's limitless capacity for meddling to be turned to what seemed to be the advantage in opposing Soviet ambitions in the region. But these ambitions, too, are gone. Israel is simply no longer relevant to the larger political canvas.

During the past decades the Arabs have showed signs of becoming considerably more politically mature; with political maturity comes assurance. The Arab world, the Palestinian leadership included, seemed posed to respond to initiatives to resolve the corrosive crisis which has beset the Middle East for so long.

With the advent into the White House of a regime which seemed considerably less ineluctably tied to Israel, real change, for the first time for decades, had a chance of coming about. The Americans entered into a dialogue, no matter how cautiously, with the Palestinians. At last it seemed as though the more mature politicians among the Palestinian leadership, who had been arguing for contact rather than confrontation, were bringing about a real shift in Palestinian policy, to match the shift in American policy.

But as so often has been the case, in the past, a wholly irresponsible act perpetrated by one of the Palestinian splinter groups destroyed the delicate mechanism of diplomatic contact and exchange with was beginning to work, however, hesitantly. There is some evidence – again not for the first time – that the Israelis had infiltrated the Palestinian group concerned. Equally it is apparent that they knew of the plan to land a boat on an Israeli beach some months before it occurred. They allowed the plan to go ahead undeterred, with cynical opportunism knowing that they would be able to draw the Americans back from their contact with the Palestinians in the light of another 'terrorist' act. That the action was clearly carried out without the knowledge of the PLO leadership was not judged to be relevant.

As a result the dialogue with the Americans was broken off. When the invasion of Kuwait occurred this episode made those amongst the Palestinian leadership who pursued a relentlessly anti-American policy take the Palestinians into support of Iraq, on the basis of that country's confrontations with American-led forces opposing its illegal occupation of an Arab neighbour.

The continued presence of the State of Israel in Palestine threatens not only the peace of the Middle East (and also eventually the stability of the Western world), but also that of the Jewish population of Israel, for whose security the state was supposedly created. If the status of Israel is not changed fundamentally its people will always be at hazard from the ever-present possibility that the day may come (some say it must come, quite inevitably) when the Arabs can no longer be held back from destroying what they persist in seeing as the affront to their historical destiny which Israel's continued existence, *as an exclusively Jewish state*, represents.

It is one thing to say that not for ever can Israel rely upon the unquestioning support of the United States, without which it cannot survive, economically or militarily, nor that of an increasingly secular Jewry overseas. But there is more than this: the Israelis are now profoundly vulnerable to the effects of adverse psychological factors which are increasingly building up inside their collective psyche and which are well on the way to destroying the moral character of the Jews of Israel themselves – if indeed that character has not already been totally undermined. The revelation of young Israeli soldiers battering the arms of Palestinians with stones and of children being shot down, has demonstrated more dramatically than anything else what has already happened to Israel's collective psyche.

This century has shown only too plainly that whole peoples and communities are as responsible for wrong-doing as are individuals and that they cannot escape the guilt which wrong-doing breeds by shifting the responsibility on to a military or political leadership. The entire German people, it has been persuasively argued, was guilty of the evil done in its name by the Nazis. It is no longer possible to argue that the acts of a government or of a ruling ideology are somehow distinct from the people governed or who acquiesce in the ideology. Collective responsibility for wrongful acts is thus unavoidable; collective guilt is a phenomenon as real as individual guilt for wrongful acts committed or condoned. Israel can be said to have demonstrated this principle strikingly in the application of collective punishments to Palestinian villages, in reprisal for actions carried out by individuals whose families and neighbours are members of the village in question, by an occupying authority which itself condones illegal acts, such as the seizure of land and the implantation of settlements. It is a fine line indeed to be drawn between such acts and the brutalities of Nazi storm troopers set on the destruction of Jewish property in the years before the Second World War.

Every Israeli who remains in Israel and everyone, Jew or non-Jew, living outside the State of Israel who condones the acts of the State of Israel shares in the guilt which must now be recognised as the most notable part of the inheritance of Zionism. This is as certain as that, in the annals of German history, every German who condoned the existence of the Nazi regime shared in the responsibility for the persecutions of the Jews and of all the other unfortunates – gypsies, Slavs, homosexuals, Ukrainians – who fell victims to it. It is a terrible indictment to level against the State of Israel, with a particularly evil precedent, but it is surely inescapable.

The appearance in recent years in Israel's political society of extreme fascistic groups, such as Kach and some of the wilder partisans of Likud and their followers, is not to be dismissed lightly nor, indeed, to be wondered at. The fact is that extremist, Arab-hating racialist politics are now deeply embedded in Israel's political consciousness and will not easily be eradicated, if indeed they can be eradicated at all.

The extremists have at least the merit of honesty. They declare, often with strident assertiveness, the reality which many more discreet and circumspect supporters of the Israeli state believe in their heart of hearts but which they know it is inexpedient to articulate. The pretence that the Palestinians do not exist, the repetition of slogans like 'A land without a people . . .' all indicate that in reality the dream of Israel remains a land cleared of Arabs ('Araberein' perhaps?), one which could declare once and for all that the population of the Jewish state is solely and only

145

Jewish. Given the nature of the Israeli state it could hardly be otherwise.

Increasingly within Israel the demand for the 'transfer' of non-Jewish, or, more precisely, of Arab populations from out of Israel into the surrounding Arab lands is to be heard. Already 'expulsions' of Palestinian activists have occurred in disregard of international law and the provisions of the Geneva Convention of 1949, of which Israel was a signatory.

The use of a term such as 'transfer' for the merciless uprooting of indigenous people from their ancestral lands is especially sinister. It demonstrates again, if demonstration were needed, how well Israel had learned the lessons taught by the Jews' own persecutors, who used the expression 'final solution' when they meant 'extermination'.

The concept of the 'transfer' of populations is one which is deeply rooted in the more dominant right-wing elements in Israeli politics. Even before the formation of the Jewish state the 'transfer' of Arab populations was canvassed as one means of ensuring the unsullied Jewishness of any state which might be created in Palestine. It was a policy adopted with particular conviction by Lehi, the predecessor of the Stern Gang, whose leaders were all committed to the idea. One of the most successful of the Stern Gang's leaders, in his later career as much as in his earlier exploits, is Yitzhak Shamir, who has never denied this fundamental tenet of Zionist belief, which is increasingly to be heard in the Knesset and in the more assertive settler communities.

Yet it would be quite wrong to assume that it is only the right wing in Israeli politics that is identified with the idea of the 'transfer' of the Arab population. More than fifty years ago David Ben Gurion, Israel's first Prime Minister, writing to his son said: 'We must expel Arabs and take their places ... and if we have to use force – not to dispossess the Arabs of the Negev and Transjordan, but to guarantee our right to settle in those places – then we have force at our disposal.'[15] The remarkable consistency of Zionist politics over the years suggests that this idea, though it may be hidden, is still alive and able to be recalled at any time. Jabotinsky promoted the same idea when suggesting, in a particularly imaginative flight, that the Arab population of Palestine should be transferred to nearby Arab

146

states, with substantial cash payments being made to facilitate their absorption.[16]

It is notable how often, in examining the origins and early history of the Israeli state and its Zionist inspiration, there will be encountered examples of brutality or organised and deliberate terror tactics directed against what have come to be described as 'soft targets'. The deliberate incitement of extreme political action, as in the case of some of the more malleable of individuals living in Jewish communities in Arab lands and, earlier still, the attacks perpetrated on civilian targets in Palestine during the Mandate are ancestral to the urban terrorist tactics which have been adopted subsequently by political groups across the world.

The declared Zionist objective, which was never concealed, of 'clearing the land' of its Arab inhabitants has an eerie echo in events taking place in south-eastern Europe today. The wholesale driving out of the Palestinian Arabs in the early days of Israel's existence, once so vehemently denied by the Israelis and their supporters, has now been so exhaustively documented that accusations of Israel's illegal behaviour are met with a shrug of indifference. Three quarters of a million Palestinians were driven from their homes. The canard that the Arab states had ordered the mass migration of Palestinians from their ancestral lands enjoyed a long currency, until it was exposed for the preposterous invention that it was. Events like the Israeli massacre of women and children at Deir Yassin ensured the effectiveness of Israel's policy of 'population transfer'.

But that this procedure should have become the policy of the Israeli state should hardly have surprised anyone. From the days of the Mandate the Zionists made no attempt to conceal their intention to drive out the Arabs. Herzl, Weizmann and Ben Gurion are all on record declaring that the indigenous population must, by whatever means, be persuaded to vacate the land and leave it to the immigrants. There was even a Zionist institution set up to organise the process. It was called, simply and directly, the Population Transfer Committee.

'Clearing of the land' was the term which Weizmann used, hailing it as 'miraculous'.[14] It stands at the head of the list of euphemisms for the cruel denial of the rights of friendless populations: 'ethnic cleansing' in the current, preferred term. 'Population transfer' is a Zionist example of malignant political double-speak; at the head of the list will stand for ever 'The Final Solution'. There is no qualitative difference between either the philosophical content of this directory of cruelty or its capacity to destroy the lives of those against whom such ruthless language, revealing an equally ruthless actuality, are directed.

So deeply rooted in the consciousness of those who have been responsible for Israel's government in the lifetime of the state is the idea of expelling Arabs from Israel that it still continues, though now those expelled are generally numbered in individual cases or, as most recently, in hundreds. It must be remembered, when judging Israel in these matters, that the state is a signatory of the Geneva Convention of which Article 49 states

> Individual or mass forcible transfer, as well as deportation of protected persons from occupied territory to the territory of the Occupying Power, or to that of any other country, occupied or not, are prohibited, regardless of their motive.

It is difficult to devise a more precisely worded prohibition of the sort of behaviour which Israel has so readily practised, secure in the knowledge that, thus far at least, its principal protector will always stand between itself and the sort of retribution which should be visited upon it, for such disregard of those very international conventions to which it is itself a party.

At the time of the foundation of the Israeli State and in the war which followed, hundreds of thousands of Palestinians were driven from their homes or, by intimidation and further threats by the Israeli authorities, were persuaded to flee. That Israel has considerable experience in the management of the 'transfer' of populations – or the expulsion of innocents from their homelands, whichever term is preferred – should not be forgotten, nor the fact that, whilst many of the earlier 'transfers' were brought about by the leaders of the Likud party, it is the Labour Party, which for so long dominated Israeli politics, which caused the greatest havoc amongst Palestinian communities.

The curious and convoluted nature of Israeli politics is the direct inheritance of its complex and disparate history. Two parties have dominated the state's affairs since its foundation. They represent the two principal streams of Israeli politics, the overtly moderate leftist Labour Party, strongly Zionist, and Likud, a coalition of right-wing elements descending ultimately from Jabotinsky's Revisionists, of which more below. Both principal parties are supported by a constantly changing constellation of small parties, ranging from Marxist on the one hand to extreme religious orthodoxy on the other. The Labour Party has, until recent years, virtually monopolised government in Israel. The influence of the kibbutz movement, for example, which had a considerable bearing on the social and political attitudes of many established migrants and on the first-born generation of Jews in Palestine, led towards the eventual formation of a succession of mildly leftward-inclined governments in the early years of Israel's existence, whose policies were similar in many respects to those of the European socialist movements from which they had derived much of their social and economic policies. But whatever might be their overt allegiance to current Western European ideologies, there remained the important and awkward fact of the confrontation with the indigenous population which was eventually to colour every aspect of government and administration in Israel itself and, later, in the Occupied Territories too. This problem was never resolved; indeed, it was never even considered by the early Zionists, and its want of resolution in fact mocked any pretensions to socialism which the Zionists maintained. Had they been true to what socialist principles were claimed to be, the resolution of the depressed political and economic condition of the Arabs should surely have been prominent in their planning. None the less the Israeli Labour Party, grafted mainly from Eastern European intellectual roots, maintained cordial links with socialist movements in the West. Such associations, indeed, did much to promote the image of the humanistic moderate socialist as one of the stereotypes of the Israeli migrant.

From the outset, however, there was another powerful element in the fractured – and fractious – polity of Israel. The right, from the earliest days, had its ardent protagonists, its leadership drawn from the terrorist gangs like Haganah, Lochamaei Herut Yisrael – better known by its leader Abraham Stern's surname – and Irgun, which were absorbed into the Israeli Defence Force after Independence and whose members retained a close sense of mutual identity and purpose. They represented, from the earliest days, an altogether more sinister influence in Israeli politics. They drew, in particular, much of their inspiration and their political philosophy from figures like

149

Jabotinsky (described by Ben Gurion as 'Vladimir Hitler'), and other pre-war activists who, as was noted earlier, were to all intents and purposes indistinguishable from the leaders of contemporary European fascist movements. Jabotinsky was the advocate of what might seem, to those who have experienced the nationalism of Germany in the 1930s and 1940s, to be a particularly obnoxious manifestation of nationalist ardour, the product very much of the time in which he flourished. He made no pretence that Zionism was other than a colonialist movement; he insisted that the native Arab Palestinians would become a minority in the land of Israel. He believed that nothing would be achieved, nor any gain sustained, without the preparedness to use, and to keep on using, force. His spirit is still very much abroad today, transmuted into an aggressive militarism by the state and a brutal supremacism, as enunciated by the extreme right wing and by some of the religious parties in the Knesset.[18] The line from Jabotinsky to Kahane and his Kach movement, from fascism to the most absolute form of Zionism, is direct and uninterrupted, but it runs via the leadership of the Likud, typified by men such as Shamir and Begin.

The invasion of southern Lebanon was a notable fulfilment of Jabotinsky's philosophy of the pre-emptive strike and the need always to maintain the Zionist state in a high degree of military preparedness and fervour. That it was also an unmitigated disaster for Israel does not alter the case.[19]

Israel's seemingly natural affinity for what most sensible people, whether of a left- or right-wing political persuasion, would consider deplorable political ideologies was well demonstrated by the Likud government under Menachem Begin's premiership, when it formed a notably unholy alliance with the Christian Phalange in Lebanon. The Israelis and their Phalange mercenaries fell upon the Palestinians in the south of Lebanon after the invasion by Israel in 1982, and later when the Israelis were foolhardy enough to advance towards Beirut. The Phalange was one of Lebanon's principal Christian groups – one of several, each seemingly more corrupt and murderous than the last – which drew its support from the Maronite community, under the leadership of the Gemayel family. The Gemayel patriarch, Pierre, had been greatly impressed with the National Socialist movement and its youth wing in particular, which he saw in action at the time of the Berlin Olympics in 1936. On returning to Lebanon he founded the Phalange which survived as a political entity long after its German, Italian and Spanish counterparts had disappeared, not to speak of the rag-bag of similar fascistic movements which were spawned in many European countries in the years before and during the war. The leadership of the Phalange devolved first to Pierre's son Bashir, a street fighter of an unimpededly ferocious disposition, and then to his brother Amin Gemayel, who became President of the Republic after Bashir's assassination.

The Phalange was staunchly anti-Muslim and successfully turned this aspect of its followers' prejudices to the confrontation with the Palestinians. Thus the centuries-long hatred of the Muslims – a more potent emotion in Lebanon than in most parts of the Middle East where Muslim and Christian communities lived relatively harmoniously together – was nurtured by the Christians, who saw their previously entrenched privileges in the Lebanese constitution being eroded. This hatred could now be harnessed to the destruction of the Palestinians. It was an ironic turn of history's wheel indeed, given that the Christians' masters in this case were Jews, to whose persecution in Europe Christian communities had repeatedly given themselves over.

The Israelis' preparedness to allow the Phalange and their supporters in South Lebanon to carry out the most heartless and cold-blooded atrocities on Lebanese civilians as well as Palestinian targets is well documented. The killing of UN peace-keeping troops, with the apparent knowledge and connivance of Israel, is a matter of record, as is the shameful massacre of civilians in the camps of Sabra and Chatila in which Ariel Sharon, then the Minister of Defence in the Israeli government, played so deplorable a role.

The right in Israel, which was eventually to be dominated by the Likud grouping, has always tended to be more explicit in its rejection of compromise with the Arabs, following the policy expressed by Jabotinsky. To this extent it is more honest than its Labour opponents who, needing the support of liberal groups in Europe and America, found it desirable to present a smiling face, speaking peace whilst hammering the Palestinians and the people of the Occupied Territories. Likud, the largest right-wing party and eventually the alternative government party to Labour, only adjusted its declared, overt antipathy to the Arabs when it achieved power. This alone made the Sadat initiative so tragic when he launched himself into his ill-fated partnership with Menachem Begin.

As the structure of Israeli society began to change so significantly with the rise to majority status amongst the population of the Oriental Jews – the Arab Jews, if you will – Likud in opposition began to extend its support among those same Orientals who, finding themselves at a considerable disadvantage when compared with the lot of the Ashkenazim, turned naturally to a party which expressed contempt and hatred for the Arabs, a group even more disadvantaged than themselves. The Arabs were represented as the source of all the Orientals' ills and relative misfortunes. It was a classical example of street-corner politics, of which the fascist and communist parties pre-war were masters, when manipulating the suppressed envy and hatred of a disadvantaged class. Ashkenazi commentators in the Israeli press responded with their own form of racist attack, describing those Orientals who supported the right wing as 'baboons'.

Latterly, and quite predictably, the Israeli right has begun to manifest two typical attitudes of proletarian regimes of the sort found in many other parts of the world; these are a strong religious fundamentalism and a marked identification with the 'beleaguered' settlers. In the case of Israel particularly this latter aspect manifested itself amongst those settlers who were established illegally in the Occupied Territories, which the right fancifully calls by their Biblical names of Judaea and Samaria. The more extreme religious enthusiasts have tended to group themselves into a series of small, vociferous, intensely inward-looking parties, often, but not always, led by charismatic teachers of rigorous orthodoxy whose hatred of the Arabs is usually only equalled, or indeed surpassed, by their hatred of each other. The settlers, like others of their kind wherever they may be found, express a determination to hold on to their land with a vehemence which is usually expressed directly in inverse relation to their legal title to its occupation.

It is a fair assumption that, on Israel's internal political economy becoming less and less sustainable – as in its present form with little doubt will be the case – the position of the right-wing parties will tend to become more extreme, less amenable to argument and more dependent on the threat or exercise of force. This will be in line not only with the conventional progress of such proletarian fascistic movements, but it will be in line with the historic ideology of the right in Israel. The right-wing alliance of Lukud and its allies has always been much more faithful to its roots in Jabotinsky's revisionism and consistent in its rejection of any compromise with the Palestinians.

The leadership of Likud has a past of political violence which is well documented. The party remains true to that past: one example must suffice. When asked what advice Shamir, its most recent leader until the recent elections, would offer to the settlers who, with the encouragement of the government which he led, had established themselves on the Occupied Territories (the 'Liberated' territories, in Begin's phrase), in absolute contravention of international statute, he said, 'Be strong.' To the Palestinians he said, with a disdain which so well exemplifies the right-wing parties' contempt for them, 'Be silent.'[20]

Shamir made it plain that he did not accept the Camp David Accords, though he was Foreign Minister at the time of their promulgation: he did not vote for their acceptance in the Knesset. Whilst the Accords are a largely futile instrument, none the less the United States, Egypt and a substantial band of European opinion is committed to the principles which they represent. Shamir disregarded them; his rejection demonstrated how little value can be put either on Israel's word or the merits of so fragile a piece of adventitious drafting.

Shamir remained constant, as does the majority of his party, to the idea of Greater Israel. Until such triumphalist ideas are eliminated from Israel's body politic, there is no hope for peace.

These two components of the Israeli state as it stands today will present those who may attempt to achieve a solution to the crisis which Israel represents in the region with two of the most crucial and most intractible factors which have to be faced and resolved. The settlers, who contain amongst their number many recent emigrants to Israel from Europe, the Commonwealth and the United States, and who have something of the fervour of the pioneer about them – a quality otherwise now significantly diminished in Israel – will probably represent the most difficult human problem. They cannot, in the nature of things, be expected quietly to assemble their belongings and to go away: whilst some of their more extreme pronouncements may be regarded with scepticism, there are undoubtedly many among them who would be prepared to fight to stay in possession of the land which they have seized or which has been handed to them by a complaisant government.

It would actually be surprising if many Israelis, particularly those who have settled in the Occupied Territories, felt otherwise than wishing to see the Palestinian Arabs gone. All settlers despise and fear the indigenes whom they have displaced. This is true in every case: whether it is the white Europeans who settled in Africa, the British who colonised Australia – and, in a particularly vicious and extreme case, hunted bands of aboriginals to destruction – or the Americans in their protracted slaughter of the Indians, history is full of similar unhappy examples. The Israelis, too, are colonials; this indeed is their misfortune, that they are probably the last example of a colonising people settling in others' land, the result of a politically encouraged migration, which has to be seen essentially as an expression of the nineteenth-century colonialist phase of history. Zionism is a particularly refined and specific form of the drive which led Europeans to implant colonies across the world. All the special pleading and specious historicism in the world will not disguise that fact.

Thus the idea of a 'population transfer' (by which of course is meant the forcible expulsion of the Arab population of Palestine) is fundamental to Zionist doctrine. It appears, quite nakedly, in countless interviews, letters, speeches, articles and books by Zionist leaders. In the period before the Second World War, as we have seen, the issue is not dissembled. Zionists, if they were concerned about non-Jewish audiences, knew that all but a very few amongst those whose opinion was worth cultivating and on whose political will they depended, would not look askance at plans to resettle a poor and generally insignificant indigenous population. It was not in the way of imperial powers of any persuasion to anguish too deeply about such matters, in any event. In the case of Palestine the Zionist declarations about the removal of the Arabs went largely unregarded, for the concerns of the Zionists were only intermittently of interest to the powers and the concerns of the indigenous Palestinians hardly at all.

There was also the consideration that, judged by the politics of the time, the proposal to resettle an inconvenient population, removing them from one location where their presence was causing problems to another location where the problem would become someone else's, was seen as entirely practical politics. In consequence, the Zionists proceeded with their clear expression of the necessity for population transfer in a sense quite naively for they were merely employing a form of political expedient entirely comprehensible to the colonial powers, whose ideology they had so enthusiastically embraced and whose language, rich in euphemisms, they readily adopted. The Zionists and their offspring, the State of Israel, were unfortunate in that they came at the end of an historical sequence, and became the last significant exponents of the idea of European colonialism. In such a context the transfer of a few hundred thousand Arabs must have seemed an entirely sensible programme to adopt.

Once again, the course of history has not dealt kindly with Israel. Zionism is an essentially European phenomenon, a point which will not have escaped the diligent reader of these pages. But the population of Israel is now wholly transformed from the structure which its Zionist founders envisaged. Now the majority of the population is Sephardic, of Oriental origin. What do the majority of the Oriental Jews believe about 'population transfer'? They have some knowledge of it, after all; they may even see themselves, having in mind the treatment which they have often received from their fellow Ashkenazi Israelis, as candidates for transfer, at some future date.

Vladimir Jabotinsky who, in addition to being the most important ideologue to have emerged in the development of a living, continuous Zionist idea, was also the most honest spokesman of Zionist objectives, made clear the essentially colonialist view which the philosophies of the Zionist movement maintained toward Palestine. 'We maintain unanimously that the economic position of the Palestinian Arabs under the Jewish colonialisation has become the object of envy in all the surrounding Arab countries.'[21] With similar revealing honesty Jabotinsky averred, 'What I do not deny is that in the process the Arabs of Palestine will necessarily become a minority in the country of Palestine.'[22] In the light of such disclosures by the man who is still the inspiration of one of the brands of politics which dominates Israel, it is easy to understand the apprehension of the Palestinians, even to this day. Jabotinsky was characteristically direct when he spoke of 'Jewish colonisation'. He also spoke prophetically for what was to become the Israeli right when he said, 'We cannot "concede" anything.'[25]

8

RELIGION, MORALITY AND THE DECLINE OF ISRAEL

It is one of the characteristics of European societies since the French Revolution that, with the decline in religious belief and the weakening of the social bonds which religion imposes, there has been a marked tendency to invest political movements with many of the elements of religious faith. The absolute acceptance demanded of their followers by Fascism, National Socialism and, especially, Marxism-Leninism, in the particular brands of social management which they represent, is in no way different from the absolute demands of faith imposed by the medieval church.

It was much the same with Zionism. The increasing secularisation of European Jewish societies, the consequence of the emancipation of the Jews and their tendency to assimilation, were matched, as noted earlier, by a response to late nineteenth-century nationalistic ideas. The secular nature of the beliefs of the founders of political Zionism was reflected in the policies enunciated by them, which underlay the development of the programme and principles by which the movement developed. However, the reduction of traditional Jewish religious belief amongst the Zionist leadership produced the same reaction as occurred amongst other similar political movements. The ideology began to assume the place of a sort of pseudo-religion, a secular faith in which the contradictions of secularism and religion were hopelessly at odds with each other. Zionism is a particularly potent example of this phenomenon.

The proliferation of communications media around the world has had a considerable effect on the religious beliefs of all sorts of communities, particularly those which are, or which feel themselves to be, disadvantaged. The insecurities of the world

157

are highlit by the reporting of events, usually of the most dismal sort, from around the globe. Orthodox religion has failed the generations of its adherants and, in consequence, all manner of 'charismatic' sects have arisen, their success fuelled by the skilful use of the media and communications and the insecurities of their followers.

Much is made of the threat which is perceived to be represented to the traditional power centres by the rise of what is commonly termed 'Muslim Fundamentalism'. The use of this term is to misunderstand the nature of Islam in its relation to the societies which it seeks to govern by the recognition of the principle of submission to a final revelation which it promotes. In a sense, *all* Islamic belief and practice is fundamental; to the Muslim there can be no occasion for a return to Islam's origins, since Islam has never deviated from them. There has been no Reformation in Islam nor indeed could there ever be one, in the sense that Christianity experienced its Reformation as a rejection of what was seen to be the corruption of the original Gospel message, not of the message itself, as much as the corruption of the Church which was charged with its promulgation.

What has happened in Islam in relatively recent times is that its political dimension, in reality inseparable from its precepts which deal with man's relationship with the Divine, has come to assume a much greater importance and exposure in a world which generally separates the political and the religious dimension of human experience. This has produced, in response, the assertion by some Muslim divines of the need to accept the totality of the Qur'an's message, to set the world's wrongs to right.

The Palestinian issue is, to the Muslim, to be seen in this context. It has become, in consequence some would say of the political world's indifference, a matter of commitment to Islamic activists who would not in other circumstances have regarded it as of such importance to them.

The involvement of religious activists in Islam in the struggle for Palestine has, inevitably, been echoed by the involvement of other religious groups which can, more accurately, be categorised as fundamentalists in that they seek a return to the literal interpretation of its revelations. In this both the Jews and the Christians differ from the Arab Muslims in one important particular: neither has the familiar access to the original text of *their* holy books which the fact that the Qur'an is written in Arabic gives to the present-day speakers of that language.

The secular nature of early Zionism somewhat masked the involvement of religious orthodoxy in the campaign for the creation of the Jewish state. As was earlier noted, this was largely deliberate as the founders of Zionism believed that a secular, non-religious approach would be more acceptable to the world opinion which they sought to subvert, than an overtly religious message. The religious dimension, was, of course, always present and could be invoked whenever it was considered expedient. It was not, however, until well into the lifetime of the State of Israel itself that a specifically Jewish fundamentalism began to be apparent as a powerful factor in the increasingly complex political fabric of the Jewish state.

Much of the overt influence of Jews who seek the most literal interpretation of the books of the Torah as history – giving them a warrant, in consequence, for the occupation of the territories in which, against the repeated demands of the international community and in defiance of international law, settlements have been established – has come from new settlers from America and, to a lesser degree, the United Kingdom. These people have been the most vociferous in their dismissal of the Arabs, in the assertion of their claims to 'Eretz Israel', and in their rejection of any settlement with the Palestinians which would require the surrender of any part of the land which, at present, they inhabit.

The concept of 'Eretz Israel', of the greater entity which, in modern political terms, would embrace, not only Palestine but much of Syria, all of Jordan, Lebanon and parts of Egypt, has always been of fundamental, even transcendental importance to the more extreme religious groups which support the creation of the Israeli state. To them, the issue of land is not a political matter, but of essential belief, its holding a duty imposed by a tribal divinity four thousand years ago. Thus, to these people the withdrawal, abandonment or dismantling of settlements in the Occupied Territories is a betrayal of the most essential tenets of their faith.

The political expression of this mentality finds itself in a number of small, strident and exceptionally vituperative political parties, in several cases led by charismatic rabbis. They have come to see themselves as power-brokers in the making and unmaking of successive Israeli governments, the tiny handful of votes in the Knesset which they control often representing the government of the day's majority.

Likud has been the most covetous of the support of these religious fragments, reflecting both their problems of securing a working majority by the Knesset and their natural sympathy with the extremist positions often adopted by the religious parties. The leadership of Likud has gone, on occasion, to extra-ordinary lengths to secure the blessing of these groups: Mena-chem Begin, it is reported, was seen actually to kneel to one of the leaders of the extreme religious fundamentalist parties, Tzri Yehuda.[1] Such deference is not, of course, applied even to the Divinity in Judaism, since kneeling or prostration have no part in Jewish ritual, unlike Christianity and Islam.

The most powerful grouping of the religious right is repre-sented by Gush Emunim[2] ('The Bloc of the Faithful') which, in its policies as much as in its name, is evocative of some of the Islamic groups which its followers so roundly denounce. Gush has been especially successful in recruiting support in the settle-ments, from recent largely non-European immigrants and, para-doxically, from the Orientals. In this last respect they have been singularly successful in appealing to the sense of disadvantage and discrimination which the Israelis of Middle Eastern origin feel in comparison with those of European background, who have traditionally been the backbone of the Labour Party's sup-port and in whose interest the affairs of Israel have largely been manipulated.

Gush Emunim, in common with other extreme parties, sets the unity of Israel as supreme above all other considerations. No other aspect of Israeli policy approaches this issue in import-ance: the position therefore of any Israeli government in nego-tiating a settlement with the Palestinians must be judged against this proposition. Unless the religious extremists can, in some miraculous way, be contained, their presence in the Israeli polity is yet another reason for distrusting any proposals for peace which are predicated upon the continued survival of the Jewish state.

Every sign of compromise with the Palestinians is, to these people, an abomination; every sign of moderation on the part of the Palestinians is seen as a danger, to be vigorously opposed and, by whatever means, discredited.

160

It is from such sources as Gush Emunim that the most frequent calls for the 'population transfer' of Arabs is to be heard.
Such proposals are couched in language which has distressing
and inevitable counterparts in euphemisms such as 'ethnic
cleansing' and 'the final solution to the Jewish problem', and
will undoubtedly increase as pressure is exerted on Israel to
take action to resolve the injustices done to the Palestinians.
Any proposals for the return of the Occupied Territories will be
countered by the demands of fundamentalist settlers for the
ridding of Eretz Israel of its 'alien' (for thus are the indigenous
Arabs described in settler rhetoric) population which lives in
what once was Palestine.

It is little wonder that, at a time when many of the ideas and
institutions of political Zionism are withering away, this type of
activist fundamentalism, calling for a literal interpretation and
absolute acceptance of ancient myths, thrives as never before.
There is little doubt that the most obvious danger to the internal
stability of Israel in the aftermath of any agreement with the
PLO will come from these extremist religious groupings and
from the more overtly fascist and racist right-wing politicians.

Much the same condition applies with the other of these
luscious and exotic growths which flourish on the tree of faith.
Christian fundamentalism, the most aptly named of the three
forms of aberrant belief to which the term is applied, is in a
particularly vigorous phase of growth and is of special relevance
in the particular context of the survival of the State of Israel as
a specifically Jewish institution.

Charismatic Christianity is, in many of its manifestations,
genuinely fundamentalist in that it believes that there is a
simple, uncomplicated faith which may be recovered from the
Gospels and which has been complicated and contaminated by
centuries of interpretation and amendment by religious leaders
more concerned to serve the society and the state than to promote the original message of Christ. The sects which are identified with this brand of Christian enthusiasm – a condition wisely
condemned by the Fathers of the Church, against whom the
Christian fundamentalists presumably represent the most forceful reaction – tend towards what they believe to be the marks
of the early Christian communities, singing, dancing and speaking in tongues.

Since they draw much of their inspiration from what they

supposed were the original communities of Christians in Jerusalem, the role of the Holy Land (a particularly Christian concept, by the way) has always been paramount. In consequence its role and political direction is of great and enduring importance to them.

The support of the charismatic or fundamentalist Christian churches has been of great importance to Israel, especially in the United States. The belief in the literal truth of the Bible, as it is written (though in a language undreamed of when its original authors and editors were at work) is the bedrock of this increasingly powerful branch of Christianity which, as the more conventional wings of the church have declined in support and influence, has grown perceptibly. The members of such churches will support the idea of the Jews as specially chosen of God, of the Promised Land and, most important, of the ingathering of the Jews to Israel as a witness of the approach of the Second Coming and the end of days. Close to these concepts is the idea, proposed also by some orthodox Jewish groups, that the world's redemption depends upon the return of the Jewish people to their homeland.

Such ideas are, of course, valuable to the politicians who seek to mobilise opinion in Israel's support, no matter how bizarre or extreme their origins. Particularly in the United States do they represent a potentially formidable and very numerous constituency. Against these often very curious views must be set the implacable hostility of some of the most extreme orthodox Jewish groups who believe that the Israeli state is an abomination and an affront to God. It is unlikely that religion, of whatever denomination, will contribute much to the just solution of the dispute or to the integration of the Jewish population of the eastern Mediterranean into a secular and peacable state.

As Zionism declines as a political influence, with the reduction of support by international Jewry and the increase in the proportion of Orientals in Israel itself, the nature of Zionism as a pseudo-religion will attenuate. The process will be accelerated by the corrosive effect which the inevitable slide of Israeli politics into a perpetual round of repression and injustice has on what many Jews themselves see as essential Jewish characteristics of compassion, concern for the individual and the relief of suffering. Whether these perceptions are accurate or whether they are accepted by the majority of non-Jews is irrelevant; the Jews' own perceptions of themselves are being gravely, probably irrevocably, damaged by the practices of successive Israeli governments. These practices are now an ingrained part of the Israeli state's character and will not change.

The need for recognition by the international community of the essential immorality of Zionism's position is, to put it no higher, overdue. Zionism has corrupted Jewish ideals, which have so significantly contributed to the culture of the Western world. In doing so it has brought into disrepute the traditional Jewish virtues which the advanced societies of the West have admired and, when it suited them, adopted. Respect for the individual and the rule of law are claimed as peculiarly Jewish concepts; these virtues have been wantonly discarded by Israel even in the few years of its existence. It is this turning aside from their traditional ethos which sets the people of Israel at great peril and denies the historic character of both Jews and Judaism.

It is telling that Chaim Weitzmann, one of the founding fathers of Israel and its first President, evidently had some apprehension of what might come. He dreamed of Israel as 'a high civilisation based on the austere standards of Zionist ethics.'[3] It might be difficult today to demonstrate with conviction the austerity of Zionist ethics, or indeed their very existence; Weitzmann himself observed, 'I am certain that the world will judge the Jewish state by what it will do to the Arabs.'[4] It would perhaps be malicious to point to the ambiguity of the last quotation and doubtless Weitzmann meant to imply that the world would expect the Jewish state to deal honourably with the Arabs. But closer to the truth of things was the belief that the Arabs would be 'the hewers of wood and the drawers of water' for the Jewish inhabitants of Palestine.

The Israelis' treatment of the indigenous Arabs of Palestine is deeply at odds with many of the perceptions which the Jews hold of themselves. One of the least rational but none the less one of the most enduring myths which have attached them-selves to Israel and to Jews generally is the assertion (one which Jews themselves have not been shy to advance) that some sort of moral superiority goes with Jewishness and, hence and by extension, to the Jewish state. The roots of this quaint idea go deep; in the Old Testament the Hebrews are proclaimed a priestly nation and, more generally still, that they are a holy people 'which shall be a light unto the nations'. Early Zionists, or at least those like Weitzmann who concerned themselves with morality, thought that the Jewish state would need necessarily to set itself higher principles of political morality than other nations. Israel, it was argued, could not be judged by the standards of the common moralities adopted – or, more usually, ignored – by less high-minded states.

This presumption of moral excellence as a characteristic of the Jewish state has been trumpeted by its leaders as much as by its foreign protagonists over the years. It has proved to be a valuable asset in developing Israel's international status and acceptance proving, if proof were needed, that if an assertion, no matter how preposterous, is trumpeted loudly and frequently enough, the world will believe it.

The fact, of course, is that Israel is no more moral in its dealings as a member of the international community than any other nation and, demonstrably, is a good deal less moral than many. The Jews are no more moral, nor less venal, than any other group. Yet many influential voices, particularly those which are identified with the Christian right, fundamentalists and the promoters of charismatic forms of religious worship, accept and promote such assertions which by their very repetition mislead the credulous and the ill-informed (in high as much as in low places) when the deceptions and repressions of the Israeli state are displayed to the world.

The psychic traumata which mark the history of the Israeli state and its treatment of the Palestinians are now profoundly rooted. With them are constellated the residue of the effects of the Jews' own persecution in Europe and the damage which these events did to Europe's own character.

It has been well argued that the particularly European tendency to persecute dissenting minorities is an expression of Europe's own besetting demons. It has been the continent's misfortune that in the period of its finest cultural flowering it has been, almost literally, bedevilled by sinister and authoritarian religious movements which have imposed a pervasive orthodoxy on the minds of Europeans. This demand for an unquestioning acquiescence in canons of religious belief untested by reason, resulted in the surging up, from who knows what hideous depths of the unconscious, of demons which needed to be propitiated by repeated holocausts of innocents. The Devil, it should be remembered, has become a peculiarly Christian concept.

It has also been rightly observed that it is the persecuted who persecute. The demons released by the European unconscious set upon the Jews in Israel, and those who support them in the world outside have fallen victim to those same demons, who have recognised the land of Israel as a rich land for their habitation. Young Israelis now beat elderly Arabs and children as readily as young stormtroopers and SS men beat elderly Jews or drove Jewish children into the concentration camps.

The transgressions of the State of Israel are manifest, flouting, as they do, international law as much as moral law. To the deportation of the inhabitants of Arab villages and towns must be added the use of collective punishment and the destruction of property of bystanders or third parties, this despite the fact that settlements in the Occupied Territories are specifically prohibited for nationals of the Occupying Power.

Israel stands condemned by its rejection of the Geneva Convention, of which it is a signatory. By the terms of the 1949 Declaration

- deportations of the inhabitants of occupied territories are prohibited;
- settlements by the nationals of the occupying power are prohibited;
- collective penalties and likewise measures of intimidation or of terrorism are prohibited.

These three provisions neatly summarise the misdeeds of Israel in respect of Palestine and its people.

The practice of expropriation of property and the intimidation of civilian communities practised extensively by Israel against the Arab population of the state and, more particularly still, against the people of the Occupied Territories, are explicitly contrary to international law. That Israeli occupation of what are whimsically referred to as Judea and Samaria is described as the 'Liberation' of those territories must inevitably recall, to anyone with an historical cast of mind, the Liberation of the Sudetenland by the Nazis in the 1930s and their subsequent liberation of much of continental Europe. It is, of course, no surprise to find that the term 'liberation' has been used in this sense by Menachem Begin, who learnt the lessons of his youthful involvement with the Bitai movement well.[5]

To describe the corruption of the inhabitants of Israel by such actions is not merely fanciful mystologising. The same deep-seated demonic fantasies which Jung detected in the early 1920s in the German psyche, which presaged the appearance of National Socialism nearly a decade later, have their parallels in the inversion of Jewish belief and custom which can now be witnessed, serving the demands of a harsh and unbending militarism.

There is no scope now for compromise. The solution to the issue of Israel and the Palestinians lies no longer in the mere acceptance of the presence of a Palestinian state, a concept which is rejected out of hand by one of the two dominant parties in Israeli politics at the present time. The solution demands the creation of a secular Palestinian state – and more besides. Nothing short of the de-Zionisation of Israel will begin to create the conditions in which peace might come to the small, troubled land at the eastern end of the Mediterranean. This is still most emphatically the case no matter what degree of recognition Israel and the PLO award each other.

9

THE ORIENTAL JEWS AND THE DE-ZIONISATION OF ISRAEL

From the foundation of the State of Israel its affairs have been dominated by the preoccupations, and indeed by the collective personality, of Jews of European origin. The characteristic institutions which have been developed in Israel are essentially European in origin and function. Israel, to all intents and purposes, is a European state transplanted into the soil of the Eastern Mediteranean.

Such a Euro-centric character to the Israeli state was indeed inevitable. The Jews of Eastern Europe, the Ashkenazim, were the founders of the state; Zionism is a peculiarly European phenomenon and the Israeli state is Zionism's supreme artefact.

But there is another, most significant, yet so far still insufficiently recognised component in the population of Israel today. This is represented by the Oriental Jews, sometimes called, in contradistinction to the Ashkenazim, the Sephardim, in Israel referred to as Edot Hamizrach or, more generally, Mizrachim, the Orientals.[1] These are the Jews who lived in Yemen, North Africa, Syria and the Levant, and Iraq; historically they included the Spanish and Italian Jews also. Their experience, both in terms of their history and of their relationship to Israel, is markedly different from that of their European co-religionists.

The Oriental Jews have not received anything like the same degree of attention, either from scholars or from political commentators, Jewish or non-Jewish, as have the Europeans, yet they are the elder of the two great congregations into which Jewry is divided. Jewish communities were established all round the Mediterranean in Hellenistic times. In the Roman period such communities expanded considerably and, during that curious era, when a multitude of mystery cults and exotic religions

167

drifted into the Roman world, leaving their mark most notice-
ably on the sect that was eventually to become the Christian
church, the Jewish communities flourished exceptionally.[2] Contrary to their later custom, the Jews of the Hellenistic world
undertook energetic programmes of proselytisation and, securing many converts from the declining cults of the ancient world,
the communities grew and prospered.[3] This was particularly
true in the time of John Hyrcanus (134–104BC), during whose
singularly blood-spattered reign forcible conversion to Judaism
was conducted on a large scale.[4] It was during the time of the
Hasmoneans, of whom John was perhaps the most repulsive,
that there could be actually said to be a Jewish *state* in Palestine.
It lasted from 152 to 37BC.

Amongst the peoples who were forcibly judaised in John's
time were the Edomites, who lived in the north-western quadrant of the Arabian peninsula and across into Sinai. It was
probably this episode and others which followed it which
planted the substantial Jewish populations in northern and western Arabia, who were still there in Prophetic times. The expulsion of those who would not accept Islam undoubtedly
introduced more stock into the Jewish communities of the Mediterranean and North Africa with which they were subsumed,
which had no historical or genetic connections whatsoever with
the original population of the Levant.

Forcible conversion was still more evidently the hallmark of
the reign of John's son, Alexander Jannaeus. During his rule the
inhabitants of the Greek cities in the Jordan Valley were Judaised
or put to the sword.[5] Even Petra, the Nabataean capital of the
people who are one of the significant elements in the ancestry
of the modern Arabs, was taken into his grip. The Hasmonean
state, representative of the family to which both John and Alexander belonged, swept over large tracts of territory in the Levant
and Syria, wiping up the non-Jewish populations as they went,
eliminating them by massacre, forcible conversion or (an ominous portent for the future) by expulsion. This brutal assertion
of a Jewish statehood, which many Jews would deny as properly
representative of their historic role in the world, swiftly
increased the percentage of the world's population which was
at least nominally Jewish, to a degree that it had never achieved
before. At the time of the destruction of Jerusalem by Titus in
AD67, the Jewish population is estimated to have reached 4.5

million.[6] This very high figure was undoubtedly in large part the product of conversion, by whatever means.

Whatever may have been the racial unity of the Hebrew-speaking tribes initially, by the early centuries of the Christian era this unity had been entirely replaced by Jewish diversity as the result of proselytism, inter-marriage and forcible conversion.

It is worth observing, incidentally, that in pre-Islamic times in Arabia, after the dubious episode of Hasmonean supremacy, there is not the slightest evidence of any sustained animosity between the Arabians of Jewish religious allegiance and those who were either pagans or Christians.

However it was that the communities came to be enlarged in this generally untypical time, rich and secure Jewish communities were widespread in the world of late antiquity; this period was undoubtedly one of the high points in the Jewish historical experience. The extent of the growth of Jewry throughout the Roman Empire was matched by the exceptional prosperity of Palestine at this period.[7]

In Roman times Judaism was not itself an illegal practice, providing the gods of Rome were given their official, largely formal, recognition. This many Jews felt able to do, using the device of private reservations which was to allow Jewish converts to Islam and Christianity in Spain, for example, to conform to the religious practices of the society amongst which they lived whilst conducting their own Jewish rituals in private. So it was in Rome. Occasionally, however, particular Emperors disapproved of the Jews and hounded them. Thus Hadrian, a devout Philhelline, seems to have had a marked dislike of circumcision – a matter about which his own tastes presumably disposed him to have strong feelings – and outlawed Judaistic practices in consequence.

The Jews of the Mediterranean cities were little affected by the destruction of the Temple in Jerusalem in AD70, other than by the influx of many more Levantine Jews into their midst. These, expelled by the Romans, moved south and joined their fellows in North Africa; others moved west from Palestine into Anatolia and no doubt formed those cells of Jews which, corresponding with the communities in the Mediterranean, were later to impress the Khazars so much in the ninth and tenth centuries.

The coming of Islam in the seventh century was a crucial time for the Jews, in those lands in which the Prophet's writ so quickly ran. There were large bodies of Jews in western and southern Arabia, living side by side with the pagan Arabs, from whom indeed they sprang. Muhammad sought their conversion; there is no doubt that many Jews accepted Islam, but others were intractable and rejected his apostolate. Muhammad always insisted that Jews and Christians, though both were patently misguided, should be treated with consideration and not coerced into accepting his message.[8]

The position of the Jews of Arabia represents a special case. During the centuries of the proselytising enthusiasm which seized the Jews of the Hellenistic world, missionaries converted a large number of tribesmen and townspeople in the Arabian peninsula. It may be that Arabians, even when they were predominantly pagan, had a predisposition to monotheism; at any event, there were substantial communities established in the Arabian cities in the late pre-Islamic period. When the Prophet brought his message to the peninsula people, the Arabian Jews found themselves in an equivocal position; as a 'people of the Book' they were tolerated, but as members of large and prosperous communities they swiftly found themselves disadvantaged when compared with their Muslim compatriots. Many converted but a large number undoubtedly migrated from Arabia, adding their seeding to the established communities around the Mediterranean and, eventually, moving into European lands. Then, paradoxically, they found themselves caught, in some cases, between the hammer of Islam and the anvil of Christianity. In general, however, they preferred living under Muslim rule which, after its first fervent years, became notably more tolerant.

Both Jewish and Christian communities were, however, kept at a social disadvantage when compared with the Muslims. This did not prevent individual Christians and Jews from achieving all but the very highest rank in many of the Imperial Muslim states which reached such extraordinary material and cultural richness in the centuries following Muhammad's death. In all the states which struggled and manoeuvred for power over the whole Muslim community, Jews and Christians were the foundation of the bureaucracy and of much of the professional class. They were often the trusted aides of the rulers, on whose goodwill they depended absolutely; to a large degree they were instigators of many of the intellectual and scientific advances for which the Muslim empires are justly renowned.

To assert that the Jews, like the Christians, were generally tolerated by the Muslim states is not to suggest that the condition of either people was ideal, or even agreeable. Non-Muslims were discriminated against, often penalised, frequently abused and generally disadvantaged. But in this they fared, if not better, probably no worse than most minorities living amongst a dominant society at any time in history. What is certain, however, is that conditions under the Muslims were vastly to be preferred to those experienced by minorities in Christian lands at much the same time. Those minorities which lived under Islam, compared with those which lived in Europe, enjoyed a relatively fruitful and productive existence alongside those who saw themselves as their masters, in the society of which they were all part.

There were occasions when mob violence, either spontaneously engendered or stimulated by the provocation of one side or the other, was directed against Jewish and Christian shops and houses in Muslim cities. But during the centuries following the spread of Islam such occurrences were exceptional. Their rareness is demonstrated by the fact that when there were such outbreaks, as in Granada in 1066, they were long remembered and their causes analysed as much by Muslim historians as by the Jews themselves.[9] Significantly the most notable attacks on Jews in Arab cities occurred after the rise of European influence in the Near East, especially during the nineteenth century. This is not the consequence of coincidence; rather it is the result of people of a Christian or Jewish persuasion seeking to ally themselves with the representatives of powers or interests with which they could identify, with, indeed, their own co-religionists in some cases.[10]

Non-Muslims had long been frequently exposed to humiliating legislation concerning dress, the riding of horses or the size and height of their houses. None the less Jews in particular achieved, and went on achieving, high status throughout Islamic lands. They usually did this, too, whilst remaining Jews in custom and religious practice.

There are records of many converts to Islam throughout the period that the Muslim empires flourished, with both Jews and Christians embracing Islam. The Muslims, like the Christians, always maintained a somewhat ambivalent attitude towards Judaism and the Jews. They acknowledged their kinship: Muslims have always felt closer to the Jews in matters of custom and belief than ever they have done to the Christians, whom they suspected were only disguised idolators, worshipping a Trinity, a conceit which sounded to them remarkably like polytheism. Jewish customs, as expressed in the Torah and later in the Talmud, are ultimately drawn from the same social and environmental circumstances as those of Islam, a way of life devised primarily for relatively small groups living on the fringes of deserts. It is as reasonable, indeed it is perhaps more so, to speak of a Judeo-Islamic culture as it is to describe the underlying religious character of much of European culture as Judeo-Christian. Christianity, at least in the form which has been dominant since the lifetime of Constantine, is the binding belief of a society which separates religion and politics (unlike Islam, or for that matter, Judaism) but which nevertheless employs religion in the service of the state. Christianity has become the creed of dominance and exclusivity in a way which has characterised neither Islam or Judaism, though the latter does seem to imply a superiority, based on the choice of God, of its followers over all other mortals. Islam sees the expression of its superiority as doctrinal, not individual.

Orientalism, the literary and artistic phenomenon which appeared so strikingly in the first half of the nineteenth century and which continued to flourish in many European societies at least until the outbreak of the Great War, paid little attention to the Near East's Jewish communities as such, regarding them simply as part of the colourful and exotic mixture of peoples which contributed to the European view of the Orient.[11] Occasionally a rabbi would be portrayed by a visiting painter, or a Jewish wedding or a procession to or from a synagogue, lovingly observed, but little was made of the separateness of the Jews in Middle Eastern societies, for there was simply little evidence of such separation.

Even Disraeli, who, when it suited him or when he felt especially romantic, dwelt proudly on his Jewish origins (to the exasperation of some of his Tory friends, who dearly wished he would not), as he travelled throughout the Levant and Egypt in all the overdressed and mannered glamour of his young manhood, paid little attention to the Jews there. He preferred, as witnessed by his literary *alter ego* Sidonia, to see himself as a scion of the 'rigidly separate and unmixed Bedouin race'.[12]

Disraeli's most developed expression of interest in the history of the Jews in Arab lands typically focusses itself on the romantic and mysterious figure of the 'Prince of the Captivity'. In his novel *Alroy*[13] Disraeli displays an engaging delight in recreating a medieval Muslim society, brilliantly assembled round the Caliph in Baghdad, and introducing a colourful tale around the leader of the Jewish inhabitants of the imperial city. The Jews of the empire were organised under their own government represented by the Nasi, the official to whom Disraeli awarded the mellifluous and evocative title of 'Prince of the Captivity'. In fact there is a historical basis for his story in that the Jewish community in Baghdad was numerous, rich and powerful; enterprise and talent, especially in the arts, jewellery, banking and the like, were thus harnessed to the service of the empire and the Jewish community was administered by its own elders, under the dispensation of the Caliph.

Naturally enough Disraeli hinted that he was descended from such a glamorous figure. Though his family was certainly Sephardic, there is not the slightest evidence to support the suggestion.

Zionism, like Disraeli, paid little or no attention to the Oriental Jews during the formative decades of its growth; its concern was exclusively with the European Jews. Many Jewish writers in the nineteenth century, when describing Middle Eastern scenes, made virtually no distinction between Jews and the Arabs among whom they lived, seeing them indeed as Jewish Arabs, just as the Christians of Syria and the Levant were recognised as Christian Arabs. Thus it was that Disraeli identifies the ancestors of the Jews from whom he believed he descended as the Bedouin of the Syrian and Egyptian deserts.

During the Nazi persecution of the Jews of Europe, the North African Jews were virtually untouched. Where Vichy France attempted to impose its anti-Jewish laws on French North Africa, these were generally ignored by local administrators. The Jews of Egypt, Iraq and Morocco in particular were prosperous and secure. In Morocco that country's distinguished monarch, Mohammad V, protected the Jews in his dominions.[14]

In many Middle Eastern countries Jews traditionally followed occupations which in times of crisis exposed them to the dislike of non-Jews. They were often the tax- or debt-collectors employed both by the state and by private landlords and capitalists to extort payments due to them; it was felt apparently that they were less likely than others to be swayed by familial or other sympathies. The appearance of the debt-collector in, for example, a Lower Egyptian village, would be an occasion for distress, even for protest and resistance. Jews were also the money-lenders, an occupation virtually reserved to them in Muslim countries as in Christian states in medieval Europe. Both believed that the Jews were forbidden to lend at interest; neither apparently realised that the prohibition did not apply to loans to non-Jews. But, in contrast, Jews were also respected in the professions, as learned men and pious teachers.

There never was, nor had there ever been, systematic and sustained persecution of the Jews in Muslim lands as there had so frequently been in Christian Europe. This is certainly true of those regions in which the beliefs of the Muslim majority, the Sunni, pertained. Broadly this meant all the Muslim states with the exception of Persian lands and those immediately adjoining Persia, which followed the Shia doctrine. In fact the lot of the Jews was generally less fortunate in Shia lands; there persecutions which almost approached the level of European intensity were, with less frequency though, unleashed against the Jews.

Until the overthrow of the Qajar Dynasty in 1926 the misfortunes of the Jews in Persia continued. With the coming of the more Western-oriented and internationalist Pahlavi regime, however, their position improved immeasurably. By the time of the late Shah's rule, Israel had become a surreptitious partner of Iran, buying oil and supplying military advice and what was to become one of Israel's principal exports, subversion and political intelligence.[15] It is one of the more cynical ironies of contemporary politics that even the regime of the Ayatollah, whilst it execrated Israel yet employed Israeli military experts – mercenaries, in a word – in its war with Iraq. Israel had quickly learnt the merit of the Arab saying 'the enemy of my enemy is my friend'.

If there was significant intolerance of the Jews in Middle Eastern states it was most actively demonstrated by the Christian-Arab communities of the Levant and Egypt and only became a matter of communal strife in the nineteenth century,

174

by which time European prejudices had begun to infect Muslim lands. The Muslims maintained a position of general if somewhat contemptuous toleration (perhaps indifference is a more accurate description) towards the Jewish communities in their midst. This attitude, however, changed, drastically and dramatically as a consequence of the emergence of the State of Israel in 1948. Suddenly an alien state was implanted in land which had, for as long as memories reached, been Arab. Worse still, the new state insisted that the first loyalty of any Jew, no matter where he lived, must be to itself. Israel is probably the only state in the history of the world that has made disloyalty to a man's native land a virtue; the point was not lost on the Arabs at the time of its foundation.

When the long campaign to achieve the creation of an exclusively Jewish state reached its climax in the events of 1947 and 1948 in the General Assembly of the United Nations, the Arab states, few in number as they then were, found themselves divided; many of them were still dominated by the colonial powers, though this influence was waning. It is important to understand that Israel, whilst it had achieved its existence as a result of mercilessly harrying a colonial power, was itself a colonial implant, as much as were the settlers in Rhodesia or the French colonies in Vietnam or Algeria.

In 1948 many Arab states were still dependent on European political and material support; as a consequence many regimes were kept in being for considerably longer than would otherwise have been their natural life-span. Only one Arab leader of international status opposed the creation of the Jewish state, vigorously and persistently; he was indeed perhaps the greatest of his generation though long past his prime, King Abdul Aziz bin Abdul Rahman al-Saud, of Saudi Arabia.[16] He had always rejected the concept of an exclusively Jewish entity on Arab soil and he warned anyone who would listen to him (and many who would not) against the policy of permitting European Jews to migrate to Palestine. But his was a lone voice and at the time Saudi Arabia did not exercise the political and financial influence which later was to be at her disposal.

In the aftermath of Israel's creation, when the men who had led the Stern Gang and the Irgun could begin their careers as servants of the new state, it was timely for them, and for the others who had brought about what was perhaps the most unlikely political coup of the century, to look about them and to take stock. One thing was starkly clear; Israel needed every mite and shekel of support and subvention from wherever they might be gleaned, for the state to survive. International Jewry, or, as described in the fanciful language employed by Zionist propagandists, 'the Jews of the Diaspora', was the first target. No Jew, those living abroad were informed, was truly a Jew if he did not migrate to Israel; but this harsh judgement might be mitigated by the transfer of as much of his substance as possible to the benefit of the state. A Jew's loyalty, those living abroad were further advised, should not be primarily to the country of his citizenship, not even to the country of his birth, but to Israel. Thus was the singular doctrine of disloyalty enshrined as part of the new state's programme for those of its constituents, as they were seen to be, who lived beyong its frontiers.

At this point the architects of Israel's polity, in a stroke of remarkable perception, determined that Israel needed a clear, implacable but preferably not too dangerous enemy, whose hostility could be demonstrated as demanding American and European support for what quickly came to be tagged 'gallant litle Israel'. The Arabs were at hand, leaderless and bemused by a world which they little understood; here was the enemy.

The Egyptian revolution of 1952 was a godsend to Israel. Gamal Abdul Nasser came to power in Cairo, young, charismatic and politically naif.[17] It was not difficult to bring about the situation in which Nasser came to symbolise the Arabs' rejection of Israel and the frustration they experienced at the world's indifference. In reality, Nasser's leadership of the Arabs amounted to very little, except for the waste of the lives of young Egyptian soldiers in a succession of engagements in which the Israelis seemed destined always to be victorious. But now the Arab world, one hundred million strong, could be represented to American opinion in particular and in the media of the world in general, as ranged against the tiny Israeli state: the little Israeli David striking out against the monstrous Arab Goliath, in the weary cliche of Middle Eastern polemic.

Nevertheless, one potentially awkward anomaly remained after the creation of Israel which, if it were allowed to persist, could make nonsense of much of the argument which Israel promoted about the perils which it faced from its brutal Arab enemy. This was the continued, placid existence of substantial

Jewish communities in a number of Arab states.[18] Many of these communities in Cairo, Alexandria and Baghdad were extremely prosperous, their members highly sophisticated and playing a full, valuable and valued part in many aspects of life in the countries in which they were citizens and of which, in most cases, their ancestors had long been citizens too. It was clearly essential that the members of these communities be persuaded, by whatever means, of the necessity to migrate to Israel; if they could not be persuaded then the case for Israel as the sanctuary for all the world's Jews would be invalidated and the entire nature and purpose of the State of Israel would be called into question. Thus, in the process, such migrations would demonstrate that they were necessary as a result of the habitual persecution to which the Jews of the Arab world were subjected by their Arab overlords, so that they would be seen to be experiencing a persecution at least comparable with that so recently undergone by the Jews of central and eastern Europe.

The story of this aspect of Israel's policy has not yet received the attention which it deserves, though it is now well documented.[19] A study of the records will show how Israel's agents infiltrated peaceful Jewish communities in several Arab capitals,[20] fomenting discord and, in the process, producing 'martyrs'. These often misguided and sadly misled individuals, having been persuaded to criminal or terrorist actions against the countries in which, up to that time, they had been living peacefully, were then the subject of prosecution which frequently led to their execution. Israeli media did not stint in its outpouring of vilification of the Arab states (in fairness matching only too convincingly the equivalent vilification of Israel by the Arabs) and drawing attention to what they chose to represent as the plight of Jewish communities in Arab cities.

As a result of this peculiarly heartless campaign, the Arabs came for the first time to regard the Jews living in their midst as somehow alien, instead of merely different, and as the source of possible subversion. It has already been pointed out that Zionist propaganda has always had one of its most receptive audiences amongst the Arabs themselves. Gradually, and often against their individual inclinations, Jews from the Arab world were persuaded to leave their homelands and set out for a Palestine of which they had only the dimmest apprehension, urged on by other Jews with whom they had only the most fragile sense of community.

When eventually they did arrive in Israel, wealthy merchants from Baghdad, doctors and teachers from Cairo and Alexandria, farmers and small shopkeepers from Algeria and Morocco, barely literate peasants from the Yemen and a host of small people from all these places, the reality of Israel did not prove kindly. The Orientals were immediately relegated to a secondary status; contemptuous and abusive terms were used to describe them and their supposed way of life by the European settlers who resented them and their supposed 'Arab' character. Even to this day, Oriental communities are described by their Ashkenazi fellow citizens as 'black'; the term is not intended to flatter.[21]

Much of the abuse levelled against them would have been at home in Germany in the 1930s when its targets would have been those very European Jews who now vaunted their superiority above the despised Orientals. These were to discover, like the Arabs, that Israel's much publicised democracy did not apparently extend fully to Jews of Oriental origin, just as it had already disenfranchised the aboriginal Arab inhabitants of Palestine. This distaste of the western Jews for the Orientals was not a new phenomenon; even in Ottoman times European Jews living in the empire had demanded the separation of their living quarters, food and worship from their Oriental co-religionists. The Oriental Jews in Israel quickly found themselves relegated to the status of the country's proletariat. The Ashkenazi, accustomed to seeing themselves as the 'true Israeli settlers', pressed the Orientals down to a level not far above that of the indigenous Arabs. They tended to find it more difficult to obtain higher educational qualifications, to move into the management levels of industry, or to obtain officer rank in the forces.[22]

The separation of the Orientals and the Ashkenazi has been perpetuated by the distribution of the communities in which they live. There is a fairly rigid separation between them which, if it can be justified by the familiar excuse of like wishing to live with like, has opened up a permanent fissure in Israeli society which it is probably now impossible to bridge. It is revealing that in Israeli parlance 'ethnic', when applied to social groupings, music, theatre and the like, means 'Oriental'; 'Israeli', on the other hand, means Ashkenazi when similarly employed.

The Ashkenazim, even those of good will towards their Oriental neighbours, have found themselves adopting unmistakably patronising attitudes (which might even be interpreted as racist by those who were not uncritically supportive of Israel) towards those of Oriental origin. It is assumed that Ashkenazi European-style culture and mores are the norm for Israeli society, that all Israelis who are not of Ashkenazi stock will aspire to the trappings of the European lifestyle. The class and racist attitudes implied in this position do not require further statement, yet Israeli protagonists will insist that Israel is neither a class nor a racist society.

The Jews of European origin, joined now by zealots from America (often the most aggressive and self-assertive of all the immigrants, particularly those who settled in the Occupied Territories after the war of 1967) and from the British Commonwealth, tended to exclude the Orientals from their society, preferring to see them occupying what were little more than disadvantaged ghettoes in the larger Israeli society. Ironically and sadly such ghettoes were of the sort which the Ashkenazim had so vehemently, and with justice, rejected for themselves in Europe. But the Orientals had a secret weapon which was to change the character of Israel very swiftly; a power which lay in the loins of the men and in the wombs of the women.

It is clear that Jews of non-European origin will be in the majority in Israel by the year 2000. This proportion will increase to the point that by the year 2015 the percentage of Jews of European or American origin is likely to be not more than 30 per cent of the population: that percentage becomes 22 per cent if the Occupied Territories are taken into account. At present the Israeli Arabs represent 40 per cent of population growth. In thirty years the Jewish percentage of the combined population of Israel and the Occupied Territories will amount to only 52 per cent, barely half the total of all the inhabitants of 'the Jewish state'.[22]

To this imbalance must be added the effect of negative migration which Israel has been experiencing since the early 1980s, whereby the state has actually lost migrants, many of those from Russia, for example, preferring to settle in America or in the West; in addition long-settled Israeli have also left, further diminishing the state's reserve of western Jews, who were its *raison d'être* and who gave it is particular 'Israeli' character. Eighty per cent of the Jews leaving Russia, about whose right to emigrate such strident protests have been raised by activists, are said to wish to travel on to the West. So dramatic has been the rejection of Israel by the Jews of Russia that America has been persuaded to limit entry by Russian Jews to the United States and strenuous efforts have been made to airlift Jews directly from Russia to Israel. Those who travel through European routes show a disturbing tendency either to stay in Europe, or, when they were still able to do so, make for an American haven.

Thus the proportion of those Jews for whom Israel was conceived to be the refuge against European persecution, has rapidly declined to the point where they will soon be in a clear minority to their despised co-religionists, the Orientals, who never sought to go there in the first place. By its own internal dynamics Israel has become a totally different entity from that conceived by the Zionists who created it. The situation affecting Israel's demographic balance is compounded by the decline in the population of world Jewry. This is especially so in Ashkenazi communities, the consequence of a low birth rate and assimilation.

As Oriental Jews move towards becoming the dominant political force in Israel, they may be expected to adopt more extreme policies, and no doubt they will be disinclined to be subject either to courteous persuasion or the measured arguments of statesmen. The anger of the Oriental Jews will be compounded by a falling off in the subventions from international Jewry which, since they are largely Ashkenazi in origin, will view with dismay the sort of society which they will see Israel becoming. Gradually – or perhaps not so gradually – the already evident trend of net emigration *from* Israel will accelerate, amongst those Jews with Western European or American connections.

Israel has made much of the necessity for Russian Jews to be facilitated to leave the Soviet Union and settle in Israel. The embarrassing need for the United States to put a stop on Jewish immigration from Russia had suggested something of a want of absolute enthusiasm on the part of the Russians to seek a life in Israel; most of them patently would wish to live in Europe or the United States. Now, however, many thousands of Jews are said to be leaving, or have already left, Russia.

Not surprisingly, the Arab states have voiced considerable concern at this development, seeing it both as a lack of support by the one-time ally and a further occasion for the settlement of European Jews on Palestinian land. But Israel itself must recognise that the migration of large numbers of Jews, mainly drawn from professional backgrounds, presents it with a serious, potentially dangerous implant. Most of the new Russian migrants are not Zionists; few of them indeed seem to be ideologically committed to Israel in any way. They will clearly find it difficult to find the sort of life in Israel to which their professional status and qualifications entitled them in Russia; accusations of rabid anti-Jewish provocation on the part of an emerging political opposition in Russia, which cannot perhaps be wholly disregarded, is clearly not of the scale which is currently being represented. The 'new' Israelis therefore are likely to find themselves setting out for life in a land for which they have little preparation. Israel may well find that by attempting to absorb these migrants, the upshot will be the creation of a dissident Jewish minority, to match the dissident Arab minority which already exists in the society. While the Russians are hardly likely to launch their own *intifada*, their absorption may well contribute to Israel's ultimate undoing.

Despite whatever may be the problems caused by the introduction of the Russian emigrants into the Israeli body politic, the Arab population of Israel will continue to grow as will the population of Oriental Jews. And in this may be glimpsed the one glimmer of hope in an otherwise dismal prospect.

It will probably never be possible for Jews of European origin to adapt themselves sufficiently to accept a secular, non-Zionist state in place of the Jewish state. It is possible, however, that two oriental peoples, or, more accurately, the two parts of the same oriental people who merely follow different religious loyalties, could find an accommodation together; after all they always did before the Europeans, in whatever form, meddled with them. The Palestinians, Muslims and Christians alike, must acknowledge that the Oriental Jews are what they have always been, Jewish Arabs: those who come from Arab lands are as much entitled to be called Arab as, in the same cultural sense, a Lebanese Christian is Arab or a Moroccan Berber or a Copt from Upper Egypt. The Orientals must in turn recognise that they and the Arabs are one people, their mutual relationship quite different in quality and much closer than their relationship can ever be with the Europeans who are living in their midst.

This consideration becomes ever more acute when some form of dialogue between the Palestinians and the Israelis is in prospect. It is a fair assumption that any policies considered or adopted by the government of Israel will primarily favour the Ashkenazi component of Israel society; it is from the Ashkenazim that the Labour Party has always drawn its most committed support and whose interest it has always set first. The Orientals will not find themselves receiving anything much more than cursory consideration in whatever new alignment may emerge from the latest situation. The election of the Labour Party to power in Israel was unfavourable to the Sephardim and nothing in the course of the Labour government's actions in the intervening period has given them any cause for optimism.

By the most subtle of ironies it is possible that the dialogue between Israel and the PLO may eventually – sooner perhaps rather than later – result in a coming together of the Palestinians and the Orientals and the recognition of the general identity of their interests. This is probably not at all what either the Americans or the Israeli governments had in mind when this process began: it may be all the better and eventually more enduring for that fact.

10

THE FUTURE OF PALESTINE

The Arabs have watched the wheel of fortune turning for millennia, for they are an ancient and patient people. They know that circumstances will one day return Palestine to them – unless a disaster of unthinkable proportions supervenes.

The world community, which gave rise to this problem, must unite to resolve it. It cannot be expected that Israel, of her own volition, will accept the de-Zionisation of the state, yet this must be the first, essential condition of any solution which stands a chance of permanence. Without such a solution, chaos and old night descend.

If this proposition is stated with some emphasis it is because the de-Zionisation of Israel is so profoundly important a precondition of a lasting solution. To create an *exclusively Jewish* state can never have been the intention of those who supported the concept of a national home for the Jews in Palestine. This was, in the light of history, an unwise and an unfair idea in the first place, but it does not contain so total an injustice as that which has deprived the Palestinians of their ancestral homeland.

In the world today it is unacceptable for a state's reason for existence to be postulated on the identity of a particular religious sect and to give members of that sect absolute rights of habitation and citizenship at the expense of the indigenes. There is simply no precedent anywhere in the world for such a construct and the Jews, as a community, cannot be so utterly different from all other communities and sects that they should deserve such a special dispensation, setting at nothing in the process the rights of others.

The objection will be made that Muslim states, for example, proclaim themselves to be sectarian in the sense that they are

183

identified as Islamic or as adhering to the precepts of Islam in their social and legal principles. But such states are all of a substantial and continuous historical lineage, their people are indigenous and they have formed the overwhelming majority of the population for centuries past, living under the various forms of Muslim or Islamic rulership. The fact of the European origin and character of the politics and people of the State of Israel makes the situation in that country entirely different.

Western politicians who become involved in any settlement which may eventually seem in prospect to undo the catastrophic consequences of their past interventions will undoubtedly urge caution, compromise and the acceptance of the realities of politics. This will, initially at least, take the form of urging respect for Israel's right to exist as a sovereign state which, once conceded, will pre-empt any question of its de-Zionisation. Yet this necessary condition, though it will be castigated as a counsel of extremism, unrealistic and untenable, must be insisted upon if ever peace is to come to a region which has suffered much for the interference of those who have ignored the imperatives of history. Unless Israel is secularised it will always represent a focus for extremism, for a myth-based chauvinism and an intolerable provocation to the majority of the peoples who surround it. It will serve as the focus too for the trouble-making of any populist demagogue, in Israel, in the Middle East, or in some yet-to-emerge power bloc.

It will be said that to attempt to impose such a condition from the outset will vitiate any chance of producing in Israel a frame of mind capable of actually achieving a settlement. It will be said that, in the first place, the 'two-state' solution – a Palestinian state existing side by side with the Jewish state – must be allowed to emerge; only at some distant point in the future might the secularisation of Israel be contemplated. The proponants of this procedure will argue that to insist on Israel's secularisation will damage the prospects for the establishment of any sort of Palestinian entity, even if it predictably falls short of the ideal.

There are great dangers in this attitude. In the first place it is wrong to equate, as so many commentators do, including those who drafted the original partition plan for Palestine, the terms 'Jewish' and 'Palestinian' (or Arab) when speaking of the two states which it is hoped would emerge from a settlement. Then, the proposal ignores the inherent risk in fixing a situation where two states, which are not in any way integrated, are allowed to become permanently polarised, one representing the 'Arab', the other the 'Jewish' ethos. It has been argued already that the two terms are not in any way comparable and that political decisions which depend on their acceptance as being of equal weight will fall to the ground.

Further, the creation of an economically weak and militarily unviable Palestinian state would represent a permanent temptation to an Israel which would retain its armoury and, even if on a reduced scale, would be able to insist upon continued United States and other international support. In the nature of affairs, it would be in a powerful position to dominate when compared with its Palestinian neighbour. Such a situation would only set in stone the antagonisms which the past four decades have brought to the Middle East, confirming the sense of deprivation and dispossession of the Arabs and the supremacist attitudes of much of the Israeli governing establishment.

Having observed this, it must also be said that one of the most disastrous influences in the politics of the region in the past forty years – especially in the past twenty years – has been the unbridled marketing of increasingly sophisticated arms and weapons systems to all its states. In this process, the Americans, the Russians, the British, French, Germans and even Third World countries which have not hesitated to climb on a particularly murderous band-wagon, have all profited greatly for the instability which the very presence of Israel in the region has provoked. In any settlement which has a chance of survival, an eventual agreement on staged demilitarisation must be an essential precondition with proper, agreed procedures for inspection and control. If Europe can foresee the prospect of demilitarisation after half a century of the intense mutual antagonism of world powers it should not be impossible to achieve similar results in the Middle East.

However, it will be crucial that Palestine shall not feel itself to be placed at a hopeless disadvantage from the outset by being forced to forsake a military capability as a precondition. It must start from a basis of parity with Israel even if both agree eventually to relinquish their capacity to wage war.

If the preceding pages of this study have meant anything at all it must be clear that if a concept of justice exists in the management and inter-relationships of human societies, then justice requires that the Palestinians be restored to their land and permitted to establish a state which can take its place in the world community. In the aftermath of the Gulf crisis, assuming that the region experiences no further catastrophies, there will be a demand throughout the Arab world on a scale which cannot be resisted for a righting of the injustice done to the Palestinians.

If such an outcome is baulked or qualified, to the extent proposed even by some of the protagonists of a solution which is intended to aid the Palestinian objective of an independent political existence, then no lasting solution will be forthcoming. Indeed the situation will become more and more fragile; it is better to face the realities now than to hope that a partial settlement (which is no settlement at all) will somehow bring peace and fulfilment to the true indigenes of Palestine as well as to the European settlers and others whom they must accommodate.

Such political ingenuity as the world possesses must now be directed towards finding the means by which Israel can with honour be induced to renounce the Zionist character of the state and the Arabs to accept the permanent presence of a large foreign Jewish population in their midst; this latter proposition would almost certainly be easier to resolve than the former, for the Arabs have never regarded the Jews as enemies, not, at least, before the creation of the State of Israel.

Ultimately the prospects for peace in the Middle East depend not upon the intervention of the Great Powers or of supranational bodies, but upon the development of an understanding between these two groups which at present may well seem hopelessly at odds with each other. But there may be some hope, in that the Oriental Jews have much in common with the Palestinians. Both were repressed and despised by their Turkish masters; in the days of the Ottomans both were required to undertake tasks which they found distasteful. The Oriental Jews, like the Palestinians, have equally little cause to love the Ashkenazim, individuals amongst whom have generally despised and frequently exploited them. The marked Ashkenazi character of Israel has forced the Orientals into the position of an underclass. They now form the proletariat of the Jewish state.

But both peoples are the victims of Zionism, the Jews hardly less than the Palestinians. The Oriental Jews were uprooted from their homes in North Africa and Iraq as a consequence of deliberate policy on the part of Israel and seldom by their own volition. Without the provocation of Zionist activists it is doubtful if many of the North African communities in particular would have left; the ineptitude of Arab politics allowed the Zionists to take the initiative and, by responding to the Zionist persecution of Arabs in Palestine by the persecution in turn of Oriental communities in the Arab states, contributed immeasurably to the creation of the need for those communities to seek the protection of the Zionist state.

If a solution to the problem of Palestine-Israel is to be found, it must be one which is first and foremost acceptable to the dispossessed population of the land, the Palestinians. Unless that condition is fulfilled, no solution has any chance of enduring. This proposition is advanced not from any sentimental concern for the Palestinians bereft of their patrimony, but simply in the firm belief that only by addressing their grievances and relieving them will the longer-term menace of a concerted military effort to destroy Israel be deflected. This is why it was earlier said that only the Palestinian people can confer the right of citizenship to anyone who would live in their land.

Once the justice of any part of the Palestinians' case is admitted, the arguments which have sustained the existence of a specifically Jewish, settler, secular, sovereign *state* in any part of Palestine falls away. The arguments based either on policy or morality for the perpetuation of the Jewish state, in any formal, sovereign form, become insupportable. Indeed one of the principal barriers to a solution in the past is this fact that once *any* part of the justice of the Palestinian case is admitted, then every part of the Zionist claim to a Jewish state in Palestine begins to disintegrate. This dilemma is clearly apprehended by the increasingly vociferous right wing in Israel itself, which now asserts the right of possession as the principal warrant for their continued presence in Palestine. They are matched by those settlers who assert a god-given right to occupy the land of Palestine.

Compromise does not come easily, it would seem, to people who involve themselves in the affairs of Palestine. Over half a century ago Jabotinsky remarked, 'We are not free agents: we cannot concede anything.' The same terms can, without doubt, be applied to the positions of the Palestinians today. Their problem, if it may be expressed in that term, is another Jabotinsky statement: 'Our demand for Jewish majority is not our maximum – it is our minimum.' It is such forthright and cogently expressed ideas of dealing with the Palestinian Arabs which inform much of the policy of the Israeli government in the phase of politics which has flowed from the election of Likud in 1979 and which was emphasised by the governments of Menachem Begin and Yitzhak Shamir.

Any prospective solution following the admittedly uncompromising position set out in these pages must also take into account the Occupied Lands on the West Bank of the Jordan river, the Hashemite Kingdom of Jordan itself, the dispersed Palestinians living in the Arab world and outside it, and those living in the refugee camps. Further, the proper concerns of Syria must be recognised, as must the restoration of some sort of stability to Lebanon, though it may prove necessary to redraw extensively the latter's frontiers. All these parties have a right to a place in the negotiations, no matter how these may be conducted or under whoever's auspices.

The process must begin with a plan for the government of a state which must replace Israel in the form in which it has developed whilst providing for the continued settlement of a substantial number of Jews. It must allow for the re-introduction of dispersed Palestinians and for the proper status for Arabs living within the boundaries of what presently constitutes the Israeli state. The simplest formula from which to proceed must envisage the creation of a federal, cantonal structure which will embrace Palestine, as defined by the federal partition plan of 1947, Israel as defined by the same process, and those parts of the Hashemite Kingdom of Jordan which would remain. Each part of the federation would have equal rights; all communities living within the federation's frontiers, of whatever religious affiliation, would be of equal status. The nature of the state would be defined constitutionally as secular and hence not denominationally Muslim, Christian or Jewish.

It may be worth recalling here the provisions of a minority plan which three countries, India, Iran and Yugoslavia, put before the United Nations at the time when plans to partition Palestine were first being discussed.

The three members proposed that an independent federal state of Palestine would be created following a transitional period not exceeding three years, during which responsibility for administering Palestine and preparing it for independence would be entrusted to an authority to be decided by the General Assembly. This time-scale would no doubt need to be reviewed.

The independent federal state would comprise an Arab State and Jewish State. Jerusalem would be its capital. This proposal would require qualification. 'State' has too definite a connotation in today's politics and it may be that a word such as 'canton' would be preferred, demonstrating membership of a larger sovereign state body.

During the transitional period a Constituent Assembly would be elected by popular vote and convened by the administering authority on the basis of electoral provision which would ensure the fullest representation of the population.

The Constituent Assembly would draw up the constitution of the federal state, which was to contain, *inter alia*, the following provisions:

> The federal state would comprise a federal government and governments of the Arab and Jewish states, respectively.
>
> Full authority would be vested in the federal government with regard to national defence, foreign relations, immigration, currency, taxation for federal purposes, foreign and inter-state waterways, transport and communications, copyrights and patents.
>
> The Arab and Jewish states would enjoy full powers of local self-government and would have authority over education, taxation for local purposes, the right of residence, commercial licenses, land permits, grazing rights, inter-state migration, settlement, police, punishment of crime, social institutions and services, public housing, public health, local roads, agriculture and local industries.
>
> The organs of government would include a head of state, an executive body, a representative federal legislative body composed of two chambers, and a federal court. The executive would be responsible to the legislative body.
>
> Election to one chamber of the federal legislative body would be on the basis of proportional representation of

189

the population as a whole, and to the other on the basis of equal representation of the Arab and Jewish citizens of Palestine. Legislation would be enacted when approved by majority votes in both chambers; in the event of disagreement between the two chambers, the issue would be submitted to an arbitral body of five members including not less than two Arabs and two Jews.

The federal court would be the final court of appeal regarding constitutional matters. Its members, who would include not less than four Arabs and three Jews, would be elected by both chambers of the federal legislative body.

The constitution was to guarantee equal rights for all minorities and fundamental human rights and freedoms. It would guarantee, *inter alia*, free access to the Holy Places and protect religious interest.

The constitution would provide for an undertaking to settle international disputes by peaceful means.

There would be a single Palestinian nationality and citizenship.

The constitution would provide for equitable participation of representatives of both communities in delegations to international conferences.

A permanent international body would be set up for the supervision and protection of the Holy Places, to be composed of three representatives designated by the United Nations and one representative of each of the recognised faiths having an interest in the matter, as might be determined by the United Nations.

The original plan proposed that for a period of three years from the beginning of the transitional period Jewish immigration would be permitted into the Jewish State in such numbers as not to exceed its absorptive capacity, and having due regard for the rights of the national rate of increase. An international commission composed of three Arab, three Jewish and three United Nations representatives would be appointed to estimate the absorptive capacity of the Jewish State. The commission would cease to exist at the end of the three-year period mentioned above. This proposal clearly would no longer pertain.

The minority plan also laid down the boundaries of the proposed Arab and Jewish areas of the federal state.

The world has moved on since 1947 when this plan was proposed, but in principle the federal solution is still the most likely to succeed in providing a lasting and secure political environment for all the peoples involved. The 1947 plan, however, would require considerable detailed amendment to take account of the changed and deteriorated situation which is the consequence of forty years of confrontation. Its most important provision, however, would need to be the recognition of the status of the Palestinian Arabs, Muslims and Christians, and their right to determine the qualifications of citizenship of those who would live in their land.

All dispossessed Palestinians who had left the land since 1947 (or their descendants) who could prove their Palestinian origins would be entitled to return and to full citizenship. Schemes of compensation would need to be set up which would reimburse those whose land or property had been seized or expropriated by the Israels, or whose homes had been destroyed by the authorities in the course of collective or similar punishments, as well as those whose property had been acquired illegally or by extortion. A form of tribunal, administered according to acceptable international practice, would be established to put these requirements into effect.

The Jewish settlements on the West Bank and Gaza would be dismantled and the settlers returned to the department of the federation in which the majority was Jewish by religious affiliation. Those settlers who wished to return to their countries of origin would be assisted to do so.

A Common Market would be established between the cantons of the Palestinian state and with those of its neighbours who wished to associate with it. For a long time the new state would be economically unviable: it would require immense subventions from abroad, from the United States, the oil-producing world, the European Community. Such subventions, however, are likely to be less burdensome than those which America has had to bear for the past forty years or which the Arab states have had to provide for the various factions which have claimed at one time or another to represent Palestine.

The adoption of a federal constitution would assist the resolution of one particular area of potential conflict: the new state's military status. Israel has opposed vehemently the creation of the Palestinian state on the ground, amongst others, that it would represent a permanent threat to Israel and that a sovereign identity, with its inevitable right to the maintenance of armed forces, is not to be countenanced. However, it has already been suggested that such a limitation of sovereignty would be provocative in the extreme, if an independent or autonomous identity were to be their objective. If, on the other hand, a federal structure is adopted, a federal military force, officered from all communities and concerned equally with the defence of the federation, becomes a wholly feasible and acceptable concept.

A necessary corollary of the conclusion that Israel be de-Zionised must be the elimination of Israel's exclusive access to nuclear weapons. In the medium to longer term no graver threat to the stability of the Middle East exists than the imbalance in military capability as between Israel and the Arab states. In whatever outcome may be anticipated (or even hoped for) it is essential that either Israel is required to relinquish her nuclear capability as part of a general process of demilitarisation or, alternatively, that the Arabs are enabled themselves to acquire nuclear weapons, to neutralise Israel's. Israel has always insisted on maintaining the edge over the Arabs in this regard and had hitherto persuaded successive American administrations to support her in this position.

Unless Israel gives up its exclusive access to nuclear weaponry, peace will be impossible. As Israel's position becomes increasingly eroded, politically and economically, the temptation to more adventure in the region will tend to be too great for it to resist. An Israel faced with bankruptcy and the loss of international support on the sort of scale which is clearly now in prospect will be more dangerous for the players than is the case already in a game where the stakes are far too high for safety.

But it is not only in the material sphere that great sacrifices must be demanded from Israel if peace is ever to have a chance of persisting in the region which its presence has so gravely destabilised during the decades of its existence. The influence of revealed religion is profoundly important in the area, whether it is viewed from the standpoint of a believer in any of the three faiths which trace their origins to this small segment of the world's surface; so much will be clear – if it was ever in doubt – from a reading of this essay this far. All three faiths have deeply entrenched positions erected around cities in the Levant, running down into Western Arabia. It is interesting, by the way, that the city, a very recent development in the systems which our species has adopted in which to live, is of such profound importance to Judaism, Christianity and Islam. Of the cities in the region of which we speak the most intractable problem is likely to attend the decision of the status of Jerusalem.

To the Israelis Jerusalem has always represented the ultimate prize; to the Arabs its loss after the War of 1967 was the ultimate disaster. Jerusalem is unique in that it is the one common denominator (other than the object of their faith) of the three monothestic religions. It is the focus of the most complex bargaining by all three; the city is clearly too important, at this stage of history at least, for it to be the exclusive enclave of any of them. Its future must be determined by all those to whom it is important, Jews, Christians and Muslims. Almost certainly such a knot into which it has become tangled can only be untied by declaring Jerusalem an international city and entrusting its government to some form of international commission. The future of Jerusalem is likely to be the most powerful component in the Israeli position – if it ever comes to this – though it is in fact of relatively little importance to them strategically or politically. Such a status for Jerusalem has always been envisaged in settlements advanced by any but the most intransigent protagonists of one side or the other. However, it must not be forgotten that Count Bernadotte, the United Nations mediator, was murdered by the Stern Gang, under Yitzhak Shamir's leadership, for urging the internationalisation of Jerusalem.

In the cantonal structure envisaged for Palestine Jerusalem would, at first sight, appear to offer a natural capital for the federation. Its international status, however, would require it to assume an additional series of functions and relationships.

One function that a de-politicised Jerusalem might with considerable appositeness discharge would be to provide the location for a permanent United Nations presence in the region. All the area's religions advance the concept of peace as high in their sacred agenda; though the United Nations is hardly pristine and while its role in the unfolding of the tragedy of Palestine has not been a happy one, yet the status of Jerusalem might provide it with an opportunity to fulfil some of its ideals and to offset some of the harm which it did, wittingly or not, so long ago.

A permanent political and administrative UN presence in Jerusalem would provide not only some guarantee for the observance of any agreement which might eventually be negotiated. It would also enable the UN to disengage itself tactfully from so definite an identification with the United States, as is the case at present. In a changing world this would surely be to the advantage of all nations.

It may be that Jerusalem's peculiar status, as the focus of so much emotional concern directed at it by the adherents of the three monotheistic faiths, would be better suited if it were not to be the capital of the new state, but that its international, inter-denominational character should be signalised by giving it an altogether distinct status. If it were to be the political capital of a state which necessarily will have many occasions, at least in the early days of its existence, for dissension and political conflict, then inevitably, its more numinous quality may be diminished. As a truly 'open city', the seat of some part of the UN and its agencies, and as a universal place of pilgrimage it could play a more useful role for humankind than would ever be the case if it were simply to fulfil a political or more narrowly national purpose.

The new state, would, of course, need to have a capital on which all its various constituents might agree. It would be difficult to find a suitable candidate if Jewish were to be set aside, but not impossible. Thus, if it were to be considered that an outward-looking symbol was appropriate then Ashkalon on the coast might serve, having the merit too (if merit it be) of striking a chord in European minds as well as in those who are native to any part of the new state. Alternatively, if it were thought that it would be better to avoid any links with even the medieval past, then a site such as Jerash, principally notable as a Roman settlement, might serve, though its Roman connections might not strike an altogether happy chord of memory in Jewish minds. A third possibility might be Jericho, of great symbolic importance to both the Arabs and Jews and, as one of the oldest 'cities' known to archaeology, an eminently suitable location for a new beginning.

Two other issues of significance to the peoples of the Levant and to the eventual peaceful settlement of the region must be addressed in the same terms and time-scale as the Israeli-Palestinian confrontation: these are the occupation by Israel of territory in the Golan Heights and the tragic collapse of Lebanon into anarchy, a condition made immeasurably more difficult of solution by the invasion by Israel in 1982. The continued presence of Israeli and Syrian forces in that country must also be addressed and resolved.

There is probably little to be done to restore Lebanon even to the admittedly very fragile status that it enjoyed before 1976. Then all was for the best in the best of all possible Lebanese worlds as far as the Christians were concerned and for some of the more fortunate or better educated Sunni Muslims. For the substantial Shia community in the south, however, life was largely a miserable grind of poverty and disadvantage. That situation would now seem to have changed for ever and any settlement in the future must take account of that fact.

It is just possible that some form of federal structure might be possible for Lebanon, though the idea is bitterly rejected by most parties at present. Historically, however, the various communities which made up what was to become the Republic of Lebanon in 1943 always dominated particular regions of the country: the Christians on the mountains, the Shia in the south, the Sunni the northern coastal region. Syria's very reasonable concern for recognition of *its* historical position must also be acknowledged; no settlement in this part of the Levant is possible without Syria's commitment to it. After all Syria stands in a somewhat more secure case in relation to much of the Levant as the successor of the Ottomans in the region (Damascus was the seat of the governorate, it will be remembered) than did ever Iraq, which did not even exist when Basra was the location for an enfeebled provincial administrative claiming control over a part of the Gulf which it could not sustain.

So far as Syria itself is concerned it is clear that Israel must withdraw from the Golan Heights, without conditions. It will be said that the Jewish settlements which lie within sight of the Golan will forever be menaced by a militant Syria; cynically, it might be said in return that since such settlements have no right to be where they are, their security, or want of it, is largely an academic issue. However, the world community is unlikely to reject such settlements out of hand and so account must be taken of them. Again, a powerful United Nations political and military presence in the region, with its headquarters in Jerusalem, would do much to ensure the compliance of all the parties to peaceful co-existence in the area.

The Kingdom of Jordan would seem, on the present evidence available, the most likely sufferer from the latest developments in the region. Jordan has had, like the Palestinians, to pay dearly for its ill-judged support of Iraq during the invasion of Kuwait: given the large number of Palestinians in Jordan who followed their leadership's espousal of the Iraqi position, Jordan's response was at least, in political terms, understandable. The country, one of the least advantaged in the area, has had to absorb some 300,000 Palestinian refugees since the ending of the Kuwaiti crisis. Its political complexion is, in consequence, radically changed.

Although Jordan will no doubt be able to restore some of its past credit of goodwill its most secure future must surely be as one of the partners in a federal Palestinian state. Jordan could add immeasurably to the state's viability, especially in its arms. What will be perceived as national interest, however, is likely to argue strongly, at least for a time, against any such development.

The invasion of Kuwait by Iraq did much to focus the world community's mind on these issues. Saddam Hussein tried to identify the settlement of the dispute of the Arabs with Israel with the settlement of his claim to Kuwait. The two issues are, of course, distinct and have no similarity of circumstance. However Saddam is right in pointing to the injustice of a world community which unites in defence of one of its own close friends and stands aside, despite the repeated condemnation of Israel's actions by the United Nations, when Israel's ruthless despoliation of Palestine is called into question.

Although the two issues must not be allowed to run into each other, like colours on an incompetent painter's palette, yet the world community will do well to attempt to face them in the same time-scale. Unless Israel is required to adopt a new status and a new policy in the world, there is no hope for peace in the Middle East, nor, for that matter, in the world at large.

It will not be overlooked that to tackle these two issues in the same chronological period will produce demand for other legacies of the late colonial period to be faced. The frontiers of the states created in the 1920s – Lebanon, Syria, Jordan, Iraq – will all require restructuring. It will be difficult to resist the argument that the Kurds, unhappily divided between Turkey, Iraq, Iran and Russia do not have the right to their own national identity. With the break-up of the Soviet Union – to be replaced eventually by who knows what alternative – it is illogical to refuse autonomy or at least cantonal status to the minorities which exist in Iran, Afghanistan and Iraq itself.

The implications for this process are of course immense. If it is agreed to allow small nations to assume their own identity in the aftermath of the break-up of the Soviet Empire then the same must apply to nations in Europe which have been demanding their separation from the countries with which they are at present often unwillingly united. It is not a prospect which will be welcomed by the majority of politicians.

Yet unless such peoples, of whom the Palestinians are the most clear and evident example, are given the opportunity to control their own destiny there can be no hope for political stability in any of the parts of the world where minorities feel themselves to be oppressed. The world, despite the evidence of what is happening in Europe, is moving away from massive political groupings; everywhere there is a sense of the need for individual freedom and expression which cannot find its life in some huge centralised political administration.

Difficult though it will be to accept, it is none the less essential in the plan envisaged here for the future peace of the Middle East that Israel recognises and accepts that the Jewish state, as such, has no future in the Middle East; that is emphatically not to say that a large Jewish population in Palestine has no future. Indeed, the opposite, it has surely been demonstrated, is the case. The profoundly courageous decisions which will be required from the present generation of Israelis must be matched by a generosity and compassion, on a scale hardly ever seen before, from the Muslim and Christian Arabs who must share with the Jewish population if any of them is to have the prospect of a real future, living in peace and allowing for future generations to grow up in some sort of fraternity.

Such a settlement will depend upon an almost limitless generosity of spirit amongst those who have ultimately to determine the outcome of the discussions which must precede any settlement. What is being asked of the Israelis will, of course, seem to be the greater: the relinquishment of cherished ideals and the possession of an exclusively Jewish state; they must be assured that by such relinquishment they will restore justice and honour to Judaism and ensure a peaceful existence for the Jewish inhabitants of Palestine into future ages. For the Arabs, sacrifices are also required, especially from the Muslims. They must accept a large foreign, Jewish population in their midst in perpetuity.

Ultimately it is a political solution, not a solution based on force, which must be achieved if the peoples of the Middle East are to live together peaceably, however uneasily that state may be achieved. The currents of politics run in diverse and irregular channels; in Palestine the strands which comprise the political fabric are more diverse, as much as anything by reason of the interference of many forces in the region's affairs, as anywhere on earth. Often those political influences which can be discerned appear to be mutually exclusive, their interests contradictory and inimical. And yet the evidence of history suggests that this may not be so, that appearances can mislead and the inflexibly entrenched position of today becomes the bargaining chip of tomorrow. The history of the Israeli state may yet prove to be a supreme example of this contradiction.

The Orientals, though at the outset they will be among the most vociferous opponents of any deal with the Arabs, possibly represent a more pragmatic and hence a more promising segment of Israeli society. They, unlike their Ashkenazi co-religionists, have lived amongst the Arabs for centuries. It would be naive, as was acknowledged earlier, to pretend that their lifestyle, as a minority amongst Muslims, was ideal, but at least compared with the lot of Jews in Christendom it was certainly tolerable. The reality is that the Orientals, the Jews of North Africa, of Yemen, Iraq and the Levant itself, are Arab Jews, whose culture, language and way of life, with the exception of their religious practice, were indistinguishable from the other Arabs amongst whom they had lived for countless generations. But it has suited the Zionists and the Ashkenazi leadership in Israel over the past decades to present the Oriental Jews as the implacable enemies of the Arabs.

It was not the Oriental Jews who erected the elaborate ideology of Jewish supremacism which has come to permeate the State of Israel. With the prevailing mood in Israel, however, they will no doubt present as unbending a front as their European co-religionists, but, being Orientals, they may also be more pragmatic, more inclined to take the long view, more ready, perhaps, to seek a settlement which allows them to remain in the Levant without necessarily demanding the perpetuation of the Zionist state as a political entity.

Even when a significant degree of political change is considered – the recognition by Israel of some kind of Palestinian entity, for example, or the return of the Occupied Territories – inevitably, the terms in which Israel has fashioned her own status are accepted by most commentators as sacrosanct. It is customary, when looking towards some sort of assured position to which the so-called 'moderate' Arabs can be called upon to accede, to accept what has increasingly come to be seen as Israel's 'right' to exist. The Palestine Liberation Organisation has indeed conceded that Israel has a right to exist. But the question must be asked as to what sort of state does this right presume Israel to be? It cannot be that a supremacist, sectarian state which elevates the position of one social group above all others is that whose right to existence is acknowledged. An apparently inviolable principle asserts that Israel must have the 'right' to exist in the form which she has determined for herself. This condition, of an exclusively Jewish state, armed to the teeth, is the entire reason for the state's existence. But it is precisely this supremacist definition of such a state built on Arab lands which is and must remain unacceptable to all Arabs, moderate or extreme, Muslim or Christian, and which ultimately will disqualify all attempts at moderation or compromise. Nothing will ever change this situation whereby Israel's existence in the form which is now accepted as one of the enduring political realities is tenable neither morally, historically nor, ultimately, politically. The qualification to the position which one generation of an Arab or Palestinian leadership might be persuaded to accept would certainly not be seen as binding on any of their successors, if they were to compromise any of the fundamental rights of the Palestinians to their land. This is why the world and Israel must determine this issue in terms which in the first place will be acceptable to the Arabs, harsh and painful though such a determination will be. No one, not even the Palestinians, can alienate their rights to their land, for themselves or for future generations.

The Jews cannot, simply as Jews, pretend to 'rights' in a homeland which so patently belongs to another people. There is no way of compromise: unless the world realises this and by whatever means persuades the rulers of Israel to give up the demand for Jewish supremacy and exclusivity, then Armageddon really does portend. But, equally, there is another principle which must also be expressed: the Jewish population now living in Israel, though they are migrants or the descendants of migrants and have not, in any sense except a very romantic one, 'returned', without question have the right to a peaceful and secure existence. As they are now resident in Palestine (or what once was Palestine), there, presumably, they must remain. Any prospective solution must face this issue, as must, indeed, the Arabs.

The status of the Jewish migrants in Palestine will present perhaps the most difficult of the issues which face any sort of settlement. Only one instrument can confer legal right to settlement in the land of Palestine to a community of newcomers: the will of the indigenous people of Palestine. They alone can admit to co-citizenship an alien people who have in truth been imposed upon them.

The presence of a state as alien as Israel to the Middle East is not, of course, unprecedented. The Crusader kingdom was such a one, planted in just the same way and in the same region with a very similar ideological authority. It lasted for less than two hundred uneasy years. For long the Muslims were disorganised and outclassed militarily by the better equipped and better disciplined Christian forces who also, as a tiny minority surrounded by a sea of enemies, were able to keep themselves at a level of belligerence quite unlike that of their opponents. They were sure of their god-given authority to free the Holy Land from the Saracen thrall; time, however, produced the conditions of their ignominious defeat and expulsion. In time, the early passionate European commitment to the Christian kingdom declined, while the Christians born in Outremer became more and more *déraciné* as they succumbed to the manners and customs of the people amongst whom they lived. The Christian states became increasingly distanced from their supply lines, which had their roots in Europe. The once seemingly inexhaustible supply of younger sons showed signs of drying up and the Christian kingdom became more and more dependent on professional military resources which were subject to influences and policies very different from those which once motivated its founders.

The kingdom's paymasters discovered other priorities and the military orders of knighthood, the strongest arm of the Christian kingdom's defence, became corrupt and self-seeking. Then a military genius emerged on the Arab side, in the person of Salah ed-Din Ayub, and the last act of the foreign Christian presence in medieval Palestine began. After the momentous Battle of the Horns of Hattin in 1187 the collapse of the kingdom was inevitable; it followed soon after, to end in shame and discord.

Such a parallel may easily be dismissed as facile and irrelevant. History, however, does not always fail to repeat itself. Israel cannot ever be certain that the Arabs may not one day become sufficiently powerful to destroy her, by force rather than by argument. She cannot be certain that those who have so unstintingly poured out their resources to keep the Israeli state viable, will continue to do so; indeed, she may very well decide that they will not. Unless the world community can persuade Israel that its exclusively Jewish character is a perpetual incitement to the Arabs, then there will be only one possible outcome. Unless wiser counsels prevail than appear to have done so far, the fears that many have expressed, of Israel invoking the 'Sampson Syndrome', whereby nuclear war is threatened or even unleashed, could be realised. The stratum of violence and malevolence which has been part of Israel's character since her foundation makes such an outcome not merely possible but even likely.

Israel's massive military potential, compounded of advanced conventional weapons, biological weapons and well developed nuclear capability, is by far the most powerful in the region. It has been most skillful in thwarting any attempts by an Arab state to acquire even a fraction of its own capability. Yet Israeli armament remains a constant provocation and a model for her adversaries; the Arabs, faced with an intransigent and militaristic enemy, with so great an armoury at its disposal, can hardly be expected to stand by impotently for ever. The Arabs will find it increasingly difficult to understand why the Western world will regard the possession of a nuclear capability in Israel as acceptable whilst the suggestion that an Arab state should aspire to a comparable potential provokes outrage.

The present population of Israel is in great peril, as much from its militaristic attitudes as from the other elements of corruption which have entered the body politic. Its nature is changing profoundly. The West has become accustomed to the idea of the archetypal Israeli as an immigrant European intellectual, working in the kibbutz by day, at night playing in a string quartet, rifle lying at his feet to drive away those who would threaten the existence of so high-minded a lifestyle. But with the diminishing importance of the European component in the population the situation becomes yet more perilous; the emergence of the Oriental Jews to dominance brings with it a fundamental change in the society.

In recent years there has come a flood of stories out of Israel all of which contribute to the belief that the country's society is in a state of moral and political degeneracy. To such dubious achievements as the kidnapping of Eichmann, the hunting of supposed enemies of Israel wherever they may be and their elimination by the country's secret services, the subversion of citizens of supposedly friendly states, and the acquisition of strategic information by illegal means, has been added a series of scandals involving large-scale corruption, financial criminality, the trade in weapons to regimes or movements with which no decent state would have dealings and, most recently, the involvement of leading Israeli service and intelligence personnel in the most pernicious of modern crimes, the promotion of addictive drugs.

All such actions are seen as being justified in terms of the paramount consideration of the survival of the Israeli state; all other considerations, all moralities are to be subjected to this supreme imperative. This, in itself, would not perhaps be notable or surprising in the life of a maverick state born and nurtured in such circumstances as was Israel, were it not for the insistence, from the earliest days of the Zionist movement to the present day, that Israel somehow has a special claim to the moral high ground, that the motivations of its leaders were always of the highest, and that Israel's assumption of moral rectitude entitled it to special consideration and the immediate, unquestioning acceptance of its acts and policies as self-evidently just. Whilst much of Israel's history reveals a degree of duplicity and profound amorality, it is only in the past decade and particularly during the period of the Likud government and the *intifada* that the mask has begun to slip and the true face of Israel's authoritarianism has become clear for all to see.

One fundamental principle of the practice of politics must be borne firmly in mind in this, as in all similar cases; all new political initiatives are denounced with the most absolute vehemence, and their acceptance most unalterably rejected, immediately prior to their acceptance. It may be too optimistic to hope that some of the suggestions contained in this document will experience the same sequence of swift rejection and eventual acceptance.

The importance to the world of securing a solution to the Palestinian problem rests not only in the wish to settle the differences with justice and honour, between two communities of great and enduring historical importance, but also in the precedent the resolution of such a conflict would portend. If it is possible, by means of the type of federal solution foreseen in this review, to resolve the Arab-Israeli confrontation, it should be possible to devise similar solutions to the disputes which have bedevilled Ireland for centuries and which now beset the Kurds in their fragmented homeland, arbitrarily divided between four powers with little goodwill between them. The hazards which now face the former Soviet Union with regard to the rights of minorities within the Soviet system might also be reduced by similar, creative political practice.

Indeed, as the world itself faces more and more serious hazards (and it must increasingly be doubted if our species has much real chance of survival, even in the medium term) it is essential, surely, that people everywhere are at least given the chance to control their own destinies. It may be that political groupings in the international sphere must get larger and hence more remote from the individual; if this is so, then it is vital that compensating structures are devised which return at least some part of direct political control to more local interests. The promotion of federal structures, even if they come about as the consequence of urgent necessity, to offset an alternative otherwise unthinkable, may be one way in which more direct control may be achieved. By its imaginative application it would be possible to bring about the fulfilment of the national destinies of peoples like the Scots or the Welsh, the Basques, Sardinians and all the other peoples which European concepts of nationalism have deprived of their identities.

It may even be that if the type of solution proposed here for Palestine could be achieved, the historic contribution of the people of that part of the Levant, now augmented by a vibrant and creative body of European immigrants, may yet prove not to be limited only to the benefits of revealed religion. But – unless a start is made which reverses the recent history of this sadly disputed land, then all other experiments can never even be contemplated. The results of the initiative between Israel and the Palestinians may match the hopes which it has already aroused, but the omens are not encouraging.

Given the theme of this book and its author's belief that it is Israel that must change fundamentally if peace is to have even a chance of survival, it would be the ultimate irony if the agreement between the PLO and the Israelis had, as its only or principal effect, the conferring of a degree of legitimacy on the State of Israel which it is this book's contention it has never enjoyed. The injustice remains, the wrong is unrighted; but what remains equally certain is that the essential rights of the Palestinian people to the determination of their own future is in no way diminished.

APPENDIX 1

THE MANDATE

The Council of the League of Nations:

Whereas the Principal Allied Powers have agreed, for the purpose of giving effect to the provision of Article 22 of the Covenant of the League of Nations, to entrust to a Mandatory selected by the said Powers the administration of the territory of Palestine, which formerly belonged to the Turkish Empire, within such boundaries as may be fixed by them; and

Whereas recognition has thereby been given to the historical connexion of the Jewish people with Palestine and to the grounds for reconstituting their national home in that country; and

Whereas the Principal Allied Powers have selected His Britannic Majesty as the Mandatory for Palestine; and

Whereas the mandate in respect of Palestine has been formulated in the following terms and submitted to the Council of the League for approval; and

Whereas His Britannic Majesty has accepted the mandate in respect of Palestine and undertaken to exercise it on behalf of the League of Nations in conformity with the following provisions; and

Whereas by the aforementioned Article 22 (paragraph 8), it is provided that the degree of authority, control or administration to be exercised by the Mandatory, not having been previously agreed upon by the Members of the League, shall be explicitly defined by the Council of the League of Nations;

Confirming the said Mandate, defines its terms as follows;

ARTICLE 1

The Mandatory shall have full powers of legislation and of administration, save as they may be limited by the terms of this mandate.

ARTICLE 2

The Mandatory shall be responsible for placing the country under such political, administrative and economic conditions as will secure the establishment of the Jewish national home, as laid down in the preamble, and the development of self-governing institutions, and also for safeguarding the civil and religious rights of all the inhabitants of Palestine, irrespective of race and religion.

ARTICLE 3

The Mandatory shall, so far as circumstances permit, encourage local autonomy.

ARTICLE 4

An appropriate Jewish agency shall be recognised as a public body for the purpose of advising and co-operating with the Administration of Palestine in such economic, social and other matters as may affect the establishment of the Jewish national home and the interests of the Jewish population in Palestine and, subject always to the control of the Administration, to assist and take part in the development of the country.

The Zionist Organisation, so long as its organisation and constitution are in the opinion of the Mandatory appropriate, shall be recognised as such agency. It shall take steps in consultation with His Britannic Majesty's Government to secure the co-operation of all Jews who are willing to assist in the establishment of the Jewish national home.

ARTICLE 5

The Mandatory shall be responsible for seeing that no Palestine territory shall be ceded or leased to, or in any way placed under the control of, the Government of any foreign Power.

ARTICLE 6

The Administration of Palestine, while ensuring that the rights and position of other sections of the population are not prejudiced, shall facilitate Jewish immigration under suitable conditions and shall encourage, in co-operation with the Jewish agency referred to in Article 4, close settlement by Jews on the land, including State lands and waste lands not required for public purposes.

ARTICLE 7

The Administration of Palestine shall be responsible for enacting a nationality law. There shall be included in this law provisions framed so as to facilitate the acquisition of Palestinian citizenship by Jews who take up their permanent residence in Palestine.

ARTICLE 8

The privileges and immunities of foreigners, including the benefits of consular jurisdiction and protection as formerly enjoyed by Capitulation or usage in the Ottoman Empire, shall not be applicable in Palestine.

Unless the Powers whose nationals enjoyed the aforementioned privileges and immunities on August 1st, 1914, shall have previously renounced the right to their re-establishment, or shall have agreed to their non-application for a specified period, these privileges and immunities shall, at the expiration of the mandate, be immediately re-established in their entirety or with such modifications as may have been agreed upon between the Powers concerned.

ARTICLE 9

The Mandatory shall be responsible for seeing that the judicial system established in Palestine shall assure to foreigners, as well as to natives, a complete guarantee of their rights.

Respect for the personal status of the various peoples and communities and for their religious interests shall be fully guaranteed. In particular, the control and administration of Waqfs shall be exercised in accordance with religious law and the dispositions of the founders.

ARTICLE 10

Pending the making of special extradition agreements relating to Palestine, the extradition treaties in force between the Mandatory and other foreign Powers shall apply to Palestine.

ARTICLE 11

The Administration of Palestine shall take all necessary measures to safeguard the interests of the community in connection with the development of the country, and, subject to any international obligations accepted by the Mandatory, shall have full power to provide for public ownership or control of any of the natural resources of the country or of the public works, services and utilities established or to be established therein. It shall introduce a land system appropriate to the needs of the country having regard, among other things, to the desirability of promoting the close settlement and intensive cultivation of the land.

The Administration may arrange with the Jewish agency mentioned in Article 4 to construct or operate, upon fair and equitable terms, any public works, services and utilities, and to develop any of the natural resources of the country, in so far as these matters are not directly undertaken by the Administration. Any such arrangements shall provide that no profits distributed by such agency, directly or indirectly, shall exceed a reasonable rate of interest on the capital, and any further profits shall be utilised by it for the benefit of the country in a manner approved by the Administration.

ARTICLE 12

The Mandatory shall be entrusted with the control of the foreign relations of Palestine, and the right to issue exequaturs to consuls appointed by foreign Powers. He shall also be entitled to afford diplomatic and consular protection to citizens of Palestine when outside its territorial limits.

ARTICLE 13

All responsibility in connexion with the Holy Places and religious buildings or sites in Palestine, including that of preserving existing rights and of securing free access to the Holy Places, religious buildings and sites and the free exercise of worship, while ensuring the requirements of public order and decorum, is assumed by the Mandatory, who shall be responsible solely to the League of Nations in all matters connected herewith, provided that nothing in this article shall prevent the Mandatory from entering into such arrangements as he may deem reasonable with the Administration for the purpose of carrying the provisions of this article into effect; and provided also that nothing in this Mandate shall be construed as conferring upon the Mandatory authority to interfere with the fabric or the management of purely Moslem sacred shrines, the immunities of which are guaranteed.

ARTICLE 14

A special Commission shall be appointed by the Mandatory to study, define and determine the rights and claims in connection with the Holy Places and the rights and claims relating to the different religious communities in Palestine. The method of nomination, the composition and the functions of this Commission shall be submitted to the Council of the League for its approval, and the Commission shall not be appointed or enter upon its functions without the approval of the Council.

ARTICLE 15

The Mandatory shall see that complete freedom of conscience and the free exercise of all forms of worship, subject only to the maintenance of public order and morals, are ensured to all. No discrimination of any kind shall be made between the inhabitants of Palestine on the ground of race, religion or language. No person shall be excluded from Palestine on the sole ground of his religious beliefs.

The right of each community to maintain its own schools for the education of its own members in its own language, while conforming to such educational requirements of a general nature as the Administration may impose, shall not be denied or impaired.

ARTICLE 16

The Mandatory shall be responsible for exercising such supervision over religious or eleemosynary bodies of all faiths in Palestine as may be required for the maintenance of public order and good government. Subject to such supervision, no measures shall be taken in Palestine to obstruct or interfere with the enterprise of such bodies or to discriminate against any representative or member of them on the ground of his religion or nationality.

ARTICLE 17

The Administration of Palestine may organise on a voluntary basis the forces necessary for the preservation of peace and order, and also for the defence of the country, subject, however, to the supervision of the Mandatory, but shall not use them for purposes other than those above specified save with the consent of the Mandatory. Except for such purposes, no military, naval or air forces shall be raised or maintained by the Administration of Palestine.

Nothing in this article shall preclude the Administration of Palestine from contributing to the cost of the maintenance of the forces of the Mandatory in Palestine.

The Mandatory shall be entitled at all times to use the roads, railways and ports of Palestine for the movement or armed forces and the carriage of fuel and supplies.

ARTICLE 18

The Mandatory shall see that there is no discrimination in Palestine against the nationals of any State Member of the League of Nations (including companies incorporated under its laws) as compared with those of the Mandatory or of any foreign State in matters concerning taxation, commerce or navigation, the exercise of industries or professions, or in the treatment of merchant vessels or civil aircraft. Similarly, there shall be no discrimination in Palestine against goods originating in or destined for any of the said States, and there shall be freedom of transit under equitable conditions across the mandated area.

Subject as aforesaid and to the other provisions of this mandate, the Administration of Palestine may, on the advice of the Mandatory, impose such taxes and customs duties as it may consider necessary, and take such steps as it may think best to promote the development of the natural resources of the country and to safeguard the interests of the population. It may also, on the advice of the Mandatory, conclude a special customs agreement with any State the territory of which in 1914 was wholly included in Asiatic Turkey or Arabia.

ARTICLE 19

The Mandatory shall adhere on behalf of the Administration of Palestine to any general international conventions already existing, or which may be concluded hereafter with the approval of the League of Nations, respecting the slave traffic, the traffic in arms and ammunition, or the traffic in drugs, or relating to commercial equality, freedom of transit and navigation, aerial navigation and postal, telegraphic and wireless communications or literary, artistic or industrial property.

ARTICLE 20

The Mandatory shall co-operate on behalf of the Administration of Palestine, so far as religious, social and other conditions may permit, in the execution of any common policy adopted by the League of Nations for preventing and combating disease, including disease of plants and animals.

ARTICLE 21

The Mandatory shall secure the enactment within twelve months from this date, and shall ensure the execution of a Law of Antiquities based on the following rules. This law shall ensure equality of treatment in the matter of excavations and archaeological research to the nations of all States Members of the League of Nations.

ARTICLE 22

English, Arabic and Hebrew shall be official languages of Palestine. Any statement or inscription in Arabic on stamps or money in Palestine shall be repeated in Hebrew and any statement or inscription in Hebrew shall be repeated in Arabic.

ARTICLE 23

The Administration of Palestine shall recognise the holy days of the respective communities in Palestine as legal days of rest for the members of such communities.

ARTICLE 24

The Mandatory shall make to the Council of the League of Nations an annual report to the satisfaction of the Council as to the measures taken during the year to carry out the provisions of the mandate. Copies of all laws and regulations promulgated or issued during the year shall be communicated with the report.

APPENDIX 1

ARTICLE 25

In the territories lying between the Jordan and the eastern boundary of Palestine as ultimately determined, the Mandatory shall be entitled, with the consent of the Council of the League of Nations, to postpone or withhold application of such provision of this mandate as he may consider inapplicable to the existing local conditions, and to make such provision for the administration of the territories as he may consider suitable to those conditions, provided that no action shall be taken which is inconsistent with the provisions of Articles 15, 16 and 18.

ARTICLE 26

The Mandatory agrees that if any dispute whatever should arise between the Mandatory and another Member of the League of Nations relating to the interpretation or the application of the provisions of the mandate, such dispute, if it cannot be settled by negotiation, shall be submitted to the Permanent Court of International Justice provided for by Article 14 of the Covenant of the League of Nations.

ARTICLE 27

The consent of the Council of the League of Nations is required for any modification of the terms of this mandate.

ARTICLE 28

In the event of the termination of the mandate hereby conferred upon the Mandatory, the Council of the League of Nations shall make such arrangements as may be deemed necessary for safeguarding in perpetuity, under guarantee of the League, the rights secured by Articles 13 and 14, and shall use its influence for securing, under the guarantee of the League, that the Government of Palestine will fully honour the financial obligations legitimately incurred by the Administration of Palestine during the period of the mandate, including the rights of public servants to pensions or gratuities.

The present instrument shall be deposited in original in the archives of the League of Nations and certified copies shall be forwarded by the Secretary General of the League of Nations to all Members of the League.

DONE AT LONDON the twenty-fourth day of July, one thousand nine hundred and twenty-two.

APPENDIX 2

UN GENERAL ASSEMBLY RESOLUTION ON THE FUTURE GOVERNMENT OF PALESTINE (PARTITION RESOLUTION)

November 29, 1947

The General Assembly,

Having met in special session at the request of the mandatory Power to constitute and instruct a special committee to prepare for the consideration of the question of the future government of Palestine at the second regular session;

Having constituted a Special Committee and instructed it to investigate all questions and issues relevant to the problem of Palestine, and to prepare proposals for the solution of the problem, and

Having received and examined the report of the Special Committee (document A/364) including a number of unanimous recommendations and a plan of partition with economic union approved by the majority of the Special Committee,

Considers that the present situation in Palestine is one which is likely to impair the general welfare and friendly relations among nations;

Takes note of the declaration by the mandatory Power that it plans to complete its evacuation of Palestine by 1 August 1948; Recommends to the United Kingdom, as the mandatory Power for Palestine, and to all other Members of the United Nations the adoption and implementation, with regard to the future government of Palestine, of the Plan of Partition with Economic Union set out below;

Requests that

(a) The Security Council take the necessary measures as provided for in the plan for its implementation;

(b) The Security Council consider, if circumstances during the transitional period required such consideration, whether the situation in Palestine constitutes a threat to the peace. If it decides that such a threat exists, and in order to maintain international peace and security, the Security council should supplement the authorization

212

of the General Assembly by taking measures, under Article 39 and 41 of the Charter, to empower the United Nations Commission, as provided in this resolution, to exercise in Palestine the functions which are assigned to it by this resolution;

(c) The Security Council determine as a threat to the peace, breach of the peace or act of aggression, in accordance with Article 39 of the Charter, any attempt to alter by force the settlement envisaged by this resolution;

(d) The Trusteeship Council be informed of the responsibilities envisaged for it in this plan;

Calls *upon* the inhabitants of Palestine to take such steps as may be necessary on their part to put this plan into effect;

Appeals to all Governments and all peoples to refrain from taking any action which might hamper or delay the carrying out of these recommendations, and

Authorises the Secretary-General to reimburse travel and subsistence expenses of the members of the commission referred to in Part I, Section B, paragraph 1 below, on such basis and in such form as he may determine most appropriate in the circumstances, and to provide the Commission with the necessary staff to assist in carrying out the functions assigned to the Commission by the General Assembly.

PLAN OF PARTITION WITH ECONOMIC UNION
PART I – FUTURE CONSTITUTION AND GOVERNMENT OF PALESTINE

A. TERMINATE OF MANDATE
PARTITION AND INDEPENDENCE

1. The Mandate for Palestine shall terminate as soon as possible but in any case not later than 1 August 1948.

2. The armed forces of the mandatory Power shall be progressively withdrawn from Palestine, the withdrawal to be completed as soon as possible but in any case not later than 1 August 1948.

The mandatory Power shall advise the Commission, as far in advance as possible, of its intention to terminate the Mandate and to evacuate each area.

The mandatory Power shall use its best endeavours to ensure that an area situated in the territory of the Jewish State, including a seaport and hinterland adequate to provide facilities for a substantial immigration, shall be evacuated at the earliest possible date and in any event not later than 1 February 1948.

3. Independent Arab and Jewish States and the Special International

Regime for the City of Jerusalem, set forth in part III of this plan, shall come into existence in Palestine two months after the evacuation of the armed forces of the mandatory power has been completed but in any case not later than 1 October 1948. The boundaries of the Arab State, the Jewish State, and the City of Jerusalem shall be described in parts II and III below.

4. The period between the adoption by the General Assembly of its recommendation on the question of Palestine and the establishment of the independence of the Arab and Jewish States shall be a transitional period.

B. STEPS PREPARATORY TO INDEPENDENCE

1. A Commission shall be set up consisting of one representative of each of five Member States. The Members represented on the Commission shall be elected by the General Assembly on as broad a basis, geographically and otherwise, as possible.

2. The administration of Palestine shall, as the mandatory Power withdraw its armed forces, be progressively turned over to the Commission, which shall act in conformity with the recommendations of the General Assembly, under the guidance of the Security Council. The mandatory Power shall to the fullest possible extent co-ordinate its plans for withdrawal with the plans of the Commission to take over and administer areas which have been evacuated.

In the discharge of this administrative responsibility the Commission shall have authority to issue necessary regulations and take other measures as required.

The mandatory Power shall not take any action to prevent, obstruct or delay the implementation by the Commission of the measures recommended by the General Assembly.

3. On its arrival in Palestine the Commission shall proceed to carry out measures for the establishment of the frontiers of the Arab and Jewish States and the City of Jerusalem in accordance with the general lines of the recommendations of the General Assembly on the partition of Palestine.

Nevertheless, the boundaries as described in part II of this plan are to be modified in such a way that village areas as a rule will not be divided by state boundaries unless pressing reasons make that necessary.

4. The Commission, after consultation with the democratic parties and other public organisations of the Arab and Jewish States, shall select and establish in each State as rapidly as possible a Provisional Council of Government. The activities of both the Arab and Jewish Provisional Councils of Government shall be carried out under the general direction of the Commission.

If by 1 April 1948 a Provisional Council of Government cannot be selected for either of the States, or, if selected, cannot carry out its functions, the Commission shall communicate that fact to the Security

Council for such action with respect to that State as the Security Council may deem proper, and to the Secretary-General for communication to the Members of the United Nations.

5. Subject to the provisions of these recommendations, during the transitional period the Provisional Councils of Government, acting under the Commission, shall have full authority in the areas under their control, including authority over matters of immigration and land regulation.

6. The Provisional Council of Government of each State, acting under the Commission, shall progressively receive from the Commission full responsibility for the administration of that State in the period between the termination of the Mandate and the establishment of the State's independence.

7. The Commission shall instruct the Provisional Councils of Government of both the Arab and Jewish States, after their formation, to proceed to the establishment of administrative organs of government, central and local.

8. The Provisional Council of Government of each State shall, within the shortest time possible, recruit an armed militia from the residents of that State, sufficient in number to maintain internal order and to prevent frontier clashes.

This armed militia in each State shall, for operational purposes, be under the command of Jewish or Arab officers resident in that State, but general political and military control, including the choice of the militia's High Command, shall be exercised by the Commission.

9. The provisional Council of Government of each State shall, not later than two months after the withdrawal of the armed forces of the mandatory Power, hold elections to the Constituent Assembly which shall be conducted on democratic lines.

The election regulations in each State shall be drawn up by the Provisional Council of Government and approved by the Commission.

Qualified voters for each State for this election shall be persons over eighteen years of age who are (a) Palestinian citizens residing in that State and (b) Arabs and Jews residing in the State, although not Palestinian citizens who, before voting, have signed a notice of intention to become citizens of such State.

Arabs and Jews residing in the City of Jerusalem who have signed a notice of intention to become citizens, the Arabs of the Arab State and the Jews of the Jewish State, shall be entitled to vote in the Arab and Jewish States respectively.

Women may vote and be elected to the Constituent Assemblies.

During the transitional period no Jew shall be permitted to establish residence in the area of the proposed Jewish State, except by special leave of the Commission.

10. The Constituent Assembly of each State shall draft a democratic constitution for its State and choose a provisional government to succeed the Provisional Council of Government appointed by the Commission. The constitutions of the States shall embody chapters 1 and 2

215

of the Declaration provided for in section C below and include *inter alia* provisions for:

(a) Establishing in each State a legislative body elected by universal suffrage and by secret ballot on the basis of proportional representation, and an executive body responsible to the legislature;

(b) Settling all international disputes in which the State may be involved by peaceful means in such a manner that international peace and security, and justice, are not endangered;

(c) Accepting the obligation of the State to refrain in its international relations from the threat or use of force against the territorial integrity or political independence of any State, or in any other manner inconsistent with the purposes of the United Nations;

(d) Guaranteeing to all persons equal and non-discriminatory rights in civil, political, economic and religious matters and the enjoyment of human rights and fundamental freedoms, including freedom of religion, language, speech and publication, education, assembly and association;

(e) Preserving freedom of transit and visit for all residents and citizens of the other State in Palestine and the City of Jerusalem, subject to considerations of national security, provided that each State shall control residence within its borders.

11. The Commission shall appoint a preparatory economic commission of three members to make whatever arrangements are possible for economic co-operation, with a view to establishing, as soon as practicable, the Economic Union and the Joint Economic Board, as provided in Section D below.

12. During the period between the adoption of the recommendations on the question of Palestine by the General Assembly and the termination of the Mandate, the mandatory Power in Palestine shall maintain full responsibility for administration in areas from which it has not withdrawn its armed forces. The Commission shall assist the mandatory Power in the carrying out of these functions. Similarly the mandatory Power shall co-operate with the Commission in the execution of its functions.

13. With a view to ensuring that there shall be continuity in the functioning of administrative services and that, on the withdrawal of the armed forces of the mandatory Power, the whole administration shall be in charge of the Provisional Councils and the Joint Economic Board, respectively, acting under the Commission, there shall be a progressive transfer from the mandatory Power to the Commission, of responsibility for all the functions of government, including that of maintaining law and order in the areas from which the forces of the mandatory Power have been withdrawn.

14. The Commission shall be guided in its activities by the recommendations of the General Assembly and by such instructions as the Security Council may consider necessary to issue.

The measures taken by the Commission, within the recommendations of the General Assembly shall become immediately effective unless the Commission has previously received contrary instructions from the Security Council.

The Commission shall render periodic monthly progress reports, or more frequently if desirable, to the Security Council.

15. The Commission shall make its final report to the next regular session of the General Assembly and to the Security Council simultaneously.

C. DECLARATION

A declaration shall be made to the United Nations by the provisional government of each proposed State before independence. It shall contain *inter alia* the following clauses:

The stipulations contained in the declaration are recognised as fundamental laws of the State and no law, regulation or official action shall conflict or interfere with these stipulations, nor shall any law, regulation or official action prevail over them.

Chapter 1 – Holy Places, Religious Buildings and Sites

1. Existing rights in respect of Holy Places and religious buildings or sites shall not be denied or impaired.

2. In so far as Holy Places are concerned, the liberty of access, visit and transit shall be guaranteed, in conformity with existing rights, to all residents and citizens of the other State and of the City of Jerusalem, as well as to aliens, without distinction as to nationality, subject to the maintenance of public order and decorum.

3. Holy Places and religious buildings or sites shall be preserved. No act shall be permitted which may in any way impair their sacred character. If at any time it appears to the Government that any particular Holy Place, religious building or site is in need of urgent repair, the Government may call upon the community or communities concerned to carry out such repair. The Government may carry it out itself at the expense of the community or communities concerned if no action is taken within a reasonable time.

4. No taxation shall be levied in respect of any Holy Place, religious building or site which was exempt from taxation on the date of the creation of the State.

No change in the incidence of such taxation shall be made which would either discriminate between the owners or occupiers of Holy Places, religious buildings or sites, or would place such owners or occupiers in a position less favourable in relation to the general incidence of taxation than existed at the time of the adoption of the Assembly's recommendation.

5. The Governor of the City of Jerusalem shall have the right to determine whether the provisions of the Constitution of the State in relation to Holy Places, religious buildings and sites within the borders of the State and the religious rights appertaining thereto, are being

properly applied and respected, and to make decisions on the basis of existing rights in cases of disputes which may arise between the different religious communities or the rites of a religious community with respect to such places, buildings and sites. He shall receive full co-operation and such privileges and immunities as are necessary for the exercise of his functions in the State.

Chapter 2 – Religious and Minority Rights

1. Freedom of conscience and the free exercise of all forms of worship, subject only to the maintenance of public order and morals, shall be ensured to all.

2. No discrimination of any kind shall be made between the inhabitants on the ground of race, religion, language or sex.

3. All persons within the jurisdiction of the State shall be entitled to equal protection of the laws.

4. The family law and personal status of the various minorities and their religious interests, including endowments, shall be respected.

5. Except as may be required for the maintenance of public order and good government, no measure shall be taken to obstruct or interfere with the enterprise of religious or charitable bodies of all faiths or to discriminate against any representative or member of these bodies on the ground of his religion or nationality.

6. The State shall ensure adequate primary and secondary education for the Arab and Jewish minority, respectively, in its own language and its cultural traditions.

The right of each community to maintain its own schools for the education of its own members in its own language, while conforming to such educational requirements of a general nature as the State may impose, shall not be denied or impaired. Foreign educational establishments shall continue their activity on the basis of their existing rights.

7. No restriction shall be imposed on the free use by any citizen of the State of any language in private intercourse, in commerce, in religion, in the Press or in publications of any kind, or at public meetings.[1]

8. No expropriation of land owned by an Arab in the Jewish State (by a Jew in the Arab State)[2] shall be allowed except for public purposes. In all cases of expropriation full compensation as fixed by the Supreme Court shall be paid previous to dispossession.

[1]The following stipulation shall be added to the declaration concerning the Jewish State: 'In the Jewish State adequate facilities shall be given to Arabic-speaking citizens for the use of their language, either orally or in writing, in the legislature, before the Courts and in the administration.'

[2]In the declaration concerning the Arab State, the words 'by an Arab in the Jewish State' should be replaced by the words 'by a Jew in the Arab State'.

Chapter 3 – Citizenship, International Conventions and Financial Obligations

1. Citizenship. Palestinian citizens residing in Palestine outside the City of Jerusalem, as well as Arabs and Jews who, not holding Palestinian citizenship, reside in Palestine outside the City of Jerusalem shall, upon the recognition of independence, become citizens of the State in which they are resident and enjoy full civil and political rights. Persons over the age of eighteen years may opt, within one year from the date of recognition of independence of the State in which they reside, for citizenship of the other State, providing that no Arab residing in the area of the proposed Arab State shall have the right to opt for citizenship in the proposed Jewish State and no Jews residing in the proposed Jewish State shall have the right to opt for citizenship in the proposed Arab State. The exercise of this right of option will be taken to include the wives and children under eighteen years of age of persons so opting.

Arabs residing in the area of the proposed Jewish State and Jews residing in the area of the proposed Arab State who have signed a notice of intention to opt for citizenship of the other State shall be eligible to vote in the elections to the Constituent Assembly of that State, but not in the elections to the Constituent Assembly of the State in which they reside.

2. International conventions. (a) The State shall be bound by all the international agreements and conventions, both general and special, to which Palestine has become a party. Subject to any right of denunciation provided for therein, such agreements and conventions shall be respected by the State throughout the period for which they were concluded.

(b) Any dispute about the applicability and continued validity of international conventions or treaties signed or adhered to by the mandatory Power on behalf of Palestine shall be referred to the International Court of Justice in accordance with the provisions of the Statute of the Court.

3. Financial obligations. (a) The State shall respect and fulfil all financial obligations of whatever nature assumed on behalf of Palestine by the mandatory Power during the exercise of the Mandate and recognised by the State. This provision includes the right of public servants to pensions, compensation or gratuities.

(b) These obligations shall be fulfilled through participation in the Joint Economic Board in respect of those obligations applicable to Palestine as a whole, and individually in respect of those applicable to, and fairly apportionable between, the States.

(c) A Court of Claims, affiliated with the Joint Economic Board, and composed of one member appointed by the United Nations, one representative of the United Kingdom and one representative of the State concerned, should be established. Any dispute between the United

Kingdom and the States respecting claims not recognised by the latter should be referred to that Court.

(d) Commercial concessions granted in respect of any part of Palestine prior to the adoption of the resolution by the General Assembly shall continue to be valid according to their terms, unless modified by agreement between the concession-holder and the State.

APPENDIX 3

THE STATE OF ISRAEL: PROCLAMATION OF INDEPENDENCE

The Land of Israel was the birthplace of the Jewish people. Here their spiritual, religious and national identity was formed. Here they achieved independence and created a culture of national and universal significance. Here they wrote and gave the Bible to the world.

Exiled from the Land of Israel the Jewish people remained faithful to it in all the countries of their dispersion, never ceasing to pray and hope for their return and the restoration of their national freedom.

Impelled by this historic association, Jews strove throughout the centuries to go back to the land of their fathers and regain their statehood. In recent decades they returned in their masses. They reclaimed the wilderness, revived their language, built cities and villages, and established a vigorous and ever-growing community, with its own economic and cultural life. They sought peace, they were prepared to defend themselves. They brought the blessings of progress to all inhabitants of the country and looked forward to sovereign independence.

In the year 1897 the First Zionist Congress, inspired by Theodor Herzl's vision of the Jewish State, proclaimed the right of the Jewish people to national revival in their own country.

This right was acknowledged by the Balfour Declaration of November 2, 1917, and re-affirmed by the Mandate of the League of Nations, which gave explicit international recognition of the historic connection of the Jewish people with Palestine and their right to reconstitute their National Home.

The recent holocaust, which engulfed millions of Jews in Europe, proved anew the need to solve the problem of the homelessness and lack of independence of the Jewish people by means of the re-establishment of the Jewish State, which would open the gates to all Jews and endow the Jewish people with equality of status among the family of nations.

The survivors of the disastrous slaughter in Europe, and also Jews from other lands, have not desisted from their efforts to reach Eretz-Yisrael, in face of difficulties, obstacles and perils; and have not ceased to urge their right to a life of dignity, freedom and honest toil in their ancestral land.

In the second World War the Jewish people in Palestine made their full contribution to the struggle of the freedom-loving nations against the Nazi evil. The sacrifices of their soldiers and their war effort gained them the right to rank with the nations which founded the United Nations.

On November 29, 1947, the General Assembly of the United Nations adopted a Resolution requiring the establishment of a Jewish State in Palestine. The General Assembly called upon the inhabitants of the country to take all the necessary steps on their part to put the plan into effect. This recognition by the United Nations of the right of the Jewish people to establish their independent State is unassailable.

It is the natural right of the Jewish people to lead, as do all other nations, an independent existence in its sovereign State.

Accordingly we, the members of the National Council, representing the Jewish people in Palestine and the World Zionist Movement, are met together in solemn assembly today, the day of termination of the British Mandate for Palestine; and by virtue of the natural and historic right of the Jewish people and of the Resolution of the General Assembly of the United Nations.

We hereby proclaim the establishment of the Jewish State in Palestine, to be called Medinath Yisraeal (The State of Israel).

We hereby declare that, as from the termination of the Mandate at midnight, the 14th–15th May, 1948, and pending the setting up of the duly elected bodies of the State in accordance with a Constitution, to be drawn up by the Constituent Assembly not later than the 1st October, 1948, the National Council shall act as the Provisional State Council, and that the National Administration shall constitute the Provisional Government of the Jewish State, which shall be known as Israel.

The State of Israel will be open to the immigration of Jews from all countries of their dispersion; will promote the development of the country for the benefit of all its inhabitants; will be based on the principles of liberty, justice and peace as conceived by the Prophets of Israel; will uphold the full social and political equality of all its citizens, without distinction of religion, race, or sex; will guarantee freedom of religion, conscience, education and culture; will safeguard the Holy Places of all religions; and will loyally uphold the principles of the United Nations Charter.

The State of Israel will be ready to co-operate with the organs and representatives of the United Nations in the implementation of the Resolution of the Assembly of November 29, 1947 and will take steps to bring about the Economic Union over the whole of Palestine.

We appeal to the United Nations to assist the Jewish people in the building of its State and to admit Israel into the family of nations.

In the midst of wanton aggression, we yet call upon the Arab inhabitants of the State of Israel to preserve the ways of peace and play their part in the development of the State, on the basis of full and equal citizenship and due representation in all its bodies and institutions – provisional and permanent.

We extend our hand in peace and neighbourliness to all the neighbouring states and their peoples, and invite them to co-operate with the independent Jewish nation for the common good of all. The State of Israel is prepared to make its contribution to the progress of the Middle East as a whole.

Our call goes out to the Jewish people all over the world to rally to our side in the task of immigration and development, and to stand by us in the great struggle for the fulfilment of the dream of generations for the redemption of Israel.

With trust in the Rock of Israel, we set our hand to this Declaration, at this Session of the Provisional State Council, on the soil of the Homeland, in the city of Tel-Aviv, on this Sabbath eve, the fifth of Iyar, 5708, the fourteenth of May, 1948.

REFERENCES

1 TO RECOGNISE A GREAT WRONG

1 See Kennett Love, *Suez: The Twice-Fought War*, Longman, 1969, for a contemporary view of the approach to the Suez crisis.
2 Middle East Economic Digest, 21 John Street, London WC1.
3 The Council for the Advancement of Arab British Understanding, 21 Collingham Road, London SW5 0NU.
4 *The Times*, 25 June 1969.
5 *The Times*, 29 September 1969.
6 Sean MacBride, *Israel in Lebanon: The Report of the International Committee to Enquire into Reported Violations of International Law by Israel during the Invasion of the Lebanon*, London, 1983.
7 See D. McDowell, *Palestine and Israel – the Uprising and Beyond*, I. B. Tauris, 1989.
8 Declaration by the Palestine National Council, 15 November 1988.
9 United Nations Resolutions: in the first 40 years of Israel's existence the General Assembly and the Security Council passed some 300 Resolutions directed at Israel. *Middle East International*, 16 December 1988.
10 See Ghazi A. Algosaibi, *The Gulf Crisis: An Attempt to Understand*, Kegan Paul International, 1993, for a remarkable overview of the Kuwait invasion and its aftermath by the author, then Saudi Arabian Ambassador in Bahrain.
11 The bibliography of the Palestine-Israeli issue is almost boundless: a useful summary from the Palestinian standpoint is represented by *Palestine Today*, published by the PLO Department of Information.
12 See, further, Chapter 9 below.

2 ZIONISM AND THE WORLD COMMUNITY

1 UN Special Committee on Palestine, 31 August 1947.
2 Ibid.
3 UN General Assembly Resolution on the Future Government of Palestine, 29 November 1947.

4 Paul Johnson, *A History of the Jews*, Weidenfeld & Nicolson, 1987.
5 See Jacobo Timerman's moving polemic on the Israeli attack on Lebanon and the revulsion felt by many Israelis at Begin's repeated exploitation of the Nazi persecutions.
6 Meyer Steinglass, 'Emil Ludwig before the Judge', *American Jewish Times*, April 1936.
7 A recurring theme in some Orthodox circles, based on Old Testament prophetic texts.
8 Peter Mansfield, *The Arabs*, Allen Lane, 1976.

3 ZIONISM AND RACE – EXORCISING EUROPE'S DEMONS

1 Paul Johnson, *A History of the Jews*, Weidenfeld & Nicolson, 1987.
2 Norman Cohn, *Europe's Inner Demons*, Heinemann, Chatto, Sussex University Press, 1975.
3 See, in particular, Martin Bernal, *Black Athena*, vols 1 and 2, Free Association Books, 1987, 1990.
4 Ibid.
5 Ibid.
6 Joseph R. Strayer, *The Reign of Philip the Fair*, LPE Princeton, 1980.
7 R. Patai and J. Patai, *The Myth of the Jewish Race*, rev. edn, Wayne State University Press, Detroit, 1989. The quotations which follow relating to the concepts of race are drawn from this source.
8 See *The Cambridge History of Islam*, vol. 1, Cambridge, 1970.
9 C. G. Jung, 'Mind and Earth', *Collected Works*, vol. 10, *Civilisation in Transition* (translated from the German by R. F. C. Hull), Routledge & Kegan Paul, 2nd edition, 1970.
10 C. G. Jung, 'Uber das Unbewusste' (1918), *Die gesammelte Werke von C. G. Jung*, Zurich, 1958–1970, X, 25.

4 LANGUAGE, PROPAGANDA AND ZIONISM

1 For a useful recent summary of the extensive scholarship on the Arabs and their origins see William Facey, *Riyadh the Old City*, Immel Publishing, London, 1991, especially chapters 2 and 3 and the notes thereto.
2 S. N. Kramer, *The Sumerians*, University of Chicago Press, 1963. Also Harriet Crawford, *Sumer and the Sumerians*, Cambridge, 1991.
3 Paul Johnson, *A History of the Jews*, Weidenfeld & Nicolson, 1987.
4 George Roux, *Ancient Iraq*, George Allen & Unwin, 1964.
5 Holman Hunt, via Herzl, in Johnson, op. cit.
6 This view is deeply entrenched amongst the orthodox; see the pronouncements of the religious parties in successive election campaigns and, in particular, the statements of Neturei Karta (Guardians of the Holy City).

7 Emile Marmorstein, *Heaven at Bay: The Jewish Kulturkampf in the Holy Land*, Oxford, 1969.
8 Stanford J. Shaw, *History of the Ottoman Empire and Modern Turkey*, vol. 1, *Empire of the Gazis*, Cambridge, 1976.
9 Bernard Lewis, *The Jews of Islam*, Routledge & Kegan Paul, 1984.
10 T. Herzl, *Der Judenstaat: Versuch einer modernen Loering der juedischen Frage*, Vienna, 1896.
11 Letter from A. J. Balfour to Lord Rothschild, the Foreign Office, 2 November 1917.
12 See Alan R. Taylor, *Prelude to Israel: An Analysis of Zionist Diplomacy 1897–1947*, Darton, Longman & Todd, 1959.
13 In Meyer Weisgal (ed.), *The Letters and Papers of Chaim Weizmann*, New Brunswick NJ and Jerusalem, Transaction Books and Israel Universities Press 1985.
14 Lenni Brenner, *Zionism in the Age of the Dictators: A Reappraisal*, Lawrence Hill, 1983.
15 For the Kastner case see Brenner, op. cit.; for the Israeli involvement in the Iran-Contra affair see, *inter alia*, Benjamin Beit-Hallahmi, *The Israeli Connection: Whom Israel Arms and Why*, I. B. Tauris, 1987.
16 Brenner, op. cit.
17 Ibid.
18 Ibid.
19 Walter Lehn with Uri Davis, *The Jewish National Fund*, Kegan Paul International, 1988.
20 Brenner, op. cit.
21 Ibid.
22 Taylor, op. cit.
23 David Hirst, *The Gun and the Olive Branch: The Roots of Violence in the Middle East*, Faber and Faber, 1977.

5 PROPAGANDA, HISTORY AND THE POWER OF MYTH

1 *The Times*, 17 October 1988.
2 British Census of Palestine 1922.
3 James L. Abu-Lughod, 'The Demographic Transformation of Palestine' in I. Abu-Lughod (ed.), *The Transformation of Palestine*, North Western University Press, Evanston, 1971.
4 Estimates by the British Mandated administration.
5 G. Dossin, *Syria*, 50, 1973.
6 Benjamin Disraeli, *Tancred, or the New Crusade*, 3 vols, Colburn, 1847.
7 Paul Johnson, *A History of the Jews*, Weidenfeld & Nicolson, 1987.
8 *Pace* Lewis in *Semites and Anti-Semites*, Weidenfeld & Nicolson, 1986, where he is abruptly dismissive of the Khazars and their connection with the Jews of Europe.
9 Arthur Koestler, *The Thirteenth Tribe*, Hutchinson, 1976.
10 See Koestler's bibliography.
11 Johnson, op. cit.

12 Ibid.
13 For an interesting overview, written prior to the creation of Israel see De Lacy O'Leary, *Arabia before Mohammed*, Kegan Paul, Trench, Trubner, 1927.
14 Israel Zangwill, 'The Return to Palestine', *New Liberal Review*, December 1901.
15 *Time*, 11 April 1988.

6 ARCHAEOLOGY AS PROPAGANDA

1 Bettina Arnold, 'The Past as Propaganda: Totalitarian Archaeology in Nazi Germany', *Antiquity*, vol. 64, no. 244, September 1990. Also ibid., 'The Past as Propaganda', *Archaeology*, July/August 1992.
2 Talia Shay, 'Israeli Archaeology – Ideology and Practice', *Antiquity*, vol. 63, no. 241, December 1989.
3 O. Bar Yosef and A. Mazer, 'Israeli Archaeology', *World Archaeology*, vol. 13 (3), 1982, p. 310.
4 W. F. Albright, 'The Phenomenon of Israel's Archaeology' in *Near Eastern Archaeology in the Twentieth Century: Essays in Honor of Nelson Glueck*, ed. James A. Sanders, Doubleday, 1970.
5 Kathleen Kenyon, 'Israelite Jerusalem' in Sanders (ed.) as in note 4 above.
6 An expression made notorious by its employment as the title of a highly contentious work by Joan Peters, Harper & Row, 1984.
7 Two important works of impeccable scholarship have recently appeared which make clear this absence of historical and archaeological evidence for the principal episodes related in the Old Testament. These are Thomas L. Thompson, *Early History of the Israelite People*, E. J. Brill, 1993, and Donald B. Redford, *Egypt, Canaan and Israel in Ancient Times*, Princeton, 1992.
8 'Jerusalem' in *Encyclopaedia of Archaeological Excavations in the Holy Land*, vol. II, ed. Michael Avi-Yonah, Oxford University Press, 1976.
9 Ibid.
10 Ibid.
11 See 'The Jerusalem City Museum' in *The Museums of Israel*, eds L. Y. Rahman and Peter Larsen, Secker & Warburg, 1976.
12 'The Israel Museum' in *The Museums of Israel*, op. cit.
13 'Jerusalem' in *The Archaeological Encyclopaedia of the Holy Land*, rev. edn, ed. Avraham Negev, Thomas Nelson Publishers, 1986.
14 'The Israel Museum', op. cit.: note 12 above.
15 See 'Hebron' in *The Archaeological Encyclopaedia of the Holy Land*, op. cit., note 13 above.
16 Redford, op. cit; see n. 7 above.
17 For general surveys by the principal excavators see Paolo Matthiae, *Ebla. An Empire Rediscovered*, Hodder & Stoughton, 1977, and Giovanni Pettinato, *Ebla: A New Look at History*, trans. C. Faith Richardson, Johns Hopkins University Press, 1991.
18 Y. Yadin, *The Message of the Scroll*, Grosset & Dunlop, 1957.

19 Y. Yadin, *Masada*, Random House, 1966.
20 Shay, op. cit.
21 H. Valladas, J. L. Reyss *et al.*, 'Thermoluminescence Dating of Mousterian "Proto-Cro-Magnon" Remains from Israel and the Origins of Modern Man', *Nature*, vol. 331, 18 February 1988.
22 Ofer Bar Yosef and François R. Valla (eds), *The Natufian Culture in the Levant*, International Monographs in Prehistory: Ann Arbor, Michigan, 1991.
23 See James Mellaart, 'The Levant, Epipalaeolithic to the Aceramic period' in *The Neolithic of the Near East*, Thames & Hudson, 1975.
24 See 'Treasure (Cave of the)' in *The Archaeological Encyclopaedia of the Holy Land*, op. cit.
25 M. Tubb, *Mitteilungen der deutscher Orient gesellschaft*, 1985. G. O. Rollefsen, *Palaeorient*, 9.2.1983 and 12.1.1986.
26 S. W. Helms, *Jawa: Lost City of the Black Desert*, Methuen, 1981.
27 See note 7 above for two of the most important recent works.
28 Kamal Salibi, *The Bible came from Arabia*, Jonathan Cape, 1985.
29 See also Kamal Salibi, *Secrets of the Bible People*, Al Saqi Books, London, 1988.
30 James M. Otway Jr, 'New Assault on Troy', *Archaeology*, September/October 1991.
31 Jeffrey H. Tigay, *The Evolution of the Gilgamesh Epic*, University of Pennsylvania Press, 1982.
32 Michael Rice, *Egypt's Making*, Routledge, London, 1990.
33 Michael Rice, *The Archaeology of the Arabian Gulf*, Routledge, 1993.

7 THE POLITICAL REALITY

1 For one aspect of this issue see *A Special Kind of State: Israel and the London 'Times'*, Hermon Books, Beirut, 1970.
2 Golda Meir, 15 June 1969.
3 *Independent*, April 1988, from Reuter, Tel Aviv.
4 General Raphael Eitan, *New York Times*, 14 April 1983.
5 See Kennett Love, *Suez: The Twice-Fought War*, Longman, 1969.
6 A. Nutting, *Nasser*, Constable, 1972, for a partisan but perceptive view.
7 See Steven L. Spiegal, *The Other Arab-Israeli Conflict: Making America's Middle East Policy, from Truman to Reagan*, University of Chicago Press, 1985.
8 *Middle East Report*, May-August 1990.
9 Benjamin Beit-Hallahmi, *The Israeli Connection: Whom Israel Arms and Why*, I. B. Tauris, 1987.
10 Ibid.
11 Golda Meir, 1972.
12 *Middle East International*, 20 November 1992; also quoted in Malise Ruthven, *Times Literary Supplement*, 11–17 March 1988.
13 *Middle East International*, 20 November 1992 recounts 'the resignation

of David Steiner, President of AIPAC after he had bragged about Zionist influences on Clinton.'

14 Rabbi Shlomo Aviner quoted in Ian S. Lustick, 'Gush Emunim: The Meaning and Impact of Jewish Fundamentalism in Israel', in *Democracy in the Middle East*, Proceedings of the 1992 Annual Conference, British Society for Middle Eastern Studies, University of St Andrews.

15 David Ben Gurion to his son, 5 October 1937. S. Flapan, *The Birth of Israel: Myths and Realities*, Pantheon Books, 1987 gives a thorough review of the origins of Zionist attempts to 'clear the land'. A more recent study by N. Masalha, *Expulsions of the Palestinians: The Concept of 'Transfer' in Zionist Political Thought 1882–1948*, Institute for Palestine Studies, Washington, 1992, gives the most complete account of Zionist aspirations and actions in this matter.

16 J. C. Jabotinsky: letter written in November 1939, quoted in Robert I. Friedman, *New York Review*, 29 March 1990.

17 James McDonald, *My Mission to Israel*, Simon & Schuster, New York, 1952.

18 Lenni Brenner, *Zionism in the Age of the Dictators: A Reappraisal*, Lawrence Hill, 1983.

19 For a damning review of the consequences of the invasion of Lebanon see, *Israel in Lebanon: The Report of the International Commission to Enquire into Reported Violations of International Law by Israel during its Invasion of the Lebanon*, Chairman Sean MacBride, Ithaca Press, London, 1983.

20 Quoted in 'Profile of Yitzhak Shamir' by Ian Murray, *The Times*, 7 April 1988.

21 V. Jabotinsky, *A Jewish State Now*, evidence submitted to the Palestine Royal Commission, House of Lords, 11 February 1937.

22 Ibid.

23 Ibid.

8 RELIGION, MORALITY AND THE DECLINE OF ISRAEL

1 Ian S. Lustick, *For the Land and the Lord: Jewish Fundamentalism in Israel*, Council on Foreign Relations, New York, 1988.

2 Ian S. Lustick, 'Gush Emunim: The Meaning and Impact of Jewish Fundamentalism in Israel', in *Democracy in the Middle East*, Proceedings of the 1992 Annual Conference, British Society for Middle Eastern Studies, University of St Andrews.

3 Chaim Weizmann, *Trial and Error: The Autobiography of Chaim Weizmann*, New York, 1966.

4 Ibid.

5 Lenni Brenner, *Zionism in the Age of the Dictators: A Reappraisal*, Lawrence Hill, 1983.

9 THE ORIENTAL JEWS AND THE DE-ZIONISATION OF ISRAEL

1 For a general discussion of the Jews in Islamic countries see Bernard Lewis, *The Jews of Islam*, Routledge & Kegan Paul, 1984. The anomalous position of the Oriental Jews in Israel is graphically documented by Shlomo Swirski, *Israel: The Oriental Majority*, Zed Books, 1989.
2 Paul Johnson, *A History of the Jews*, Weidenfeld & Nicolson, 1987.
3 R. Patai and J. Patai, *The Myth of the Jewish Race*, rev. edn, Wayne State University Press, Detroit, 1989 for what is by far the most comprehensive survey of Jewish proselytism in late antiquity.
4 Johnson, op. cit.
5 Ibid.
6 Patai and Patai, op. cit.
7 Johnson, op. cit.
8 Lewis, op. cit.
9 Ibid.
10 It is in this light that the outbreaks of anti-Jewish feeling in North African towns in the nineteenth century, for example, must be judged.
11 See Edward W. Said, *Orientalism*, Routledge & Kegan Paul, 1978.
12 For Disraeli's fascination with a highly romanticised Orient see, in particular, *Alroy* and *Tancred*. For his sense of his own Jewish identity see his speech on the admission of Baron Rothschild to the House of Commons in 1847. Robert Blake, *Disraeli*, Eyre & Spottiswoode, 1966.
13 Benjamin Disraeli, *The Wondrous Tale of Alroy and the Rise of Iskander*, 3 vols, Saunders & Otley, 1833.
14 See Marion Wolfson, *Jews in the Arab World*, Faber and Faber, 1980, citing *Jewish Chronicle*, 10 June 1977.
15 See Benjamin Beit-Hallahmi, *The Israeli Connection: Whom Israel Arms and Why*, I. B. Tauris, 1987.
16 David Holden and Richard Johns, *The House of Saud*, Sidgwick & Jackson, 1981.
17 See, *inter alia*, Erskine Childers, *The Road to Suez*, MacGibbon & Kee, 1962; Sir Anthony Nutting, *Nasser*, Constable, 1972.
18 A revealing study of one important Sephardic community, that of Baghdad, its transmission to Israel and its subsequent experience, is related in Chaim Raphael, *The Road from Babylon*, Weidenfeld & Nicolson, 1985.
19 In particular, Marion Wolfson, op. cit.
20 For example, Abbas Shiblak, *The Lure of Zion: The Case of the Iraqi Jews*, Al Saqi Books, 1986.
21 See Swirski, op. cit.
22 G. N. Giladi, *Discord in Zion*, Scorpion Publishing, London, 1990.
23 Swirski, op. cit.

INDEX

Note: References to Arabs, Jews, Judaism and Palestine have generally been omitted as they are ubiquitous.